"Here's a book to make you stop and think. For me, Robin Parry's chapters on the Trinity (even if they had not been in a book on worship) are well worth reading in their own right. He is extremely lucid in handling a difficult and mysterious subject. I found my own spirit was stirred by simply reading those excellent central chapters . . . This is a book well worth reading and one which I wholeheartedly recommend."

—Terry Virgo
New Frontiers, UK

"This is an academic book wonderfully disguised in language most in our churches would understand. I cannot recommend this work highly enough. Pastors, worship leaders, and mature Christians must read this and practice the sort of trinitarian worship Parry recommends."

—Myk Habets
Lecturer in Systematic Theology,
Carey Baptist College, New Zealand

"Bloody good!"

—Andrew G. Walker
Emeritus Professor of Theology, Culture, and Education,
King's College, London

Worshipping Trinity

Worshipping Trinity

Coming Back to the Heart of Worship

ROBIN A. PARRY

Second Edition

CASCADE *Books* · Eugene, Oregon

WORSHIPPING TRINITY
Coming Back to the Heart of Worship. Second Edition.

Copyright © 2012 Robin A. Parry. All rights reserved. Except for brief quotations in critical publications or reviews, no part of this book may be reproduced in any manner without prior written permission from the publisher. Write: Permissions, Wipf and Stock Publishers, 199 W. 8th Ave., Suite 3, Eugene, OR 97401.

Previously published by Paternoster, 2005

Cascade Books
An Imprint of Wipf and Stock Publishers
199 W. 8th Ave., Suite 3
Eugene, OR 97401

www.wipfandstock.com

ISBN 13: 978-1-62032-171-3

Cataloguing-in-Publication data:

Parry, Robin A.

Worshipping Trinity : coming back to the heart of worship. Second edition / Robin A. Parry.

xx + 204 pp. ; 23 cm. Includes bibliographical references.

ISBN 13: 978-1-62032-171-3

1. Trinity. 2. Worship. 3. Liturgics. I. Title.

BV4817 P37 2012

Manufactured in the U.S.A.

Permissions

To Keith Getty

—Thank you for your ongoing commitment to writing theologically rich worship songs. They are a gift of God to his people.

Contents

Foreword 1

SOMEONE ONCE TOLD ME that congregations learn so much of their theology from the songs of worship they sing. In other words, the lyrics we write and choose for congregational worship actually have an effect on people's view of God. As a songwriter and lead worshipper, that scared the singing daylights out of me.

Since then, I've made a point of posing the same question to most Christian leaders and theologians I happen to meet: Where are the major theological gaps in our songs of worship? Or, to rephrase it, what should we be singing about that we aren't? I've had many different responses, and each one is a helpful eye-opener as to how we might paint a fuller picture of God and his story in our gathered worship. But the answer I've received time and time again is this—that we need more of a sense of "Trinity" in our worship.

Then on this quest I met Robin Parry, the author of this book. I was soon to discover, over a series of large cappuccinos, that this man had a great big theological bee flying around his worshipful bonnet. And it was the very same neglected theme that was worrying him—the lack of a Trinitarian grammar of Father, Son, and Holy Spirit in so much of our gathered worship. I was also to discover that not only does Robin have a great gift for thinking about such grand themes, but he also has a very clear and original way of expressing them to others.

The thread of teaching running through this book is this: it is essential that our worship reflects Trinity, because the one true God we worship is Father, Son, and Holy Spirit. As well as applying this teaching to our gathered worship meetings, Robin so helpfully shines vital light on how every aspect of Christian living is connected with Father, Son, and Holy Spirit.

I know of many, many lead worshippers and songwriters on the same quest as myself—to paint the fullest and most wholesome picture of God we can through the way we prepare congregational worship. This book is an extremely valuable resource for all of us—for any pastor, leader, or worshipping heart who likes to think about these things. In these pages, Robin punches us in the stomach (theologically speaking), gives us a few moments to get our breath back, and then teaches us some nifty moves so that we can defend ourselves better in the future—and even throw a few theological punches of our own. Get your gloves on—this is an extremely helpful book.

—Matt Redman
Songwriter and lead worshipper
September 2004

Foreword 2

ONE THING IS FOR sure—today *we are what we sing*. From the phrases of
the preacher to the prayer of the student; from the testimonies of the young
people to the concerns of the parent. From the catchphrase to the content,
from the in-vogue discussions to the glaring omissions, what we choose to
sing infuses our thinking, our living, and takes on a wholly greater significance than we might ever have imagined. One thing is for sure—today we
are what we sing.

So if our desire is to fully worship "God" and to translate this highest
calling into authentic living, it only makes sense that we must have an authentic picture of who our God is in the first place. This is what we should
be expressing when we sing as a community of believers: the great truth,
the humbling thoughts, the enriching wonder, the daily challenges that will
sing through our heads throughout the week and pour out into our conversation and choices and minute-by-minute relationship with God.

In *Worshipping Trinity*, Robin Parry has given us a terrific resource
with which we can see a clearer picture of the God we worship—Father,
Son, and Holy Spirit. He humbly makes us aware of the blind spots of our
contemporary worship movement and encourages us to move forward as
authentic worshippers of the true God of the Bible so that, when we wor-
shipfully sing, we are what we have been created to be.

—Keith Getty
Hymn writer, co-writer of "In Christ Alone."

Acknowledgments

I AM NOT AT all sure what it was that first drew my attention to the issue of the Trinity in contemporary Western evangelical worship. I think it was that I was just becoming interested in Trinitarian theology and so my radar was subconsciously scanning for such things. Whatever it was, the matter seemed to accelerate from 0 to 60 mph in my mind in no time at all and became something of a passion. I have been greatly encouraged along the way by many who seem to think that I am indeed "onto something" and that I have something important to say.

I ought to emphasize very clearly here, because I do not mention it in the book, that I am committed to the view that "worship" is not just about what Christians do when they get together on a Sunday morning. Worship is about the whole of life lived in adoration of the Lord God (Rom 12:1). Worship is as much about what we do at home or at work as it is about what we do on a Sunday morning. However, the public worship of groups of Christians is intended to bring to clear expression the adoration that permeates the rest of life. When public worship is not in harmony with the lives of the community then it is hypocritical and is unacceptable to God (e.g., Isa 1). However, I am simply going to take all that for granted in what I write here. When this book speaks about "worship" it refers to acts of public or private devotion (including singing, praying, and listening to God). I would not want any reader to suppose that I think that so long as we get the words right in our songs and prayers then we can do as we please in the rest of life!

It is impossible to list all the people who have fed into this book because I seem to babble on about the topic to people wherever I go and draw off the insights of more people than I can remember. However, certain people have had a clearer influence. First of all, I must mention all the theological brains that have kindly looked at the material to check that it is orthodox and accessible and all those who chatted through the ideas with me. Special mention should be made of Andrew G. Walker, Julie Canlis, Graham Buxton,

Acknowledgments

John Witvliet, R. Kendall Soulen, Lizzie Shipp, and the fine gentlemen of the Salt & Light Theological Forum. I would also like to extend thanks to all the worship leaders and songwriters who offered reflections on the material or the ideas. Special thanks go to Matt Redman, Phil Simpson, Simon and Gaynor Shaw, and Nathan Fellingham. Also to Stuart Townend who played at the launch of the first edition and has kindly recommended the book since. I am deeply grateful to all those who took part in organizing the Trinity week at The King's Bible College and Training Centre in Oxford. The principal at the time, Aled Griffith (now a pastor in Derby, UK), really took hold of the vision and ran with it. Thanks to the creative arts teams from Oxford, London, and Basingstoke who did inspirational work (some of it described in chapter 9). I also extend heartfelt thanks to the wonderful students at the college who really encouraged and challenged me. Thanks go also to my former and still beloved church in Worcester and especially to Rick Thomas for reading the whole manuscript and valuing the place of theology in the life of the church—not all charismatic leaders would be so positive about what I do. I'd like to thank Keith Getty and Matt Redman for writing the forewords to the book (and for Keith's ongoing encouragement over the years since the first edition came out!), and to Brian McLaren, Alan Torrance, Bishop Graham Cray, Jeremy Begbie, and Bishop John Inge for their kind endorsements (and also to those who subsequently published reviews of the first edition, a couple of which are included in the front matter of this edition). This foreword would be incomplete without a mention of Tara Smith and Jeremy Funk, who edited the first and second editions respectively. Also I am most grateful to my speedy typesetter Patrick Harrison whose work is, as always, very professional and elegant. Finally, thanks go to my family. This is the first and only thing that I have ever written (love letters excluded) that my wife Carol has read—even if only in part (theology is not her "cup of tea"). I am deeply grateful to her for the feedback she gave me and for her unwavering support. Thanks also to my two beautiful girls—Hannah and Jessica—for being really sweet (mostly). Hannah tested the new (and slightly controversial) Appendix B for understandability—apparently I passed (bar a couple of typos). I'd also like to mention my tripodic cat, Monty. It's not that he did anything of relevance; it's just that he is very sweet and deserves a mention.

—Robin Parry
August 2004 (with changes, January 2012)

one

Theology and Worship Up a Tree, K-I-S-S-I-N-G

IT WAS ONLY AN experiment, really. I was pondering just how Trinitarian contemporary charismatic worship really is. Being a charismatic (of the mild-mannered variety), I find that such things matter to me. I randomly selected one of my worship music CDs—a CD that, at the time, was one of the best-selling Christian CDs in the Western world—and took a look at the content of some of these popular worship songs.[1] It's a good CD with some great songs, but reading the lyrics was something of an eye-opener: there was no mention in any of the songs of either God the Father or the Holy Spirit. All the songs were addressed either to "Jesus" or to an anonymous "God" or "Lord." Yikes! thought I. This led me to wonder just how much of the biblical story got into the songs. I looked again. There was no mention of God's dealings with Israel, nor of the incarnation of Jesus, nor the ministry of Jesus, nor the resurrection, nor the ascension! Only one song mentions the cross.[2] There was a great balance on the CD of songs of intimacy and transcendence, but that seemed to be the only balance. Although I approved of most of the individual songs, the *combination* found on the album was seriously inadequate for Christian worship.

1. The CD was Michael W. Smith, *Worship* (Reunion Records, 2001).

2. Rosalind Brown, commenting on certain contemporary songs, writes that "these texts have made a transition from hymns that root us in the biblical story, out of which we respond to God, towards hymns which may assume but do not articulate that biblical foundation, focusing instead on the singer's personal need and response . . . These self-focused hymns lack formative power since their roots are not in the Christian story" (Brown, *How Hymns Shape Our Lives*, 10).

I found myself feeling somewhat disturbed. You need to understand that what originally made me look at the CD was that I had just got home from a Sunday morning meeting at my church at which neither the Father nor the Spirit had received even as much as a passing glance. The leader opened the meeting with a call to worship: "We've come together this morning to meet with Jesus." We then proceeded to sing numerous songs all directed to "Jesus" or "You, Lord." Clearly, in the context of the meeting, the "Lord" in "You, *Lord*" was also Jesus. There were numerous prayers all directed to Jesus. The sermon waxed eloquent about Jesus, but his Father and his Spirit didn't get a look in. Then there was a call to respond in faith to the gospel with a prayer that went something like this: "Dear Lord Jesus, I am sorry that I have sinned against you. Thank you for dying for me so that I could be forgiven. Please forgive me and come and live in my heart. Amen." I went home feeling rather uneasy—not simply because this had happened, but also because everyone else seemed utterly oblivious to it. It simply hadn't struck anyone else as odd.[3] And why didn't it? I vividly recall a sermon illustration used some years ago in the church. The visiting preacher took a frog and placed it in a pan of cold water and slowly heated the water until it boiled. The point was that if you turn up the heat slowly, the frog doesn't notice and will hang around while getting boiled alive! I hasten to add that the illustration is in fact mythical, and the frog that the preacher boiled was not a real one. (Although, interestingly, this fact was not revealed until later, and yet we all sat smiling uncomfortably as the guy boiled what we took to be a real frog—fuel for psychology books there).[4] I suspect that slowly but surely there has been a shift away from full Trinitarian worship towards worship that is often in practice "unitarian." This shift is not uniform, it is not the same in all evangelical churches, it sometimes waxes and wanes, and it has hardly reached boiling point, but I want to blow the whistle and say, "FROGS OF THE WORLD, UNITE! We're being boiled alive here! Let's leap out of the pan before the bubbles start rising!" One simply has to ask the painful question, at what point does worship cease to be *Christian* worship and become simply Christians worshipping?

3. I ought to add that it is not usual for my former church's worship to be quite this un-Trinitarian.

4. Although this is an apt illustration of the idea that gradual degradation is not perceivable, and the point that it illustrates is obviously true of human nature in all sorts of situations: a real frog will (apparently—I haven't tried it myself!) jump out when it gets too hot (cf. http://www.godandscience.org/doctrine/froglegs.html/).

The basic idea behind this book is very simple: *worship is about God and God is the Trinity, therefore worship is about the Trinity.* Christian worship, in other words, is worship focused upon the God who has revealed himself through Christ to be Father, Son, and Holy Spirit. This book is a journey of exploration into the implications of that simple thought.

THE TERRIFYING TRINITY

Now the doctrine of the Trinity is one of those Christian beliefs that we all affirm but which, in our more honest moments, we often think is rather perplexing and somewhat remote from ordinary life. Those in mainstream churches that follow the Christian year can almost hear the vicars, priests, and ministers groan inwardly when Trinity Sunday draws nigh—that dreaded week of the year when they are supposed to dispel the confusions surrounding the Godhead! Understandably, the prospect is sometimes anticipated with all the joyous expectation of a turkey waiting for Christmas dinner. Those preachers in churches that don't follow the Christian year thank the Lord for small mercies and avoid sermons on the Trinity like one avoids a dog with rabies.

It seems to me that there are a couple common problems with Trinitarian faith as one finds it among Christians. The first is that, as we've already hinted, many Christians do not understand Christian teaching on the Trinity. This is primarily because it is not properly integrated into our general church life and thought in worship, sermons, and lived faith. But it is also in part because the Trinity is almost never spoken of directly. The Trinity, most crucially, needs to saturate our praise, but it also needs to be explained from time to time. In twenty-eight years as a Christian I have never heard it taught in a church context—whether in a sermon, a house group, an Alpha course, a post-Alpha, or whatever.[5] I gather from speaking to people around the UK in nonconformist and/or charismatic churches that my experience here is not untypical. The impression we give people is that the doctrine is a complex, abstract, philosophical concept unrelated to Christian life. When I speak to ordinary Christians about it, I am sadly unsurprised to find some who are well-intentioned "heretics" without even realizing it.

---

5. With the exception of hearing myself speak on the Trinity in church contexts.

Let me tell you a story. I was once asked to speak to a small group in a church, and I decided to do something unusual: I decided to do an "Idiot's Guide to the Trinity." I was amazed that not one single person had ever been taught this very basic Christian doctrine before. But more amazing still were the comments made by a couple who had become Christians through the church ten years earlier. They had been along most weeks since then on Sundays and had also attended midweek house group meetings; they had done the Alpha course; they had done Alpha follow-up; they had completed beginners' courses on the Christian faith and attended numerous church camps. They explained to me that they had always thought that in Old Testament times only God the Father existed. Then, with Jesus's conception, God the Son was created, and finally, on the day of Pentecost, the Holy Spirit came into being! In ten years of an involved church life nothing had ever suggested to them otherwise! Although I kept my face deadpan, I had to peel the eyebrows of my inner man off the ceiling when they finished their tale. They were more than happy to give up the misunderstandings, but I was staggered at what their experience suggested about their church's worship. I realize that not many Christians have views as far off the beaten track as this couple's used to be, but I have come across a fair few who hold to heretical views without being aware of it. That, however, is just the first problem.

The second problem is that those who do "understand" the contours of Christian claims about the Trinity often don't see *why* the doctrine matters. Let me illustrate the problem. Many Christians will tell you that Jehovah's Witnesses are "unsound" because they reject the doctrine of the Trinity. They do indeed reject it. *So what?* Why is that a problem? Have a think about that. You may say, "Well, they're wrong." True, but we're all wrong about some things. Why is the Trinity so important? If you are struggling to answer that question, then you are not alone. For many of us, the Trinity is one of those things we believe in, but that seems unconnected to the rest of our life and faith. The general impression among Christians, therefore, is that the Trinity is an abstract doctrine that matters in theory but not in practice.

Catholic theologian Karl Rahner issued this challenge: suppose the doctrine of the Trinity turned out to be false, and we had to drop it as a belief—how much difference would it make to our Christian beliefs and practice? Tragically, says Rahner, often very little. In practice we are often no more than what he called "mere monotheists" rather than fully Trinitarian.[6]

6. Rahner, *The Trinity*, 10–15.

Trinity should be related to our other beliefs like hydrogen is related to water. Take the "H" out of H_2O and you no longer have water. Take the Trinity out of Christian faith and practice and you no longer have Christian faith and practice. In this book I want to help explain why Christians have lived and died defending the idea that God is triune. *It matters.* Before we can directly consider worship and the Trinity, we need to get a clearer grasp on this God we are worshipping.

I have been guided in my thinking by several foundational convictions, the first being that the notion of God as Trinity is a central element in Christian life and faith. Berten Waggoner, National Director of the Association of Vineyard Churches USA, writes, "The God we worship is a trinitarian God. We know no other God than the one revealed in Jesus Christ—Father, Son, and Holy Spirit . . . The Triune God is the boast of the Christian faith."[7] All the branches of the Christian church—Orthodox, Catholic, and Protestant—affirm the doctrine, and it is at the core of all the ecumenical creeds of the early church. The doctrine is biblically rooted and, although its full unpacking and clarification took several hundred years, that process was merely a legitimate development of what is there in Scripture. In this book we will look at some of the fundamental aspects of this belief and why it matters so much.

GOOD THEOLOGY MATTERS FOR GOOD WORSHIP

My second foundational conviction is that Christian theology is not an interesting exercise in abstract speculation but is intimately connected to Christian living and worship. Good theology matters for good worship. Some Christians reject this view. I know a man who used to declare that he could write all the theology he knew on the back of a postage stamp . . . IN CAPITAL LETTERS! And he wasn't lamenting; he was boasting! He was saying that he hadn't been sidetracked by the irrelevant work of the theologians. Negative attitudes towards theology among Christians are not that uncommon. Let me make a confession. For a while, as a teenager, I was heavily influenced by what is known as the "Word of Faith" movement, better known to its opponents as the "Health and Wealth" movement. Within that movement I often encountered hostility to what "theology" taught. The preacher would set up "what the theologians say" and "what God says" in opposition and then challenge the congregation to reject theology and

---

7. Waggoner, "Leading Trinitarian Worship," 5.

trust God instead. Theology, we were told, is a sinful exercise designed to undermine faith. To suggest that theology had something to contribute to good worship would be like suggesting that shredded beef had something to contribute to a veggie burger! Of course, the preacher had never actually read anything by these "evil theologians" and seemed quite unaware that every time he opened his mouth to speak about God he was talking theology himself (and often rather dubious theology).

I can understand the worries of anti-theological Christians, and it is certainly the case that *some* of the things that *some* theologians have taught have been somewhat off the wall. However, the answer to "bad theology" is not "no theology" but "good theology." Christians want to speak about God, and if you want to do that there simply isn't a "no theology" option.

But even if we concede that all Christian have to do some theology, many feel that the ideal is to do as little as possible. The motto is: "All we need is 'the simple gospel.'" The worry is that "the theologians just make everything so unnecessarily complicated." The underlying conviction is that theology is not related to the ordinary lives of Christian believers. However, while it is true that one can be saved by faith in "the simple gospel" without having a very deep understanding of it, it simply doesn't follow that God doesn't want us to seek to grow in our understanding, to think about our faith, and to love him with our minds.

Although very few Christians are called to be academic theologians, all Christians are called to think theologically. My conviction is that theology is relevant to Christian living. Theology that does not have some cash value for a life of obedient worship is, at best, of secondary interest.[8] Good theology, whether it is academic or not, is theology done for the blessing of the people of God. As we shall see, the Trinity is central to Christianity, and understanding it is necessary for healthy Christian worship, faith, and life.

I also used to think that sorting out your doctrine and sorting out your worship were two quite separate things. I thought that both were important, but the connection between the two never really struck me. Now I see that "right belief" about God is intimately connected to "right worship" because believing right things about God is an important component in honoring God appropriately. This is why Christians speak of right belief about God as *orthodoxy*, which literally means "right glory." If we are to give God the

---

8. Maximus the Confessor (580–662)—a Christian monk, not the guy in the *Gladiator* movie—apparently wrote, "Theology without practice is the theology of demons" (I have not yet tracked down the source of this quote, hence "apparently").

glory he deserves, we need to think and speak rightly about God. Thinking right about God involves having a Trinitarian framework for thinking about God. The Trinity should be at the core of our worship because the God who is at the heart of worship is Trinity. Right belief about the Trinity is important *precisely because* it is so crucial to appropriate worship.

WORSHIP SHAPES OUR SPIRITUALITY

My third foundational conviction is that our spirituality is usually shaped more by the experience of communal worship than it is by preaching and teaching. Please do not think that I am running preaching and teaching down—I believe in the importance of both. My point is simply that the way we think about God and relate to God is influenced enormously by our experience of God in communal worship. Let's put it this way: where do we learn how to pray and worship? Where is our school of spirituality? Where do we pick up good and bad habits for our individual relationships with God? In public worship, of course! That is where we learn the language of praise and the way to speak of and to God. We may not consciously be copying those around us; often we simply absorb the patterns of speech, the intonation, the words to use, the appropriate physical gestures and postures, and so on just by being immersed in an environment in which others are worshipping. The public worship we experience often sets the limits and possibilities of our worshipping worlds.

Songs, particularly in evangelicalism, are especially formative. "We are far more likely to find ourselves humming something we sang in church when we go home than we are to find ourselves meditating on a phrase in the sermon," observes Rosalind Brown. "Words set to music engage the emotions and lodge in the memory. The refrains of hymns and choruses are even more likely to stick in the mind, simply because they are sung more frequently."[9] John Wesley wrote of hymns that "I would recommend [the hymnbook] to every truly pious reader: as a means of raising or quickening the spirit of devotion, of confirming the faith, of enlivening his hope, and of kindling or increasing his love to God and man."[10]

Let me introduce a notion that may prove helpful for understanding the role of worship in shaping our Christian faith. Michael Polanyi, a Christian

9. Brown, *How Hymns Shape Our Lives*, 21.

10. John Wesley, Preface to the 1780 handbook, paragraph 8; quoted in Brown, *How Hymns Shape Our Lives*, 6.

philosopher and scientist, spoke of knowledge that we simply absorb by a kind of "osmosis" without even realizing that we have done so. This is what he refers to as "tacit knowledge." Most Christians simply imbibe a theology through the way that they worship. The songs, Scripture readings, prayers, and rituals (and even the most nonliturgical, charismatic churches have rituals) form the bricks and mortar of the congregation's spirituality and faith. The knowledge we gain through worship is not merely information but a practical knowledge. Think about riding a bike. There are some things about riding a bike, such as how to balance on it, that can only be learned by riding it and not by reading the *How to Cycle* manual. When we learn to ride a bike we are not paying attention to all the different things we need to do—try that and you'd never learn. We internalize all that we need to know through participating in the practice of cycling and then intuitively we just know how to do it, even if we would have trouble explaining it. This kind of knowledge could be called participatory knowledge. Susan Wood argues that regularly taking part in Christian worship is essential for Christian spiritual formation. We may not pay conscious attention to all the individual elements of the faith that we sing or act out in worship, but we are immersed in the practice of communal devotion to God. We internalize the shape of the faith through the sights, sounds, smells, tastes, and feel of the whole experience. Liturgy, says Wood, creates an environment that, when we indwell it, shapes our vision, relationships, and knowledge of God in Christian ways. The knowledge of God we gain in worship is not the knowledge one can learn from a book but the participatory knowledge that comes from being involved in a relationship.[11] And how does all this relate to theology?

> The truths are lived and practiced in worship before they are expressed dogmatically. For example, the church baptized in the name of the Father, Son, and Spirit and prayed to the Father through Christ in the power of the Spirit long before it developed a doctrine of the Trinitarian relationships in the fourth-century Councils of Nicaea (325) and Constantinople (381). The relationship between dogma and worship, however, is reciprocal. In addition to worship giving rise to doctrine, doctrine, on the other hand, ensures right worship.[12]

11. Wood, "The Liturgy," 110.

12. White, *Whatever Happened to the Father?*, 18–19.

So theology springs from right worship but theology also, in turn, guides and ensures right worship. There is a circular relationship between the two as healthy worship and theology support each other. In this book I want to focus on how theology can guide the kind of worship that in turn shapes people spiritually.

Worship that has a deep Trinitarian structure and syntax will form congregations who will think about God in Trinitarian ways and relate to God in Trinitarian ways even if they have never had the doctrine of the Trinity formally explained to them. Trinitarian worship teaches people the grammar of God so a preacher can say, "God is a Trinity . . . you know what I mean!" and people will immediately see that they do know (roughly) what the preacher means, even though they may never have articulated the concept to themselves fully.

This point is of crucial importance. In what follows I am going to spend quite a bit of time explaining the doctrine of the Trinity and arguing that it is important. It is crucial that some people in the church have a good, clear grasp of such thinking—including leaders, songwriters, and those involved in leading worship. As we will see, those who lead worship need to think long and hard about how to make worship more Trinitarian. However, I do not want to argue that all Christians need to ponder the Trinity in quite the same way. If we can shape worship and preaching in Trinitarian ways, our congregations will pick up a tacit knowledge of the Trinity. They will instinctively relate to God as Father, Son, and Spirit. They will pick up habits of speaking correctly and worthily about the Lord. They will be lovers of the Trinitarian God even if they haven't ever worked out exactly how all the "*i*"s are dotted and the "*t*"s are crossed. Those who shape public worship do need to think clearly and plan carefully to facilitate a rich and rounded encounter with the Christian God week by week. Members of the congregation, however, don't have to be aware that this is what is happening. They can carry on as usual—turning up to worship God together.

If what I have said is true, then we need to consider the consequences of not having richly Trinitarian worship.

Christian worship is the primary place where people internalize the Christian system, where they learn the language of faith, where they are able to find their voices in song and prayer and proclamation and sacrament. When people are deprived of a rich and subtle language about God, it deprives them of their legitimate theological and spiritual inheritance.

Very diluted theology in worship songs and prayers leads to spiritually impoverished worshippers. We need to ask whether we are being fed a diet of wafer-thin mints when we need beef burgers. Some contemporary worship songs are the theological equivalents of wafer-thin mints, and although there is an important place in life for wafer-thin mints—they can be the great finishing touch to a meal—that place is not as a staple diet. If most of our songs are of the wafer-thin mint variety, then we will shape believers who are spiritually wafer-thin; spiritually anorexic.

What I have said so far should not be heard as an argument against formal teaching on the Trinity in churches. Far from it! Rather, if we get our Trinitarian worship in order then we will find that our congregations will absorb all the key elements of Trinitarian faith before we even get as far as explaining it. So that when we do formally explain the Trinity it will resonate with people, and we will simply be helping them clarify what they already believe. However, if our worship is disordered then the message from the pulpit that "the Trinity matters" is completely undermined by the weekly experience of worship in which it clearly matters very little. The occasional sermon on the Trinity cannot compensate for week after week of communal worship that has had all the Trinitarian life and color washed out of it.

It is important to emphasize that I am not arguing that the reason we should get the theology right in our worship is so that we can teach good theology to our churches! That is precisely the wrong way around. What I am suggesting is that we get the theology in our worship right so that we can worship God more appropriately. Right worship is the reason for doing right theology, not vice versa.

This view of communal worship calls attention to the crucial importance of the job of the person or people preparing and leading public worship. The songwriters and worship leaders of today play an enormous part in shaping the faith and life of the church of tomorrow. This is an awesome responsibility. Those who shape worship are the *de facto* theologians of the church, whether they want to be or not. If you are reading this book and you have any influence over the worship of a congregation, then you are a VIP—but with this privilege comes great responsibility. Your job as a worship facilitator is to provide the context in which the Spirit can draw people into a rich encounter with the blessed Three-in-One. You don't have to force the people to worship, but you do have to facilitate and guide the worship that the Spirit elicits from the people. The songs that you choose;

the Scriptures that you read, the prayers that you pray, and the way you connect them all together make a vast difference.

Consider songs again. Pete Ward says that Christian worship songs, especially in evangelical worship, provide a kind of narrative for a journey of worship.[13] The songs structure our desire for God through their use of symbolic language, which gives content to our desire. The words of the songs will provide the focus for our thoughts about God and thus influence the shape of our love for God at any particular moment in worship. Each song, and each collection of songs, has its own rendition of the Christian story. Ward's focus is more on songbook collections, but the same insight is valid for a collection of songs pulled together for a specific worship occasion. The songs significantly contribute towards the narrative that structures the shape of any particular encounter. So the encounter will differ depending on the songs chosen. In churches that use a formal liturgy, the combination of song and liturgy will structure the worship journey, and the liturgy sets constraints on how far songs can control the encounter. In churches that do not have a liturgy, however, the burden of guiding the encounter falls heavily upon the songs. In many charismatic churches, the songs play the dominant role in shaping the worship-encounter.

Think now about one of the purposes of worship being the offering of devotion and gratitude from the church to the triune God. If songs shape that offering event, then what kinds of songs will facilitate an encounter with the Trinity? If we are cast upon the mercy of our songs in worship, then which songs will show us mercy? What kinds of songs should our songwriters be producing? How should worship leaders go about selecting songs that will make the congregation aware of this Trinity? These are important questions, but sadly they are rarely asked, let alone answered. We will devote chapter 7 to thinking about these questions.

The same question could be asked about prayer. How can we pray the Trinity? How can the Father, the Son, and the Spirit so infuse our spiritual lives that when we speak to God we weave back and forth between the persons of the Trinity, fully aware that the one with whom we speak is not just some faceless "God" but is the Father, the Son, and the Spirit? In chapter 8 we'll think about that question.

Chapter 9 tackles another conspicuous absence in much Christian worship—lament. The Bible is full of brutally honest and painful laments that were used in both individual and communal worship. So why is it that no matter how the congregation are feeling our worship gatherings seem to

---

13. Ward, *Selling Worship*, ch. 12.

be so unrelentingly happy? Something is not right with this picture. I suggest an approach to thinking about lament in Trinitarian ways—lamenting to the Father, through the Son, in the Spirit—and I make a case for reincorporating lament into our public worship.

Are there other resources in Christian worship that can fund a fully Trinitarian spirituality? In chapter 10 we will look at how Bible reading, dance, sermons, the arts, and, most importantly, the Eucharist can serve to bring the people of God to a greater awareness of the Trinity. These are the questions that those working at the coalface of worship will want to address, and the temptation is to jump straight into these more practical issues. But chapters 2 through 6 carefully lay the foundations for the practical outworking that follows. My hope is that this book will model how good theology can contribute to good worship. Chapter 2 is a story. It briefly tells the biblical story of creation, fall, and redemption from Genesis to Revelation. However, somewhat unusually, it tells the story as *God's* story—showing how the three persons relate to every act of God in the world. This approach reveals how Christian faith is integrally Trinitarian. Chapter 3 looks at the Christian life from conversion to our resurrection at the return of Christ, taking in issues like mission, church, and holy living to show how every aspect of Christian living is connected with Father, Son, and Spirit. Chapter 4 examines the basic shape of Christian faith in the Trinity and why it matters so much. Although none of this is directly connected with worship, these chapters are essential background and also provide the theological fuel for new songs and prayers. If you are a songwriter and wish to write more Trinitarian songs, chapters 2 through 4 will set you off on the right foot.

While chapters 5 and 6 are both theological, they also address worship and prayer. In chapter 5 we will see that in order to understand what we are doing when we worship and pray we must understand it in Trinitarian terms. Jesus is in heaven right now worshipping and praying to the Father. Christian worship is nothing more, nor less, than the Spirit enabling us to join in with Christ's worship of the Father. Christian prayer is nothing more, nor less, than the Spirit enabling us to join in with Christ's prayer to the Father. In this chapter we will explore the important implications of this revolutionary Christian understanding of worship. Chapter 6, finally, argues that Christians must offer worship to the Father, the Son, and the Spirit. After considering the practical questions concerning how to make our worship more Trinitarian in chapters 7 through 10, the epilogue reflects on how we can avoid Trinitarian worship becoming a fad that—like Teenage Mutant Ninja Turtles—is ubiquitous and then, as suddenly as it appeared, is gone again. Worship of the Trinity must not fall victim to the changing fashions of Christian worship, so we need to anticipate the danger in advance and take steps to guard against it.

For those who are interested, I have added two appendices. The first is a set of daily Trinitarian prayers for each day of the week. I wrote these for my family to use and some readers may find them helpful. The second briefly addresses the thorny and contentious issue of the use of masculine language for God. Is the Trinity "two men and an it"?

Worshipping the Trinity is the centre of Christian devotion. My hope is that this book will be used by the Spirit to bring us closer to the heart of worship. "To the best of my powers I will persuade all people to worship Father, Son, and Holy Spirit as the single Godhead and power, because to him belong all glory, honor, and might for ever and ever. Amen."[14]

14. Gregory of Nazianzus, *On God in Christ*, 31:33.

two

The Trinitarian Geography
of the Biblical Story

FOR MANY CHRISTIANS, THE Trinity has become like something akin to their appendix: it is there but they are not sure what its function is; they get by in life without it doing very much; and if they had to have it removed they wouldn't be too distressed. They believe that God is Trinity because that is what the Bible teaches (or because that is what their church teaches), but if they had to explain what difference the Trinity made to Christian living and thinking they'd be left wallowing in a pool of their own silence. I know, because I have been there. For me the Trinity was an item on a checklist of "things to believe." I could go down the list and tick off all the items.

Creation? Yes.

Fall? Yes.

Salvation through Christ's cross and resurrection? Of course.

Trinity? Naturally.

And so on.

After my conversion to Christianity I never doubted the truth of the doctrine of the Trinity, but it was no more than a single marble in a drawer labeled "Christian beliefs." In my "Christian beliefs" drawer the Trinity rolled around among all the other belief-marbles, occasionally bumping up against others but remaining essentially unconnected to them. If, for some reason, the Trinity marble had fallen out of the drawer, it wouldn't have had a significant impact on the other marbles in there because it wasn't connected to them in any way. Is it any wonder that I was somewhat lost for words when I tried to figure out exactly why the Trinity was supposed to be so important? For me, in spite of what I may have claimed, the Trinity was an appendix—present but nonessential. I am not surprised that many Christians secretly suspect that theological reflection on the Trinity is an escapist pastime for those who don't wish to get dirty with the grime of real life and who are bad at mathematics (1+1+1=1!).

If we stop for just a moment and think about my predicament, it should strike us as very weird. Think about it. Christianity is a God-centered religion. If God is Trinity, then it follows that Christianity is a Trinity-centered religion. We would expect the Trinity to be related to every area of Christian faith and practice. So why is it that for so many of us it remains a disconnected marble rolling around in a space of its own? If we are to see why the Trinity is the heart of Christian faith, and not its appendix, we need to reconnect it to the other marbles in the drawer. This chapter will briefly sketch an outline of the core story of the Bible, showing how every part of that story has the triune God at the centre. I want to show that Christian beliefs are not loose marbles in a drawer but like the spokes of a wheel with the Trinity as the hub. Every spoke is linked to the hub in such a way that were the hub to be removed, the whole wheel would fly apart. If we can begin to grasp the centrality of the Trinity, it will become blindingly obvious why the early church thought it was such an important issue. These early Christian thinkers who spent so much time arguing about the Trinity were not armchair theologians sitting in ivory towers—they were mostly church leaders dealing with pastoral issues. And the Trinity was not something they discussed for a hobby in their spare time, when they put up their feet at the end of the day—it was at the heart of their vision of Christian discipleship, worship, and mission. If the Trinity is to become fixed again at the centre of our worship then it is essential that worship leaders, songwriters, pastors, teachers, preachers, and small group leaders understand how the Trinity fits at the heart of Christian faith.

It will be helpful in what follows to begin with a simple image to guide us on our way. There are many illustrations of the Trinity, and all of them have strengths and weaknesses. While no illustration is perfect, as long as we don't get too precious about them they can be helpful. One such illustration was used in the second century by a church leader named Irenaeus (c. AD 130–200). He said that the Word (i.e., the Son) and Spirit were like the *two hands* of the Father. The weakness of this image is that it depersonalizes the Son and the Spirit (hands are not persons, not centers of consciousness and will). The image is still helpful, however, for understanding God's work in creation and redemption. Everything that God does is the work of the *whole Trinity*. When God acts, he does so through his two hands. The Son and the Spirit work together to achieve the Father's will, just like the hands of a sculptor work together to shape a sculpture. Throughout this chapter we will see God's two hands at work in every act of the Father.

THE BIBLICAL SUPER-STORY

Christians are increasingly remembering that the Bible is not simply a list of things-to-believe and do, or a collection of timeless blessed thoughts that one can dip into at random. On the contrary, the Bible is a single story that runs from creation to new creation, from Genesis to Revelation. Robert Webber writes that, "This story is the good news (*evangelion*). In worship we signify it (*leiturgia*); in evangelism we proclaim it (*kerygma*); in fellowship we experience it (*koinonia*); in our ministry to each other and in our service to others we live it (*deaconia*). It is the very heartbeat of who we are."[1]

The Trinitarian dimension of this story, however, has not been highlighted. The Bible has what Chris Cocksworth, bishop of Coventry, calls a "Trinitarian geography," and we need to tell that biblical super-story in such a way that this comes into focus. Let's turn now to sketch some of the important elements in a Trinitarian telling of the story. So let's take the advice of Sister Maria and "start at the very beginning." After all, as the good lady said, it's "a very good place to start."

TRINITY AND CREATION

In the beginning there was nothing at all. Nothing, that is, except God—Father, Son, and Spirit existing in an eternal dance of love. Here is a holy mystery that defies the grappling hooks of our understanding. We can say little before we are compelled to stand in reverent silence. But God chose to create, and this brings us to the doctrine of creation. Any Christian can tell you that the doctrine of creation is important—our cosmos is no mere accident, but the loving and purposive work of the one true God. But

---

1. Webber, "Is Our Worship Adequately Triune?"

remember that this one God is Trinity. What happens when we try to bring the one God into focus so that we can see the Trinity at work?

The Nicene Creed begins with the words, "I believe in one God, the Father, the Almighty, maker of heaven and earth." St. Paul made the same point when he said in his first letter to the Corinthians: "for us there is but one God, the Father, *from whom* all things came and for whom we live" (8:6a). The eternal Father is the origin-point of creation. However, Paul goes on to add the words: "and there is but one Lord, Jesus Christ, *through whom* all things came and through whom we live" (8:6b). This Christian modification of the Jewish understanding of creation marks a fresh Christian understanding of God and of the world.

The early Christians were good monotheistic Jews who were as zealous as any good monotheistic Jews in the first century to defend the unique sovereignty of Israel's God. For them there was only one creator God, Yhwh,[2] who alone was worthy of worship. So it comes as something of a seismic shock to see that, across the different streams of the early movement of Christ followers, Jesus of Nazareth was being acclaimed as sharing in Yhwh's creating work! Consider first St. Paul: "He [Christ] is the image of the invisible God, the firstborn over all creation. *For* by him all things were created: things in heaven and on earth, visible and invisible, whether thrones or powers or rulers or authorities; all things were created by him and for him. He is before all things, and in him all things hold together" (Col 1:15–17). This is astonishing! Jesus is described as "the firstborn over all creation." The firstborn son was, in Jewish society, the heir to the family inheritance and the preeminent child in the family. Paul explains in what sense the Son is the firstborn: "for by him all things were created." That is

---

2. The name of God, in Hebrew, is composed of the consonants *Yhwh* (vowels, though pronounced, were originally not written down in Hebrew). By the time of Jesus it had come to be felt that God's name is so very holy that it must *never be spoken.* Thus, when a Jewish person is reading the Hebrew Bible and comes to the name Yhwh, he or she will *say* the word "Adonai" (Lord) in its stead. That is why English translations render Yhwh as LORD (in caps). However, I think it very important to highlight that the God of Israel has revealed a *name* ("Lord" is a title, not a name), and thus I will sometimes refer to Yhwh. I have also changed any instances of LORD in the NIV to Yhwh. Out of respect for Jewish tradition I will not attempt to add the vowels to the name. In this regard, Christians would do well to note that Jesus himself and the New Testament writers followed the standard Jewish practice of never mentioned the name *directly* but instead referencing it indirectly by means of substitute words such as *Lord.* Once one sees this it is blindingly obvious that the name Yhwh stands at the *heart* of New Testament conceptions of God. See especially Soulen, *The Divine Name(s) and the Holy Trinity.*

to say, he is the "firstborn" *because* he created all things (and not because he was created first).

The book of Hebrews says, "In the past God spoke to our forefathers through the prophets at many times and in various ways, but in these last days he has spoken to us by his Son, whom he appointed heir of all things, and *through whom he made the universe*. The Son is the radiance of God's glory and the exact representation of his being, sustaining all things by his powerful word" (Heb 1:1–3). Here we see God (the Father) creating everything in the universe through the Son.

Now consider the stunning opening to John's Gospel: "In the beginning was the Word, and the Word was with God, and the Word was God. He was with God in the beginning. *Through him all things were made*; without him nothing was made that has been made" (John 1:1–3). Notice how John emphasizes that every . . . single . . . created thing (without exception) was created by God (the first person of the Trinity) *through the Word* (the second person, i.e., the Son—see 1:18). Clearly the Word did not create himself, so obviously the Word is uncreated. That is why John can write not only that the Word was "*with* God [the Father]" but also that the Word "*was* God [the Son]" (1:1).

It is important to see that the work of the Son in creation did not finish with the original act of bringing the cosmos out of nothing "in the beginning." We have seen how in Colossians Paul says that "in him [Christ] all things hold together" (1:17), and the book of Hebrews goes on to add that the Son is "sustaining all things by his powerful word" (1:3). That is to say that at every moment the universe exists it does so only because it is held in being by the Son. Every breath you draw and every beat of your heart is possible only because of the Son's ongoing creative grasping and ordering of the cosmos. Were he to let go, creation would collapse back into the nothingness from which it arose. So the early followers of Jesus were clearly teaching from a very early date that God the Father was indeed Creator and that he originated and sustains the world through the Son. But what of the Spirit?

The seeds of a Trinitarian understanding of creation are there in the very first chapter of the Bible, even though it is only in retrospect that we can see them. In Genesis 1 we read about the one creator-God who created the heavens and the earth. And how does God create? By speaking his creative words: "And God said, 'Let there be . . .'" As we have seen, John's Gospel develops our understanding of the Word through which God creates by showing us that this Word is actually an extension of God's being—what we now refer to as God the Son. But Genesis 1 also speaks of the breath/wind/spirit of God in creation: "In the beginning God created the heavens and the earth. Now the earth was formless and empty, darkness was over the surface of the deep, and the Spirit of God was hovering over the waters" (Gen 1:1–2). The Hebrew word translated "Spirit" in the NIV above is the word *ruaḥ*, and it can mean "wind" or "breath" as well as "spirit." This is God's very own divine Breath/Wind/Spirit hovering over the waters of the unformed earth as God prepares to shape it to make it habitable (days 1–3) and then fills it up with a rich variety of creatures (days 4–6). Genesis 1 doesn't make much of the activity of the divine Spirit in creation, but we can see it perhaps as God's life-giving presence brooding over the primeval world ready to animate it. After God has formed the man from dust in chapter 2 we read that, "the Lord God . . . breathed into his nostrils the breath of life, and the man became a living being" (Gen 2:7). Here God imparts his very own breath into his creation and brings it to life. The idea of God's Spirit/Breath as a source of life for creation is found elsewhere the Old Testament. For instance, the psalmist says of the creatures, "When you hide your face, they are terrified; when you take away their breath, they die and return to the dust. When you send your [Breath] Spirit, they are created, and you renew the face of the earth" (Ps 104:29–30). Yhwh thus creates both through his structuring word (the second person) and through his animating breath (the third person), almost as if when he utters his word he expels his breath in the very same action: "By the word of Yhwh were the heavens made, their starry host by the breath of his mouth" (Ps 33:6).

The Spirit is not merely the life giver "in the beginning," as if his work in creation was somehow finished way back then. Notice that the quotation from Psalm 104 above is about the Spirit's ongoing life-giving work in creation and ongoing renewal of the face of the earth. The breath of God is still present throughout creation, saturating it like water saturates a sponge. Thus the psalmist can say: "Where can I go from your Spirit? Where can I flee from your presence? If I go up to the heavens, you are there; if I make my bed in the depths, you are there. If I rise on the wings of the dawn, if I settle on the far side of the sea, even there your hand will guide me, your right hand will hold me fast" (Ps 139:7–10).

So God the Father is involved with creation right now, through his Son, who holds it together and his Spirit who animates it. Lady Julian of Norwich (1342–1416) beautifully expresses the idea in terms of divine love:

> In this vision he showed me a little thing, the size of a hazelnut, and it was round as a ball. I looked at it with the eye of my understanding and thought "What may this be?" And it was generally answered thus: "It is all that is made." I marveled how it might last, for it seemed it might suddenly have sunk into nothing because of its littleness. And I was answered in my understanding: "It lasts and ever shall, because God loves it."[3]

The Spirit is not simply the ubiquitous life-giving presence of God at work in the beginning and at every moment since, but the Spirit is also the one who draws and nudges creation towards its God-given goal. God did not make the cosmos as a finished product, such as a statue, that was intended to remain forever unchanged. On the contrary, he created it like a garden—full of potential to be drawn out over time. Eden was a work in progress to be tended by the humans and extended to the less hospitable areas beyond its bounds. The Spirit is one who guides creation to its glorious goal. This work of drawing creation towards its future destiny will come to light clearly when we consider the role of the Spirit in birthing the new creation.

TRINITY AND HUMANITY: DUST WITH A DESTINY

The climax of God's creative acts in Genesis 1 is the creation of humanity on the sixth day. The first poem in the Bible is uttered by God as he contemplates the creation of humans and then executes his plan (Gen 1:26). But what are human beings? The Bible teaches that humanity was created in the "image of God": "Then God said, 'Let us make humanity in our image, in our likeness, and let them rule over the fish of the sea and the birds of the air, over the livestock, over all the earth, and over all the creatures that move along the ground.' So God created humanity in his own image, in the image of God he created him; male and female he created them" (Gen 1:26–27).

Notice that God says "let *us* make humanity in *our* image." And notice that "our image" is further clarified as "the image of *God*." In context God can only be speaking to himself (not to the angels, nor other gods, nor the

---

3. Julian of Norwich, *Showings*, chap. 5, vision 1.

earth), and it is very unusual that he speaks using the plural. Perhaps the author was simply employing what we might call a "royal 'we.'" Nevertheless, in the light of the revelation we now possess, we see that the God who spoke is the Trinity, and we can perceive a richer meaning in the "us" and the "our" than even the original (human) author was able to. The "us" is Father, Son, and Spirit. But once we see that the God whom we image is Trinity, we need to ask what it means to be in the image of the Trinity. Well, a few things stand out from the context of Genesis 1 about the image of God.

First, several biblical scholars have argued convincingly that the garden of Eden is presented in Genesis as a temple in which the presence of the deity dwells. All temples in the ancient Near East had the image of a god—an idol—at their center. However, Yhwh forbids the creation of any images of himself, in part because he has already created his own image—humanity! God forbids the creation of idols partly because idols are dumb and powerless (Isa 41:21–24; 46)—nothing other than a human being could represent the living God in the earth. This is an absolutely stunning thought and gives humans a very high place in creation. It needs to be emphasized that the difference between Creator (Yhwh) and creature (the image) is not to be collapsed. The Bible is very clear that humanity is not God (Isa 40:6ff.). However, humanity is the *icon* of God and we need to be careful not to miss the magnitude of this claim either. I suggest that we use an analogy that, as with all analogies, has its weaknesses but will be useful later when we think about the incarnation. Think of Yhwh like a hand, and think of humanity like a rubber glove that has been molded to reflect the shape of that hand. The hand is not the glove, but the glove does represent the hand in certain ways (though not in all ways).

Second, immediately after creating humans in his image, "God blessed them and said to them, 'Be fruitful and increase in number; fill the earth and subdue it. Rule over the fish of the sea and the birds of the air and over every living creature that moves on the ground'" (Gen 1:28). Here God delegates his kingly rule of the world to a humanity filled with his divine breath. While it is grossly misleading to suggest that God only works in the world through humanity, God did plan, in part at least, to rule creation *through humanity*. This divine rule mediated through humanity is connected to the idea of humans as the "icons" of Yhwh: humans are to mediate Yhwh's kingly presence to the rest of creation. So, in context, the image of God is tied up with the idea that humans are those who rule the world as stewards on behalf of the Lord. I suggest that the "image of God" is not to be thought of a special *part* of a human being (e.g., our mind or our soul or our spirit) or a certain *capacity* (e.g., our capacity for rational thought, for creativity, or for language, etc.) but as a *divine calling.*[4] God calls humanity to the task of imaging him. Humanity may be dust (Gen 2:7) but we are *dust with a destiny.*

I want to add a little speculation of my own at this point.[5] I suggest that the Word himself was the primary model for humanity. It is God the Son who, according to the book of Hebrews, is "the radiance of God's glory and the exact representation of his being" (1:3). The Son is the one who has always mediated the rule of the Father in creation, and human dominion of the earth is, I suggest, a pale reflection of the Son's eternal rule. To be made in the likeness of the Son is, then, to be created in the image of God—for the Son himself is God and is also the exact representation of the Father. This also means that to be in the image of the Son is to be indirectly in the image of the Father. To that I would add that such imaging is only possible in the power of the Spirit.

Third, notice the wording in Gen 1:27: "So God created humanity in his own image, in the image of God he created him; *male and female he created them.*" This passage speaks of humanity and the image of God in the singular, and yet within that humanity and that image there is differentiation between male and female. This, combined with the fact that the commissions to "fill" and "subdue" creation require male and female working together, suggest that *relationship* is integral to what it is to be in the image of God, and that the marriage relationship is the model par excellence of this relational image bearing.[6] It is only in relationship that humans are able to work out the task of imaging God. If this is so, then we see here a dim analogy with the relational God in whose image we are.

The biblical story moves on to narrate the tragic fall of humanity into sin and the consequent expulsion from the source of eternal life in Eden

---

4. Of course, the call for humanity to image God does require that humans have certain capacities (such as reason, imagination, language, love, etc.). But my suggestion is that those things, without the divine call, do not constitute the "image of God." Being human is not simply about our biology—it is a *calling*, a *task*, a work in progress. For Christians, only Jesus is currently completely human: a perfect image of God. The rest of us are en route.

5. I ought to add that I subsequently discovered this idea in the work of St. Athanasius and he's one of the most important Christian theologians of all time . . . Phew!

6. Smail, *Like Father, Like Son.*

(Gen 3:22–24). The image of God in humanity is distorted (though not erased), and the relationships between human and human (3:7, 16; 4), humans and their environment (3:17–19), and humans and God (3:8, 23–24) are fractured. Using the rubber-glove analogy, we could see the glove as being torn and crumpled. The basic shape is still present for those who look carefully enough to see, but it is also warped and misshapen. The rest, as they say, is history. But God, in his covenant love for the world, would not abandon it to sin, chaos, and death and sets in motion a plan, conceived before the world began, to restore what was broken.

ISRAEL IN THE STORY OF SALVATION

The plan was to choose a single human couple that would be a second Adam and Eve—the origins of a restored human race. And so it was that God called Abraham and his wife Sarah. God made a covenant with a childless and landless couple and promised that they would have many descendants who would possess the land of Canaan (Gen 12:1–3). God would bless them and be their God. It is crucial to realize that God's plan was never to elect this man and his descendants (Israel) *instead of* the rest of humanity. It is not that God ever thought, "To hell with the rest of them! I'll just save this elect group of Israel!" On the contrary, a key point of the election of Abraham and his descendants was that through them God would bless the *whole* world (Gen 12:3). But God's unexpected way of saving the whole world begins with one man and his descendants.

And so it was that the nation of Israel, God's new people, his new humanity, descended from Abraham and Sarah. God rescued them from slavery in Egypt and made a covenant with them at Mount Sinai. He promised to be their God and to be present with them, but they had to obey his laws and statutes (Exodus 20). Thus Yhwh, in faithfulness to his promise to Abraham, brought his people to a new Eden in the land of Canaan, and there they were to live in obedience, and enjoy the consequent blessings of the divine presence among them. Stop for a moment and reflect on the parallels between Israel and Adam. God created Adam and placed him in Eden's garden to manage it. Adam enjoyed the divine presence and blessings, but he was also under orders to keep God's single commandment (do not eat from the tree in the middle of the garden). Similarly, God creates Israel, the new humanity descended from Abraham, and places them in the land of Canaan to manage it. They were to enjoy the divine presence and blessings but were under the covenant commandments that they must not disobey. The story of Israel was the story of Adam reenacted, and tragically the fall of Adam was also recapitulated in the fall of Israel. You don't have to read the Old Testament for long to see that Israel, just like Adam, disobeyed the laws of Yhwh, and just as the divine punishment of humanity climaxed in its expulsion from Eden (and thus from the source of eternal life), so the sin of Israel reached its climax in the exile in Babylon—away from the promised land.

Now God's plan was that he would save sinful, fallen humanity through Israel (Isa 42:1–7). Israel was to live in perfect obedience to the law of God and to model to the rest of the world a life of obedience and divine blessing (Deut 4:6–8). The nations would see and marvel and would be drawn to worship Yhwh with Israel in Jerusalem (Isa 60:1–16; 66:12, 18, 23). But Israel itself needed to be saved from sin (Isa 42:22–25; 46:8–13; 48). How can Israel be a light to the nations while living in darkness? (Isa 42:16, 18–25). But, odd as it may sound, God's plan had not gone astray. God always knew that Israel would fall into sin and would need to be saved. Israel shares with all other people the same sin-inclined human nature that makes perfect obedience to God's law a psychological impossibility (Rom 8:7–8). The problem was not with the law of God but with the sinful inclinations of those who had to live under it (Rom 7:7–20). God knew Israel would fail, but this was actually part of the plan—it prepared the way for Jesus.

The climax of the story of salvation comes with Jesus. Before we look at Jesus, we need to set the context in the biblical super-story. The prophets of Israel looked at the huge gap between what God had called Israel to be and their dreadful state of constant disobedience and exile. What hope could there possibly be? They looked to the future and spoke of a divine rescue. They said that God, in faithfulness to his covenant, would deliver Israel from exile and would bring her back to the land (Isa 43:5–7, 14–21). This return of Israel from the metaphorical death of exile was portrayed as a resurrection from the dead (Ezekiel 37). Yhwh would circumcise their hearts (Deut 30:6) then put his Holy Spirit in them and *enable them* to fulfill his laws (Ezek 36:26–27). This would be a new covenant (Jer 31:31–34). Then, at last, Israel would be the light to the nations that God had always intended, and all the nations of the world would come to worship Yhwh at the temple in Jerusalem (Isa 2:1–4). Wars would cease, idolatry would end (Isa 45:20–25), and a new age would begin. As time went on, many Jews began to think of this new age as beginning with the actual resurrection of the dead, a final judgment, and eternal life for the Spirit-filled people of God.

Into this picture fit the various images of messiahs (*mešiah* is Hebrew for "anointed one") found amongst the Jews at the time of Jesus. Many Jews looked for a new king like David, sent by Yhwh to rescue Israel from her enemies. This ruler would bring the new age to birth and would rule the world from Jerusalem. Others thought of the Messiah as a new High Priest who would purify the temple and restore acceptable worship. Jesus came to fulfill both messianic roles, though in unexpected ways.

Jesus's task was to be the Messiah of Israel and thus to save Israel. By saving Israel he would be putting God's plan back on track and save the whole world. As King and High Priest, Jesus is the representative of the whole nation of Israel. In his person and life he stands before Yhwh on behalf of the nation. In a representative sense, *he is Israel.* This is a hugely important point that lies at the heart of what I want to say about Jesus and the Christian life later. In the life of Jesus, the story of Israel is replayed on a miniature scale. Jesus lived in perfect obedience to God's covenant with Israel. He was the perfect Israelite. He was obedient Israel. In him, for the first time ever, Israel—in the person of her representative Messiah—fulfils her part of the covenant with Yhwh. On the cross Jesus takes upon himself the covenant curse of exilic death that Israel had experienced (Deut 28:15–68; Gal 3:13). In Jesus's resurrection, God is bringing Israel back from exile as the prophets had foretold. Jesus's resurrection is the fulfillment of the return from exile. The new age had begun! Then, just as the prophets had said, the Spirit was poured out on the Jewish people of God at Pentecost (Joel 2:28–32; Acts 2) and those from Gentile nations started coming to worship with Israel (Acts 10).

Now, in the light of the above sketch, we can see how Jesus relates to the whole of humanity. Recall the parallel that we drew between Israel and Adam. By playing out Israel's story in his own person, Jesus is actually also playing out the story of the whole human race. His obedience to Yhwh is not simply succeeding where Israel had failed, but it is also succeeding where Adam had failed. His execution was not merely bearing the curse of Israel's exile but also the curse of humanity's expulsion from Eden and the death that followed on its heels. His resurrection is not simply the return of Israel from exile but also the resurrection of the whole of humanity and, indeed, of the whole of creation. In Christ, the human story of expulsion, death, and re-creation is enacted.

However, there was something odd and unexpected about the dawning of the new age of eternal life. Instead of the whole world being involved in judgment, resurrection, and the outpouring of the Spirit (as many Jews had expected), it is the Messiah who experiences the final judgment (on the cross) and resurrection (on the first Easter) in his own person. This is the new age, but it is the new age writ small. It is the early Jewish Christ-believers who receive the Spirit of the new covenant on Pentecost, and it is the early Gentile Christ-believers who represent the nations coming to join Israel in worship. But it is clear that most people have not yet experienced the in-breaking of the new age. The present evil age is still very much with us, and we must await a future judgment and resurrection. However, that future has already been played out in the person of Jesus. It has already happened *in him*. The new age had dawned in the midst of the darkness of this age. It remains the case that many Jewish people today have still not entered into the experience of return from exile in their Messiah; many Gentiles have not yet entered into the experience of being grafted into the commonwealth of Israel, of receiving the Spirit and worshipping Yhwh. The new humanity of the new age is currently restricted to the *ekklēsia*[7]— the community of those Jews and Gentiles who have been united to the Messiah Jesus by the Spirit. In Christ, the *ekklēsia* is the new humanity (Eph 2:15). But even the *ekklēsia* only tastes the powers of the age to come (Heb 6:5). Followers of Christ still sin, still get sick, and still die; resurrection and eternal life are still awaited; the salvation of "all Israel" (Rom 11:26) and the full pilgrimage of the nations (Rev 21:22–27) lie in the future. For the time being we only experience these promises in small doses in the community of Christ.

Having seen a sketch of the big picture, we are now better placed to look at it again with Trinitarian eyes.

---

7. *Ekklēsia* is the Greek word usually translated as "church" in the New Testament. I have avoided the word "church" in this context simply because it has so many associations, gathered through the past two millennia, that it may hinder our attempts to understand the New Testament. I also try to avoid using the word *Christianity* (though not *Christian*) when speaking of the early Christ believers for the same reason. However, if understood in light of footnote 3 in the next chapter, I have no problems with it.

TRINITY AND THE STORY OF JESUS[8]

Pre-incarnation

"Before" God the Son became human in the person of Jesus, he existed in an eternal relationship of loving communion with the Father and the Spirit.[9] Nowhere is this clearer than in the intimate prayer of Jesus to his Father after the Last Supper. Here we snatch a glimpse of a glory shared in the Father's presence by the Son "before the world was made" (John 17:4–5). "No one has ever seen God," says John, "but God the One and Only, who is at the Father's side [i.e., the Son], has made him known" (John 1:18). "No one has ever gone into heaven except the one who came from heaven—the Son of Man" (John 3:13), and thus Jesus is uniquely qualified to reveal the Father precisely because he alone is the "exact representation of his [God's] being" (Heb 1:3) and has shared this glory in the Father's presence.

We have already seen that before the incarnation the Son and Spirit were also involved in bringing about and sustaining creation. The Old Testament is not explicit about the Trinity because it was only in the incarnation that it came into focus. However, in hindsight Christians can see that all of God's work in the world before the incarnation must have been through his two hands. Certainly the Spirit as an agent of God's presence and work in the world—God's "arm" or "hand"—is clear in the Old Testament (e.g., Num 11:17, 29; Judg 11:29; 15:14–15; Zech 4:6; Isa 63:10). So the Christian, seeing with clearer eyes than those present at the time and even than those writing about the events in Scripture, may look back to the great events in Israel's history, such as the exodus from Egypt, and look for hints of the activity of the Spirit. With Christian eyes we can see, for instance, that the pillar of cloud and fire that accompanied the exodus generation was the presence of the Spirit. We may also look for the work of God's creative "Word" and his "Wisdom" in the Old Testament, which were also the agents of Yhwh's activity. With Christian eyes we can see here the silhouette of Christ, the *Logos* (Word) and *Sophia* (Wisdom) of God. The early Christian community was not slow to see pre-incarnate

---

8. For a wonderfully rich Trinitarian theological understanding of Jesus, see Thomas F. Torrance's two volumes, *Incarnation* and *Atonement*.

9. I put "before" in scare quotes because if God is timeless (and I am inclined to think that God is), then in the divine life there is no *temporal* before and after (not in any literal sense). But there can still be non-temporal modes of "before" and "after."

manifestations of the eternal Son in the story of Israel. With caution we may follow suit.

Incarnation

It is with the coming of Jesus that the Trinity comes into clearer view. Obviously the place of God the Son is clear enough, for it was he who was "made flesh" (John 1:14). A very common motif in the writings of Paul is that of the Son who "laid aside his majesty" and came amongst us as a man. "Your attitude should be the same as that of Christ Jesus: Who, being in very nature God, did not consider equality with God something to be grasped, but made himself nothing, taking the very nature of a servant, being made in human likeness" (Phil 2:5–7). Here Jesus in his pre-incarnate state (his "pre-Jesus state," we could say) was in very nature God. The issue in the text is Christ's attitude to this equality with God. He did not think of his equality with God (the Father) as a matter of being served but as something to express in service to others, and so he came in the humble service of humanity as a human. The Word voluntarily chose to become incarnate as Jesus out of love for his Father and for the world.

One crucial aspect of Christian teaching about the incarnation is that Jesus was genuinely and fully human, even if he was not merely human. As John's Gospel puts it, "the Word *became* flesh" (John 1:14). Christ was as human as we are. Like us, he experienced real temptation (Heb 4:15), tiredness (Mark 4:38), hunger (Luke 4:2), thirst (John 4:7; 19:28), mental and physical pain (Mark 14:32–33; 15:17–19), and real death (John 19:30).

So the place of the Son in the story of Jesus is fairly obvious. But what about the role of the Father? Christ came into the world as a human because he was *sent by his Father.* This theme is repeated over and over again in John's Gospel (e.g., John 6:38–40; 17:18; 20:21). The first person of the Trinity always seems to be the initiator in God's relation to creation, and thus it is no surprise to find that the Father initiates the incarnation out of his great love for humanity. But we should not think that the Son comes reluctantly, out of a sense of begrudging duty. He came because he loves his Father and also because he is the Good Shepherd who loves his sheep and lays down his life for them (John 10:11). Christ and the Father are completely united in purpose. So the Father *sends* and the Son *is sent.* But what of the Spirit?

Faced with an angel who has just told her that she will give birth to the Messiah of Israel, an astonished Mary replies, "How will this be . . . since I am a virgin?" The angel answered, "The Holy Spirit will come upon you, and the power of the Most High will overshadow you. So the holy one to be born will be called the Son of God" (Luke 1:34–35). It was the Spirit who enabled the Son to become human in the womb of Mary. Without the work of the life-giving Spirit there would have been no incarnation.

But why is the humanity of Christ so important? Well, the answer to that will become clear gradually over the rest of this chapter and the next. However, to make a start at getting our heads around it, let's return to the analogy of the rubber glove that we introduced in the discussion of the creation of humanity in the image of God. You will remember that I likened humanity to a glove that was created in the image of a hand but that had been torn and crumpled by sin. The incarnation is God's mission to restore the image of God in humanity—to mend the glove—and, by so doing, to mend the whole of creation. What happens in Jesus is that the hand of God himself, he in whose image the glove was made in the first place, puts on the glove. In Jesus, something absolutely unique in the history of the world takes place. You see, in creation there was the hand and there was the glove (the image of the hand), but the hand never put the glove on. The glove represented the hand in the world but it was never more than a glove—an image of the hand. God heals the damaged glove by putting his own hand into it and reshaping the glove around it. Jesus is the "hand" of God in the "glove" of humanity, healing and restoring the damaged image.[10] However, you may find St. Athanasius' alternative analogy more helpful. He wrote that

> The Word of God came in his own Person, because it was He alone, the Image of the Father, Who could recreate man made after the Image . . . You know what happens when a portrait that has been painted on a panel becomes obliterated through external stains. The artist does not throw away the panel, but the subject of the portrait has to come and sit for it again, and then the likeness is re-drawn on the same material. Even so it was with the All-holy Son of God. He, the Image of the Father, came and dwelt in our midst, in order that he might renew mankind after Himself.[11]

---

10. All analogies have weaknesses. The one is no exception. Handle with care.

11. Athanasius, *On the Incarnation*, chap. III, 13–14.

Ministry

The public ministry of Jesus began after his baptism in the river Jordan by John the Baptist. This event was a revelation of the divine Trinity—the Father spoke from heaven of and to his Son and then bestowed the divine Spirit on him.

> Then Jesus came from Galilee to the Jordan to be baptized by John. But John tried to deter him, saying, "I need to be baptized by you, and do you come to me?" Jesus replied, "Let it be so now; it is proper for us to do this to fulfill all righteousness." Then John consented. As soon as Jesus was baptized, he went up out of the water. At that moment heaven was opened, and he saw the Spirit of God descending like a dove and lighting on him. And a voice from heaven said, "This is my Son, whom I love; with him I am well pleased." (Matt 3:13–17)

Viv Thomas writes, "This is a wonderful moment in the story of salvation. I feel like I am on the edge of the Grand Canyon and can only see for two meters. Yet, I can hear the echo of the vastness by which I am placed."[12] Then Jesus, empowered by the Spirit, enters the wilderness to be tested by Satan before beginning his ministry. Jesus is the person anointed with the Spirit par excellence and is thus enabled to function as the "anointed one" (*mešiah* in Hebrew; *Christos* in Greek). To him God gives the Spirit "without measure"! (John 3:34). It is in this capacity, as the Lord of the Spirit, that he will be the one who, after his ascension, will "baptize" people in that Spirit (John 1:32–34). But, for the time of his ministry, the Spirit could not be given because Jesus was not yet glorified through his death-resurrection-ascension (John 7:38–39).

When we think of the ministry of Jesus, we tend to think of two outstanding aspects of it: his *words* and his *works*. If there are two things any school child could tell you about Jesus, they are that he was a great teacher and that he was reputed to do wonderful miracles. The words of Jesus are not merely the words of the Son spoken with an unprecedented authority (Matt 7:28–29) but also the words of the Father (John 14:10). Jesus said that the words he spoke he spoke not on his own authority but on that of his Father—he spoke only what he heard from his Father: "For I did not speak of my own accord, but the Father who sent me commanded me what to say and how to say it. I know that his command leads to eternal life. So whatever I say is just what the Father has told me to say" (John 12:49–50).

12. Thomas, *Paper Boys*, 37–38.

And it was the Spirit who opened the hearts of some of Jesus's listeners (and some of the readers of the Gospels) to understand and believe his teaching. The Spirit enables the words of Jesus to mediate life to his hearers—"The Spirit gives life; the flesh counts for nothing. The words I have spoken to you are spirit and they are life" (John 6:63). So it is that to hear Jesus is to hear the Father through Jesus as the Spirit enables us.

Jesus's miracles are clearly works performed by the Son, but they are more accurately seen as the works of the Father performed through Jesus by the power of the Spirit. In John's Gospel Jesus often says that he comes in his Father's name (e.g., John 5:43) and that the works he does are actually the works he sees his Father doing: those that the Father has commanded him to do (John 14:11). He does nothing but on the Father's initiative: "I tell you the truth, the Son can do nothing by himself; he can do only what he sees his Father doing, because whatever the Father does the Son also does" (John 5:19). In this way Jesus exegetes the invisible Father (John 1:18) so that seeing Jesus is like seeing the Father (John 14:9). The invisible God becomes visible in the words and works of Christ. And what of the place of the Spirit? It is the Spirit who enables Jesus to perform the miracles he does: "But if I drive out demons by the Spirit of God, then the kingdom of God has come upon you" (Matt 12:28).

But what Christians often miss is that Jesus's life was lived both as the life of the divine Word in our midst, perfectly revealing the Father, and as a perfect human life. So, on the one hand, the signs and actions of Jesus point to him as the one in whom the God of Israel was personally present with his people. Jesus was no mere glove—he was the hand itself in the glove. Thus Jesus performs the saving actions that the Old Testament had said that Yhwh himself would perform on Israel's behalf. On the other hand, he walked in the power of the Spirit as a human being or, to revert to the glove analogy, he lived his life as a whole and perfectly shaped glove and not as a torn and crumpled one. Jesus was the one who kept the covenant fully and was thus the perfect Israelite. Indeed, in his role as the King of Israel (the Messiah/Christ) he represented the whole nation of Israel before Yhwh, and thus in his life he played out the role of the nation of Israel-fully-keeping-the-covenant. Paul would spread the focus further still and speak of Jesus as the Second Adam, who fully obeyed where Adam had disobeyed (Rom 5:12–21). In Christ's life the covenant relationship between God and humanity (and not simply God and Israel) is perfectly lived out. That, by the way, is how our relationship with God is so secure—because the covenant between God and humanity/Israel is fulfilled between God and the

Messiah, both of whom are perfectly loyal to the relationship. We share in the Messiah's obedient and stable covenant relationship with the Father.

What makes things a little confusing is that the hand (Christ's divine nature) and the glove (Christ's human nature) act as one, because they are united in the one person of Jesus. Thus the very same actions are the actions of a perfect human being full of the Spirit (a restored glove), and they are also the actions of God the Son (the hand) acting *as* God on earth.

Cross

Lady Julian of Norwich wrote, "when I see the cross I see the Trinity." Sadly, the story of the cross is sometimes told without any reference to the Father or the Spirit—as though only Jesus was involved in the saving work that took place. The picture is of the Son looking down from heaven, seeing the predicament of humanity, deciding to come down and die for us, and then doing just that. The danger of making Jesus the sole initiator in salvation is that a very distorted image results when the Father is introduced into the picture. I have met Christians who believed that God the Father simply wanted to punish humanity—but luckily Jesus loved us and leaped up from his throne saying, "Please, dad, don't punish them . . . I love them. Punish me instead." In this view, the Father agreed and sent Jesus to the cross in our place. This picture of the cross, in which a loving Jesus saves us from a wrathful Father, is a nasty distortion of Christian faith. Sadly, however, it is not terribly uncommon. One possibly finds cultural echoes of this distortion in the fate of Neo (the "Messiah"), when in the film *The Matrix Revolutions* he creates peace between the wrathful machine-mind (the Father) and vulnerable humanity by offering himself in a cruciform pose to absorb the virus that is Agent Smith (he who knew no sin became sin for us . . .). Now he is "at the right-hand side" of the Machine, and we await his return! Is God the Father like that? No! Scripture presents an entirely different picture in which the Father loved the world so much that he sent his Son (John 3:16). The Father is not reluctant to forgive and is certainly not itching to punish sinners. The Father longs to reconcile the world to himself and he initiates the plan of salvation to achieve this goal (2 Cor 5:18–19; Rom 5:8).

We often focus on the sufferings of Christ on the cross, but how often do we stop to think about the sufferings of the Father? Scripture says that God's love for us was *so great* that he *even* gave up the one who was most precious to him—his only Son (John 3:16). By speaking in this way the

Bible is alerting us to what the Father gives up at Calvary. Some recent theology has paid special attention to this theme. Jürgen Moltmann writes of how "the Son suffers in his love being forsaken by the Father as he dies. The Father suffers in his love the grief of the death of the Son."[13]

The Son is clearly the one who dies in our place as our representative. Here the real humanity of Christ is so important. The Bible speaks in the language of God "handing over" or "delivering up" Jesus to death. Just as sinful humanity was "delivered up" to judgment and wrath (Rom 1:18ff.), so the Father "did not spare his own Son, but gave him up for us all" (Rom 8:32). God "made him who had no sin to be sin for us" (2 Cor 5:21) and thus Christ became accursed at Calvary (Gal 3:13). But it is not simply the Father who "delivers up" his Son. Paul also speaks of "the Son of God, who loved me and *gave himself* for me" (Gal 2:20). The Father and Jesus are united about the decision that Jesus should die for us. Christ took on our humanity and, though he did not sin, he experienced our broken and cursed state on the cross—exhausting the consequences of our sin and then, in the resurrection, healing what had been broken by rebellion and death. If Christ were not divine, he could not *save* us, but if he were not human he could not save *us*.

The alienation, curse, and God-forsakenness that fracture our relationship with God and cripple our human existence are, on the cross, taken into the very life of God himself and overcome. "My God! My God! Why have you forsaken me?"

> The ["division"] in God [at the cross] must contain the whole uproar of history within itself. Men must be able to recognize rejection, the curse, and final nothingness in it. The cross stands between the Father and the Son in all the harshness of its forsakenness. If one describes the life of God within the Trinity as the "history of God" (Hegel), this history of God contains within itself the whole abyss of godforsakenness, absolute death, and the non-God . . . All human history, however much it may be determined by guilt and death, is taken up into this "history of God," i.e., into the Trinity . . . There is no suffering which in this history of God is not God's suffering; no death which has not been God's death in the history of Golgotha.[14]

---

13. Moltmann, *The Crucified God*, 245 (italics mine). I ought to add a warning that God is very different from human beings and that we cannot know exactly what it means to say that God "suffers." Such language, as all language about God, needs to be approached cautiously and carefully.

14. Ibid., 246. The warnings of the previous footnote apply to this quotation too.

But what is the Spirit doing on Good Friday? I think that a good case can be made for the following claims. First, he is enabling Jesus to face the ordeal ahead just as he enables believers to face their cruciform suffering with Christ. Second, it is through the eternal Spirit that Jesus offers his death without blemish as an acceptable sacrifice to the Father (Heb 9:14). This is perhaps because the Spirit enables Jesus to live the sinless life that allows him to be the spotless, sacrificial Lamb of God. Alternatively, perhaps the "eternal Spirit" is like the "eternal fire" on the altar in the temple on which sacrificial animals were offered (1 Esd 6:23). On this view, the sacrifice of Christ is somehow made effective through the Spirit's work. Third, on the cross the Spirit was sharing in the sufferings of Christ, groaning with Christ as he identified himself with the broken creation, moaning as a woman in childbirth bringing Christ to new life in resurrection (Rom 8:19–27).[15] Finally, the Spirit also is the one that works in the lives of those who hear the foolish message of the cross so that they can perceive the wisdom of God in it. The Spirit opens sin-blinded eyes to see the "folly" and "weakness" of the cross as being God's wise and powerful way of saving the world (1 Cor 1:18—2:16).

Resurrection

It was God the Father who raised Jesus from the dead, and he did it through the Spirit. Sometimes Christians speak as if Jesus raised himself from the dead, but the New Testament very rarely speaks in such terms—and when it does so, it is clearly only on the authority of the Father that the Son can be said to raise himself (John 10:18). The New Testament almost always attributes the resurrection of Jesus to God the Father (e.g., Acts 2:24). "And if the Spirit of him who raised Jesus from the dead is living in you, he who raised Christ from the dead will also give life to your mortal bodies through his Spirit, who lives in you" (Rom 8:11). "He who raised Christ from the dead" is clearly God (the Father). But it is just as clear that it was through the life-giving Spirit that he did this, and it is through the same life-giving Spirit that he will raise believers at the last day. As with every other divine act, the resurrection is a Trinitarian event—indeed, it is an event within the very inner-life of the Trinity.

---

15. We shall develop this idea at more length in the chapter on the Trinity and lament.

Ascension

The ascension is the climax of the story of Jesus, and as such it plays a crucial role in New Testament thought. In the ascension we can see the one man, Jesus, ruling from heaven in a dual capacity—as a glorified human in the image of God exercising dominion and also as the divine Lord, Yhwh himself. I'll unpack that claim briefly.

First, the ascended Jesus rules from heaven as the *Second Adam*. Recall that Jesus is the representative of Israel and of humanity itself. Humans were created in the image of God (the Son?) to mediate God's rule over creation. The image of God is restored by the resurrection, and humanity is ruling again at the right hand of God in the ascension bringing the story of salvation to completion in Christ.[16] What may surprise you about this is that the ascension to God's right hand in biblical thought, or so I propose, is still tied up with Jesus's *humanity*. I tentatively suggest that this is seen in the use made of Psalm 8 in Hebrews 2. Psalm 8 is a classic text about the created status of humanity: "You made him a little lower than the heavenly beings and crowned him with glory and honor. You made him ruler over the works of your hands; you put everything under his feet." This amazing role for humanity as the ruler of God's works is exactly the role that the New Testament attributes to the ascended Jesus. Look very carefully at the following passage from Hebrews.

> It is not to angels that he has subjected the world to come, about which we are speaking. But there is a place where someone has testified: "What is man that you are mindful of him, the son of man that you care for him? You made him a little lower than the angels; you crowned him with glory and honor and put everything under his feet" [Ps 8]. In putting everything under him [i.e., humanity], God left nothing that is not subject to him. Yet at present we do not see everything subject to him. But we see Jesus, who was made a little lower than the angels, now crowned with glory and honor because he suffered death, so that by the grace of God he might taste death for everyone. (Heb 2:5–9)

The human condition is that of having been created by God, in God's image, to have dominion, yet finding that sin has frustrated this destiny. The psalmist, however, celebrates that divine calling of "man"/"son of man"

---

16. One ought to acknowledge the missing step in the theology—that the destiny of humanity is transferred first to the nation of Israel and then to Jesus, the Messiah of Israel. So the resurrection is first the return of Israel from exile and the ascension is the restored reign of Israel before it is the restoration and reign of humanity.

as still in place. Looking around, though, the writer of Hebrews observes that "at present we do not see everything subject to him" (i.e., to humanity). What we do see is Jesus—the representative human who has embraced total solidarity with humanity (2:9–18)—"crowned with glory and honor" and thus restoring human dominion in his own person. By tasting death for everyone, he brings "many sons to glory" (2:10), enabling them to share in the renewed glory bestowed upon humanity.

Christians often think of Jesus's human life as effectively ceasing with the cross. On this view, the resurrection and ascension of Jesus show him getting back into his previous role as Word of the Father—still God but no longer a man. But that is simply false! Christ is *still human now* and ever shall be. Even his role of ruling creation is, stunning as it may sound, his role as the Second Adam. And with the restoration of humanity the rest of creation is resurrected (Rom 8:19–21).

At the same time as the rule of Christ from heaven is the rule of a restored humanity in the image of the divine Son, so it is also the rule of the divine Son himself who does not merely rule *on behalf of* God but rules *as* God. The ascension is the return of the divine Son to the place he occupied before the incarnation (John 6:62), to the glory and throne he shared with the Father from before the creation (John 17:4–5). Thus the ascended Jesus is the one who has the name above every name (i.e., the name of "Yhwh") and the one who, when every knee in creation bows in worship on the last day, receives the worship due to Yhwh alone (Isa 45:23/Phil 2:9–11). The book of Revelation portrays the ascended Jesus sitting upon *the very same throne* as God (22:1, 3), taking God's titles to himself (1:8/1:17; 21:6/22:13) and receiving the worship of all creation (Rev 5). Yet again we see that the ascended Jesus *is Yhwh* ruling from heaven.

Jesus' rule, then, is both representative (he rules as a glorified human) and unique (he rules as Yhwh and is thus the object of the worship of the rest of creation for all eternity). When we are resurrected and glorified we will rule with Christ, sharing in the reign of the restored humanity (Rom 8:17; 2 Tim 2:12; Rev 20:6; Eph 2:6). But we will forever be subordinate to the rule of Jesus, the divine Word, before whom angels bow in endless adoration. To return to the rubber glove analogy, the eternal Son was originally "the hand" of God—the model upon which "the rubber glove" of humanity was based. This analogy is intended to suggest that there are similarities between the eternal Son and humanity in the image of God (it wouldn't be an image otherwise), but there are also dissimilarities. The glove is not and never will be the hand. In the incarnation, the hand puts on the damaged glove and replays the human story to guide it out of the mess (Rom 8:3)—in his life there was perfect obedience to God; on the cross the damaged glove is melted down in the fires of death; in the resurrection the glove is remolded; and in the ascension the glove is restored to its proper function of mediating God's rule in creation. In his humanity our humanity is restored, but he remains the second person of the Trinity and in this way differs from every other human past, present, and future. In this capacity he is the proper object of worship, for when we worship him we worship one who does not simply represent God (as a mere human would), but one who is himself also the very God he represents! Mind blowing stuff!

The great proof that Jesus has ascended to the right hand of the Father and brought human history to its climax is Pentecost. Jesus received the Spirit and then poured out the Spirit on the *ekklēsia*. As Peter said on the day of Pentecost, "Exalted to the right hand of God, he [Jesus] has received from the Father the promised Holy Spirit and has poured out what you now see and hear" (Acts 2:33). The Spirit, in other words, comes to us *from* the Father, *through* the Son. In the Old Testament and Jewish tradition it is only ever God who pours out the Spirit, so Jesus, in his capacity as dispenser of the Spirit, is exercising his divine lordship. Now that Jesus has been glorified by death-resurrection-ascension, the Spirit is available to all who call upon the name of the Lord (Acts 2:38–39).

The ascended Christ fulfils Psalm 110, which speaks of the King as "a priest in the order of Melchizedek." Melchizedek, the mysterious ruler of Jerusalem that Abraham met (Genesis 14), was both a priest and a king—and the ascended Jesus also fulfils both roles. He has entered into the throne room of God the Father and there acts on our behalf as High Priest—interceding for us, offering his sacrificial death before the Father, and worshipping the Father. We shall explore Christ's role as High Priest more carefully when we think about the Trinity worshipping in chapter 5. But the reign of this priest-king still awaits a future consummation—he must rule *until* he has put all his enemies beneath his feet (1 Cor 15:25–28). To this future we now turn.

TRINITY AND THE FUTURE REDEMPTION OF CREATION

Christians believe that at the end of the age, God will judge the world. Those who have confessed Christ will be rescued while those who refuse the gospel invitation of life in Christ will remain in death and experience the full consequences of a life lived in rebellion against God. But the God to whom the world is accountable is the Trinity. The Father is the ultimate judge of humanity, but Jesus says that the Father has delegated the act of judgment to him (John 5:22–23, 27). Jesus mediates God's judgment just as he mediates God's creation and God's salvation. The Spirit brings this future judgment of God into the present and, in a sense, "judges the world" (John 16).

The goal of God's salvation is not saving disembodied souls for heaven but redeeming all creation in all its physicality. The Father will do for our bodies what he did for Jesus' body and, more than that, he will do for the whole physical universe what he did for Jesus' body. That is to say that the destiny of the world is resurrection—new creation (Rom 8:18–23). If Christ's bodily resurrection means anything at all, it means that Yhwh is committed to the physical world he has created. The world Yhwh created was not junk, and Yhwh will not junk it. This new creation is the act of Father, Son, and Spirit. It is God who makes all things new, but he does it through Christ's own incarnation, death, and resurrection by the Spirit. Only because of the cross-resurrection is death defeated. Only thus can our bodies and the universe be "raised immortal." Without the Son there is no new creation, for if Christ was not raised we are dead in our sins and without hope for a future after our death (1 Cor 15:16–19). But Christ has been raised by the Spirit and, as with Christ, it is the Spirit who raises us. The new age will be (and now is) the age of the Spirit, in which God is present amongst his people in ways never before experienced.

Yhwh puts his Spirit in believers now as a deposit guaranteeing our future resurrection (Eph 1:13–14). The Spirit in us is like a nuclear bomb that is leaking radiation, except that in the Spirit's case that "radiation" is the very life of Yhwh himself. For the time being the Spirit in us leaks eternal life into our mortal lives, but when Christ returns the Spirit in us will "explode" and rip through our bodies with "atomic," resurrection power and we shall be transformed in the twinkling of an eye (1 Cor 15:51–55).

Christ will return, the dead will be raised, and the enemies of sin and death defeated at the cross will be put under Christ's feet, making his victory complete (1 Cor 15:25–28). Paul speaks of how all things in heaven and on earth will be "summed up" in Christ (Eph 1:10) and reconciled to God (Col 1:20). Then he will hand over the kingdom to God the Father and God will be "all in all" (1 Cor 15:28). *This* is the Trinitarian future of the world.

three

The Trinitarian Geography
of the Christian Life

WE HAVE SEEN HOW the Trinity is important to the biblical super-story—
but what about the normal day-to-day life of Christians? The Christian life
involves meeting with other Christians for fellowship, prayer, and worship.
We engage in mission to bring the gospel to a world in darkness, we read
the Bible and seek to live lives that honor the Messiah. What has the Trinity
got to do with those kinds of things? In this chapter we will begin to see how
the Trinity is intimately connected to every aspect of the Christian life—
from the cradle to the grave and beyond. While chapter 5 will specifically
discuss worship and prayer, the goal of this chapter is to bring the Trinity
into focus at the heart of the Christian life—to highlight the relevance of
the doctrine and to provide some fuel for more overtly Trinitarian songs
and prayers. We begin with the Christian birth.

TRINITY AND BECOMING A CHRISTIAN

Becoming a Christian is a deeply Trinitarian experience—even if we aren't
overtly aware of it. To see why this is so we need to appreciate our spiritual
condition before conversion.[1] According to the Bible, we are so blinded
to spiritual truth when we are outside Christ that we can't see the glory,
power, and wisdom of God in the gospel (1 Cor 1:18ff.; 2:14). Paul explains
that the "god of this age [i.e., Satan] has blinded the minds of unbelievers,

1. The following does not discuss the situation of those brought up as Christians, but
rather of people who convert to Christ.

so that they cannot see the light of the gospel of the glory of Christ, who is the image of God" (2 Cor 4:4). Our minds are so warped by sin that left to ourselves we are hostile towards God (Rom 8:5–8). We are spiritually "dead" (Eph 2:1) and powerless to recognize our predicament, let alone do anything about it. So how is it that people do come to repentance and faith in Christ? Because of the work of God: Yhwh, Christ, and the Spirit. Perhaps we could picture becoming a Christian as follows: *The Father draws us close to his own heart (having reconciled us in Christ's death) by stretching out the hand of his Spirit, which draws us to the hand of his Son. Then, grasped between the hands of Spirit and of Son we are drawn to the Father and held in a Trinitarian embrace.*

Reconciliation with Yhwh occurs only through Christ and his work on the cross (Col 1:20). Nobody comes to the Father except through the Son (John 14:6), but we cannot even come to the Son unless the Father draws us (John 6:65)—and the way in which the Father does that is by working in our hearts and minds by his Spirit (1 Cor 2:6–16). It is the Spirit who enables us to see the truth of the gospel, to believe and to repent. He is the one who causes the blindfold of sin to fall from our eyes. So it is not as though God does his bit towards salvation by sending the Messiah to die and then we chip in with our contribution by repenting and trusting. Of course, the message of the good news requires a response of repentance and trust, but even that response is God's gracious gift to us!

Having put our trust in the Lord Jesus and turned away from our former way of life, we are baptized into Christ's body, the *ekklēsia*,[2] "in the name of the Father and of the Son and of the Holy Spirit" (Matt 28:19). In the New Testament it is more common to speak of being "baptized into Christ" or "in the name of Jesus." However, even this needs to be understood in a Trinitarian way, because to be initiated into Christ is to come to relate to Father and Spirit as Christ relates to them. Thus even our initiation into the Christian community by baptism is an initiation into a renewed relationship with the triune God.

The essence of becoming a Christian is that God the Father sends the Spirit of his Son to dwell in us as a sign that we belong to him (Gal 4:6). A Christian is one who has been baptized by Christ in the Holy Spirit into the body of the *ekklēsia* (Mark 1:8; 1 Cor 12:13). There is much we could say about this, but all we need to note here is that this Spirit-baptism, or what

---

2. In this chapter I will use "church" and *ekklēsia* interchangeably, but my use of both terms needs to be understood in the light of the comments in note 5.

John calls being "born of water and the Spirit" (John 3:5), is a fully Trinitarian experience.[3] The Father gives the Spirit to us by giving him to Christ, and then Christ pours the Spirit out upon us.

The Messiah and the Father are in heaven, but both are in us *through the Spirit*. It is because of the interpenetration of the Father and the Son in the Spirit (Greek *perichorēsis*) that the Spirit within us is the "water" that conducts the "electricity" of the presence of Father and Son to us. As God's Spirit, he pours out love for the Father in our hearts (Rom 5:5), enabling us to cry out "Abba! Father!" (Gal 4:6; Rom 8:15–16). As the Spirit of Christ he reveals Christ to us and teaches us the way of Christ (John 15:26; 16:12–15).

The earliest Christians knew much about charismatic experiences of God's empowering presence, and they understood those experiences in proto-Trinitarian ways. Every experience of God is Trinitarian—there is no other way to experience God; there is no other God to experience.

So I am not recommending an approach more concerned with getting our theology right than with knowing and encountering God. I am saying that we need a theology that helps us understand our experience of God and relate to God more adequately. Charismatic experience and good theology should go hand in hand.

TRINITY AND THE EKKLĒSIA

People in the modern Western world increasingly tend to think of religion as a private thing—something between "one man and his god(s)." Often such attitudes can creep into Christian congregations, and the focus becomes *my* relationship with God, Jesus as *my* personal savior (or therapist?), *my* ministry, *my* calling, *my* prayer life, *my* lifestyle, *my* worship experiences, and so on. As a teenager, I thought the pinnacle of spirituality was to be able to survive on my own with God "in the desert"—without any need of other believers. The super-spiritual Christian was the loner, Clint Eastwood "Christian with no name" who wanders into the town, blows the people away with his double-barreled relationship with God, and then leaves again,

---

3. I ought to say that I affirm the importance of the Pentecostal experience of the empowering of the Spirit and the role of gifts of the Spirit. I would, however, refer to such power encounters as being "filled with the Spirit" rather than being "baptized in the Spirit." It is impossible, in my view, to be a Christian and not to have been baptized in the Spirit (1 Cor 12:13). However, I do not want to make an issue of this (partly because I may be mistaken), so any Pentecostal must feel free to simply adapt the way I state things.

having led the locals to aspire to the giddy heights of his loner spirituality. Presumably church is only necessary, then, for weaker Christians (i.e., most of us) who still need encouragement from other humans!

This view of the Christ-following life is up the creek without a paddle and is the spiritual equivalent of handing a drowning man a concrete life-jacket! The *ekklēsia* is not simply a club of like-minded people who meet until they are strong enough to go it alone. Nor is it about being part of a social club of like-minded individuals. Being a follower of Jesus is all about being part of God's community. The *ekklēsia* is the family of God sharing one Father, the body and bride of Christ, and the temple of the Holy Spirit. God's plan has never been to save lots of individuals who will all relate to him individually with "Jaaaayy-zus" as their personal savior! God's plan has always been to create a human community of people who love God and love each other. That is what humanity was all about in creation. That is what God's new humanity of Israel was all about. That is what the *ekklēsia*—the community of restored humanity in Jesus, composed of Messiah-believing Jews and Gentiles—is all about. Being a Christian just *is* being part of that new humanity in Christ. So the Clint Eastwood "Christian with no name" is not a model of spirituality to aspire to but an ugly mutant in urgent need of help.

The *ekklēsia* is a Trinitarian creation. To see how this is so, let's begin with the biblical metaphor of the *ekklēsia* as the body of Christ. When we become Christians, we are baptized into Christ's body in the waters of baptism and the cloud of the Spirit (1 Cor 10:2). Christ is a single human being with a single body that is currently seated at the right hand of the Father. As we have seen, Christ represents all humanity before God. All humanity "in him" participates in whatever he is before God. Christians are those who are placed "into Christ" by the Spirit, such that what Christ is the church also is "in him." So if the Messiah has one unified body, then "in the Messiah" the *ekklēsia* is one, unified body—a single organism with many parts that play different roles but function together as one.

This has implications for thinking about Christian unity today. The unity of the *ekklēsia* is not something humans must bring about, because it is something that God has already achieved "in Christ." In this Second Adam God has brought into existence one new humanity in which all the old social divisions are abolished. There is neither Jew nor Greek, slave nor free, male nor female in Christ (Gal 3:28). The challenge for the church is to live out in practice what we already are in Christ. The *ekklēsia* lives caught between the present evil age and the age to come, tasting, but not fully enjoying, the powers of the kingdom of God. This means that we do not live in the fullness of the unity that we have in Christ. Paul faced tensions and divisions within some of the communities he planted, and he had to challenge the believers in those communities to live in ways consistent with the new reality brought into existence with Christ. Sadly, as is clear for all to see, Christian unity is not something that just happens automatically. So at the heart of New Testament ethics there are Messiah-shaped, community-strengthening virtues to be cultivated (love being the highest of them), and there are also sinful, community-eroding vices to be actively avoided (dissension, strife, anger, gossip, and so on). We need to actively seek to maintain the unity of the Spirit and not to simply lie back and let it all happen (Eph 4:3).

The image of the *ekklēsia* as the body of Christ is related to another image—namely that of the temple of the Holy Spirit (1 Cor 3:16–17). The link is this: Christ himself is the fulfillment of the old covenant temple that was based in Jerusalem. The temple was the most sacred place on earth—the place in which heaven and earth kissed each other. With the coming of Jesus, the kiss of God's presence found its deepest expression not in a building but in a person. The Messiah's body is the true temple of God—the location of the divine presence of the Spirit (John 1:14; 2:19–22). As Christ's body is the temple of the Spirit, so too the *ekklēsia* (1 Cor 3:16–17) and its individual members (1 Cor 6:19) are the temple of the Spirit "in Christ." The *ekklēsia*, in other words, is the community in which God lives by his Spirit because it is the body of Christ. "In him [Christ] the whole building is being joined together and rises to become a holy temple in the Lord. And in him you too are being built together to become a dwelling in which God lives by his Spirit" (Eph 2:21–22).

Let's consider two more metaphors for the church—God's holy nation and God's family. We need to recall from the previous chapter that Jesus the Messiah is the one who represented the whole nation of Israel before God. If Christ is the King of Israel, and represents the nation of Israel, then the Gentile wing of the *ekklēsia* is joined to Israel by being "in him." This means that the Gentile wing of the *ekklēsia* participates in Israel's identity as God's chosen people, his holy nation, his royal priesthood (1 Pet 2:9).[4]

---

4. This is the case even if 1 Peter was addressed specifically to *Jewish* believers in Jesus rather than to Christians in general. On the addressees of 1 Peter see Liebengood, "Don't Be Like Your Fathers."

Moreover, this participation of the Gentile wing of the *ekklēsia* in Israel does not displace God's covenantal commitment to the Jewish nation as his people.[5] Just as Israel knew Yhwh as Father (Hos 11:1), so Christians relate to God as Father and to each other as brother and sister. The *ekklēsia* is the family of the Father, the holy people of God.

In our lives together we are placed "in Christ" by the Spirit and so relate to God the Father "in" the Son, by the Spirit. We relate to Christ as the head of the body and we know the Spirit's indwelling, empowering, and gifting. Being *ekklēsia* is about as Trinitarian as you can get!

Many contemporary theologians see the community of the Trinity as a model for God's community of the *ekklēsia*. In God one finds mutual love between persons-in-relationship who recognize the equality and also value the differences of "the others." Although human relationships can never reach the unity of being one finds in God, they can be a dim analogy. Orthodox theologian John Zizioulas says that the Christian community is called to be "an image or sign of the Trinity"[6] while Colin Gunton writes

---

5. Thanks to Dr. David Rudolph for helping me get this paragraph sorted out. I need to clarify here: It is often said that the "church" is the *new Israel* that replaces the old, biological Israel. This is a belief known as "replacement theology" or "supersessionism," according to which "Christianity" replaces "Judaism" in God's purposes. I think such theology is radically mistaken. See Soulen, *The God of Israel and Christian Theology* for a helpful analysis and alternative. My own view is that the distinction within humanity between Jews and Gentiles is not a temporary phase in God's purposes but remains central to the divine intentions. God's ultimate purpose, as we see in Israel's prophets, is for Israel and the nations to be united as equals in the worship of the one true God. But this unity and equality does not eliminate difference; there are still Jews and Gentiles. In Christ, God brings about a new community in the midst of Israel and the nations—the *ekklēsia*—a community composed of Messiah-believing Jews and Gentiles. In this new community Jews and Gentiles are united and equal (Gal 3:28) but this does not mean that they are "the same." Jewish Messiah-believers remain Jewish and do not become Gentiles. And Gentile Messiah-believers remain Gentiles and do not become Jews (something Paul was very keen to emphasize in, for instance, Galatians). Getting to the point: I maintain that the church is an anticipatory microcosm of the future age in which Jew and Gentile, while remaining Jewish and Gentile, are renewed in the Spirit and united as one. So the church is *not* the new Israel and the Jewish people remain God's covenant people. Rather, the *ekklēsia* is a community that is an imperfect foretaste of the unity of end-time Israel (Christ-believing Jews) and the end-time nations (Christ-believing Gentiles). In this community, Christ-believing Gentiles get to become part of the *commonwealth* of Israel and thus to participate in the blessings of Israel. This states my view more precisely than the main text does The best overview of this theology is Mark Kinzer's wonderful book, *Postmissionary Messianic Judaism*.

6. Zizioulas, "The Doctrine of God the Trinity Today," 29. See especially Zizioulas, *Being as Communion*.

that God's plan was "through the work of Christ and the Spirit to create, in time and space, a living echo of the communion God is in eternity."[7]

Trinitarian thinking has led to a reaction against over-institutional views of church. Pete Ward uses the dynamic, relational, liquid view of God as the basis for moving beyond "solid church" to what he calls "liquid church":[8] "If God is seen as a flow of relationships among Father, Son, and Holy Spirit, then we have here a significant boost to a more fluid kind of church . . . The vision of church as networks of relationship and communication suddenly takes on a powerful symbolic significance in the light of these ideas."[9] Churches should seek relational unity *but not uniformity.* The Trinity provides a model of diversity-in-loving communion, which the *ekklēsia* must seek to image, albeit in a dim way, in the world. Graham Buxton writes that "The idea . . . is not that of belonging to a church, or sharing in some form of overt Christian activity, but of being incorporated into a dynamic and relational organism which has its origin in the trinitarian life of God himself."[10]

The Trinitarian model of the *ekklēsia*, significantly, leaves room for much flexibility in how we organize our communities—for there is no single right way of "doing church." However, it does provide some limits to legitimate expression of Christian community. Feminist theologian Catherine LaCugna writes:

> The trinitarian doctrine of God, as the basis for a trinitarian [doctrine of the church], might not specify the exact forms of structure and community appropriate to the church, but it does provide the critical principle against which we can measure present institutional arrangements. Very simply, we may ask whether our institutions, rituals, and administrative practices foster elitism, discrimination, competition, or any of several "archisms," or whether the church is run like God's household: a domain of inclusiveness, interdependence, and cooperation, structured according to the model of *perichorēsis* [see chapter 4, below, on this term] among persons.[11]

---

7. Gunton, *Father, Son, and Holy Spirit*, 198.

8. I am very happy to use the word *church*, but it needs to be understood in the light of my comments in note 5.

9. Ward, *Liquid Church*, 54–55

10. Buxton, *Dancing in the Dark*, 61.

11. LaCugna, *God for Us*, 402.

TRINITY AND MISSION

When I became a Christian I was taught that mission was something that God commands, but that *we* do. The truth is that mission is first and foremost *God's own* mission. God sends himself before he sends his *ekklēsia*. There is a centrifugal force in God's very being as the Son and the Spirit spiral out from the Father to bring healing to the world. Mission is, first of all, God sending his Son in the power of the Spirit to reconcile the world to himself and *the mission of the church is nothing less than the gift of sharing, by the Spirit, in the Son's mission to the world on behalf of the Father.*

After the resurrection John tells us that Jesus appeared to the fearful disciples and said: "'Peace be with you! As the Father has sent me, I am sending you.' And with that he breathed on them and said, 'Receive the Holy Spirit. If you forgive anyone his sins, they are forgiven; if you do not forgive them, they are not forgiven'" (John 20:21–22). This is a classic mission text from Scripture—but notice how the mission of the church is really just a sharing in God's own mission. The Father sent Jesus on a mission to the world, and it is that very same mission in which the *ekklēsia* participates. The Spirit is given to the disciples to empower them for this task. The Holy Spirit is passionate about mission, and he is the one who empowers and guides the Christian community, choreographing our mission in the world. Through the Spirit-enabled *ekklēsia*, Christ continues to work and to teach in the world.

The church is the weak instrument God has chosen to use to continue his awesome work of reconciling the world to himself. Notice how Paul sees his own apostolic ministry as a sharing in God's reconciling work in Christ: "God was reconciling the world to himself in Christ, not counting men's sins against them. And he has committed to us the message of reconciliation. We are therefore Christ's ambassadors, as though God were making his appeal through us. We implore you on Christ's behalf: Be reconciled to God" (2 Cor 5:19–20).

Mission (which includes, but is much broader than, evangelism) is the church becoming, in the Spirit's power, the instrument of Yhwh's work of saving the world through Christ.

TRINITY AND HOLY LIVING

Christian ethics is about participating in the Son's holy obedience to the Father with the help of the Spirit. It is the Father who desires our holiness

(Eph 1:4; Rom 8:29), it is Christ who breaks the power of sin and makes holiness a possibility, and it is the Spirit who applies the power of the cross of Christ to our lives to make us holy. Let's flesh this out a little.

What Christ is, the church is "in him." Christ, the perfect human being (Heb 4:15), fully obeyed the Father and kept the covenant commandments of Yhwh. Where Adam and Israel failed, he succeeded (Rom 5:12–21). And it wasn't just about keeping the commandments in a technical sense—Christ lived his life out of a heart of love for his Father and the world. His obedience was the overflow of a character shaped by the Spirit and the divine Word. Obedience to God takes on a different shape when seen in the light of the Christ, whose yoke is easy and whose burden is light.

When St. Paul discusses Christian ethics he begins with what Christians *already are* "in Christ" and works from there. For instance, in Romans Paul says that those who have been baptized have been united with Christ in his death and burial (6:1–4).

> We were therefore buried with him through baptism into death in order that, just as Christ was raised from the dead through the glory of the Father, we too may live a new life . . . For we know that our old self was crucified with him so that the body of sin might be done away with, that we should no longer be slaves to sin, because anyone who has died has been freed from sin . . . The death [Christ] died, he died to sin once for all; but the life he lives, he lives to God. In the same way, count yourselves dead to sin but alive to God in Christ Jesus. Therefore do not let sin reign in your mortal body so that you obey its evil desires. Do not offer the parts of your body to sin, as instruments of wickedness, but rather offer yourselves to God, as those who have been brought from death to life; and offer the parts of your body to him as instruments of righteousness. For sin shall not be your master . . . [T]hanks be to God that, though you used to be slaves to sin, you wholeheartedly obeyed the form of teaching to which you were entrusted. You have been set free from sin and have become slaves to righteousness . . . Just as you used to offer the parts of your body in slavery to impurity and to ever-increasing wickedness, so now offer them in slavery to righteousness leading to holiness. (Rom 6:4, 6–7, 10–14, 17–19)

Notice how he argues. FACT: our old self that was enslaved to sin has been crucified with Christ and buried, so sin no longer has control over us. COMMAND: so do not surrender yourself to sin as if you were still enslaved to it. Elsewhere Paul tells his converts to "put to death" acts that belong to their sin-damaged humanity (Col 3:5). He reminds them that in baptism they have "taken off the old self" and "put on the new self" which is Christ (Col 3:9–10). In the light of that he tells them to clothe themselves in compassion, kindness, humility, and the like (Col 3:12ff.). As we noted when thinking about church unity, there is a difficult balance to maintain here between a focus on what God has already achieved to enable us to be holy and the active role we must take in cooperating with the Spirit's work in us to shape our actual living in godly ways.

For Paul, sinful living by Christians is simply a lie—living as if we were still sin's slaves when in fact the cross and resurrection make obedience a real possibility for the believer. Sadly, Paul's converts regularly fell far short of such a lifestyle—as Christians through the ages often have. In our lives we clearly do not enjoy the full outworking of victory over sin yet (1 John 1:8). Our motives are still mixed and we can still be hardened against God by sin (Heb 3:13). The challenge to Christians is to be what we already are in Christ.

> So I say, live by the Spirit, and you will not gratify the desires of the sinful nature. For the sinful nature desires what is contrary to the Spirit, and the Spirit what is contrary to the sinful nature. They are in conflict with each other, so that you do not do what you want. But if you are led by the Spirit, you are not under law.
>
> The acts of the sinful nature are obvious: sexual immorality, impurity and debauchery; idolatry and witchcraft; hatred, discord, jealousy, fits of rage, selfish ambition, dissensions, factions and envy; drunkenness, orgies, and the like . . . But the fruit of the Spirit is love, joy, peace, patience, kindness, goodness, faithfulness, gentleness, and self-control
>
> Those who belong to Christ Jesus have crucified the sinful nature with its passions and desires. Since we live by the Spirit, let us keep in step with the Spirit. (Gal 5:16–25)

We are well aware that we experience the pull of our sin-damaged humanity battling with the desire of God's Spirit within us. Paul points out that if we belong to Christ, the sin-distorted nature is crucified and dead. It does not have an irresistible control over us any longer. Let's return to the rubber glove analogy of the last chapter—we suggested that the crumpled and torn glove of our sinful humanity was melted down on the cross (Rom 8:2) and in the resurrection was remolded. If we belong to the Messiah, that new rubber glove, that new creation, is ours. Paul tells the Galatians that they should surrender to the Spirit within them—if they do so they will find that they are not living by the desires of their old way of life. Instead, the fruit of the new-humanity-in-Christ will be formed in them by the Spirit: love, joy, peace, patience, kindness, goodness, faithfulness, gentleness, and self-control. The Spirit is working to transform us from one degree of glory to another (2 Cor 3:18), to forge in us the character of the Messiah. And all of this is in accord with the will of the Father that we be holy (Eph 1:4; Rom 8:29).

In summary, ethical living is not about us pulling ourselves up by our own moral bootstraps. Rather, it all begins with the Father, who longs to re-shape our warped humanity so that we can be holy. To that end he reaches out to us with his two hands. The Son took our humanity upon himself and lived in perfect obedience yet absorbed the consequences of our damaged human nature on the cross. At Calvary he mysteriously breaks the power of sin and death over humanity so that those who are "in him" do not have to be enslaved to sin any longer. The Spirit then works within the community of believers to reform their actual lives so that the fruits of the Messiah's work at Calvary work out in practice.[12] As Gordon Fee puts it, "the coming of the Spirit means not that divine perfection has set in, but 'divine infection.'"[13] The place of the believer is to co-operate with God in this work—to walk in the Spirit and resist the temptations that come our way, to confess our sins and await patiently the completion of our ethical transformation when the Lord returns.

TRINITY AND READING THE BIBLE

Reading the Bible is an important part of opening ourselves up to the Lord to be shaped by him. The Trinity is connected to the Bible in various ways.

Obviously the Bible speaks *about* the God, the Messiah, and the Spirit—they are the *subject* of the book. In particular, the whole Bible speaks of the Messiah—the Old Testament looks forward to his coming (Luke 24:27) while the New Testament reflects on the significance of his coming. The Bible bears witness to the actions of the Trinity in history.

---

12. A pastorally helpful book on Christian transformation is Greg Boyd's *Seeing Is Believing: Experience Jesus through Imaginative Prayer*. It is a protest against a try-harder approach to ethical transformation and makes a case for the place of imagination in opening ourselves up to the Spirit's renewing presence. For an excellent guide to how we should rethink holiness in Trinitarian terms see now Noble, *Holy Trinity: Holy People*.

13. Fee, *God's Empowering Presence*, 816.

More than that, the Bible records specific words spoken by the Father (e.g., Luke 9:35), by the Son (e.g., Rev 2–3), and by the Spirit (e.g., Rev 22:17).

Further still, the Bible is a gift from the Father to his people, crafted by the Holy Spirit working through human authors. Perhaps we should say that the Father, through the Spirit, provided his people with the Bible to point them to Christ and, through Christ, to himself.[14]

But the Trinity is involved not simply in the creation of the Bible, but also in the very reading of it within the life of the *ekklēsia*. In the Scriptures the church can hear the words of the Father, of the Son, and of the Spirit afresh as God continues to speak to his people through them. The place of the Spirit is especially crucial when the *ekklēsia* reads the Bible. The Spirit is the one who can cause faith and conviction to arise within us as we hear the words of Scripture. He can make "our hearts burn within us" as the text becomes transparent and we no longer see the mere words on the page but hear God himself through those words.

The Spirit will also guide the *ekklēsia* to correctly understand the word of truth. We must not to get confused here—the Spirit will not guarantee that everything you think a passage means when you read it is a correct interpretation. Some people seem to think that any understanding of the Bible that they dream up while reading it must be a Spirit-inspired interpretation. Their mistake is partly rooted in a lurking notion of the "loner Christian," which sees the Spirit's work focused primarily in the individual believer. I suggest that we should think of the Christian *community* as the primary location of the Spirit's work of opening up Scripture. There is something of a virtuous spiral here because the Messiah, by the Spirit, shapes the church, through the words of Scripture, to be the kind of community that can better hear the words of Scripture. What I mean is that when things are going right, God shapes the community through Scripture in such a way that when it reads Scripture again it hears God more clearly still. Sadly, things often go wrong as churches can and do resist the Spirit and the word.

---

14. We need to add that this trust in the Bible must include a faith that God was working through the leaders of the church in the early centuries as they discerned the books that should be included and excluded from the canon of the New Testament. So there can be no simplistic opposition of Scripture and tradition because faith in Scripture requires a confidence in tradition (even if many Protestant Christians do not always realize this).

Christians do not worship a book. That would be bibliolatry. The triune God is the only object of worship and the supreme authority in the *ekklēsia*. However, God's authoritative word is mediated to us in and through the Bible and so the Bible is the "rule" by which the church is to seek to live. But historically Christians have not been "Bible only" people, as if it were possible or desirable to ignore Christian tradition. We need guidance to read the Bible wisely. The great ecumenical tradition of the church is crucially important because it reflects the way in which the Spirit has guided the church to read the Bible. Have you ever heard someone say, "Oh, you just read the Bible through *tradition*. You can't see the truth. The Spirit shows me what it really means"? This kind of comment is usually quite unhelpful, because tradition very often reflects the wisdom of the Spirit imparted to previous generations. In other words, to ignore tradition could be an act of *resisting* the Spirit rather than being led by the Spirit. We interpret the Bible today in the light of Christian interpretations of the past because we recognize the work of the Spirit in opening up the text for the community. This is not to say that the traditions of the churches cannot ever be mistaken—they are fallible and are forever accountable to God. However, they should be accorded great respect.

TRINITY AND ETERNAL LIFE

Eternal life is the gift of the Father made *through* the Son *in* the Spirit. And forget about playing harps on clouds forever and ever. Think of eternal life not so much as a *quantity* of life (though it is ever-lasting), but as a *quality* of life given to us by God. The nearest that the Bible gets to a definition of it is a comment Jesus made when praying to his Father: "Now this is eternal life: that they may know you, the only true God, and Jesus Christ, whom you have sent" (John 17:3). Eternal life is the quality of life that is knowing God. And if you think that is profound, then this will blow your mind: the eternal life we have is *God's own life in us*—the Holy Spirit. Jesus offers us a "spring of water welling up to eternal life" (John 4:14). This life-giving water is the Spirit himself (John 7:38–39), who will animate our resurrection bodies (1 Cor 15:44). So, in a very real sense, the destiny of humanity is to participate in the life of the Trinity.

The ascended Jesus, in the words of Graham Kendrick's song "Meekness and Majesty," "lifts our humanity to the heights of his throne." That is to say, while being fully divine, he remains fully human and ever shall do. In the incarnation, life, death, resurrection, and ascension, the Messiah brings humanity into the very triune life of God. Theologians often call this *theosis* or "deification." Just think about it: the Father, the Son and the Spirit are all existing in perfect communion, but the Son has united human nature and divine nature in his person so that humanity is now joined in Christ to the very inner life of God. The divine Spirit that flows through Christ's veins will flow through ours. This is not to say that humanity and deity are confused or blurred together in Christ. The early church was clear that Christ had two distinct natures (human and divine) united in one person, so that our sharing in the life of God will never erase the difference between Creator and creature. However, it does fulfill the destiny for which humans were originally created as the icon of the Trinity. We will never be any more than human, but Christ invites us to buck our ideas up about what "being human" means.

Conclusion

In a nutshell, we can't make full sense of our conversion, of our baptism, of our experiences of God, of our place in the church, of mission, Bible reading, or the eternal life God has given us unless we understand them in a Trinitarian way. In chapter 5, when our focus moves explicitly to worship, we shall look more carefully at a Trinitarian view of prayer and worship and find exactly the same thing. What I hope to have persuaded you of so far is that thinking of the Christian life without Father, Son, and Spirit makes about as much sense as thinking of a sentence without words or of a square without four sides. A Christian life without the Trinity is not a Christian life at all.

four

The Shape of Trinitarian Faith

Now, the catholic faith is this,
That we worship one God in Trinity, and Trinity in Unity.

—ATHANASIAN CREED

WHY DID THE EARLY Christ believers start relating to God and speaking of God in Trinitarian ways? It was not because some bored Christian sat down one day and thought to himself, "Hmmm. What weird and utterly confusing new way can I dream up for speaking about God?" Belief in the Trinity grew out of the disciples' experience of God in their encounter with Jesus. That experience of Christ and the experience of the Spirit amongst early believers were both interpreted in the light of the Jewish Scriptures (which Christians now call the Old Testament), and this set in motion shifts in the understanding of God that were of profound significance.

It took some time for the church to think through the implications of Jesus' ministry, death, and resurrection, as well as his giving of the Spirit, but all the DNA of a full-grown doctrine of the Trinity was contained in that divine revelation in Christ. We shouldn't imagine that Peter, when he first met Jesus, exclaimed, "Goodness me! You must be the second person of the blessed Trinity! Perhaps you could sign my papyrus!" There simply was no concept of the Trinity before Jesus came. Yet within a very short time after the ascension we find Christians worshipping Jesus alongside the Father and insisting that in so doing they were not worshipping two gods but the one God of Israel. From the very beginning of the *ekklēsia*, the early communities of Christ-followers worshipped Jesus. Furthermore, the worship of Jesus seems to have been present in almost every version of the early Jesus movement that we know about. Yet we often fail to appreciate just how surprising that fact is. You would have expected that any good Jew would have perceived the worship of Jesus as idolatry (and the earliest Christ-believers were almost all good Jews). However, the Christians felt that their worship of Jesus was compatible with their monotheism because in some way they saw Jesus as sharing in the very identity of Israel's one covenant God.[1] The Christians began speaking of Christ existing before his birth and becoming incarnate as a human being. They began to speak of him doing the kinds of things that Yhwh does—such as creating the world, judging the world, raising the dead on the last day, and giving the Spirit. They began taking texts from the Scriptures about Yhwh and saying that these texts were actually fulfilled in *Jesus* (e.g., the use of Isa 45:22–23 in Phil 2:9–11)! They even occasionally referred to Jesus as "God" (John 1:1; 20:28; Heb 1:8). In the very practice of worshipping Christ and in the ongoing Spirit-guided reflections on Jesus we see the seeds of Trinitarian thought that took generations to mature into a full-grown tree. It was not really until the end of the fourth century that the church felt able to spell out exactly how best to do justice to the revelation of God in Christ, but all the key components of later Trinitarian belief are present in the New Testament. It is important to emphasize that the later Christian creeds aim only to "bring out" the teachings of Scripture and not to add to them.

The creeds are declarations of what the Christian communities believe. They grew from the practice of baptism. It was a very early practice to baptize people "in the name of the Father and of the Son and the Holy Spirit" (Matt 28:19; *Didache* 7:1–3). Baptismal candidates were instructed in Christian beliefs prior to initiation into the faith, and it seems that such instruction took a Trinitarian form. It was from this that the creeds of declaration developed ("I believe in one God, the Father Almighty . . ."). Very quickly, and alongside this, there grew up a tradition of candidates for baptism making a three-fold confession of faith prior to immersion. In the fourth century the priest would interrogate the candidate, asking, "Do you believe in God the Father?" and the candidate would reply "I believe," after which he or she would be immersed once. Then the priest asked, "Do you believe in our Lord Jesus Christ and his cross?" After confessing "I believe," the candidate was immersed again. Finally the candidate was asked, "Do

---

1. For more on this theme see the essays in Bauckham, *Jesus and the God of Israel.*

you believe also in the Holy Spirit?," and after an affirmative answer there was a final immersion. As time went on the questions put to baptismal candidates grew more elaborate, but the Trinitarian structure was maintained. Creeds used in public worship grew from this instruction in the faith and the interrogation at baptism. What is worth noting is that when the early church set about summarizing the content of the faith for new converts, that summary had a *Trinitarian form*.

It's often the case that we get a clearer understanding of our beliefs when questions and debates arise that force us to sit down and ask, "what exactly do I mean when I say such and such?" A vague, fuzzy idea about what we believe on some topic becomes much clearer when we are forced to think about it and explain or even defend our view. It was the same with the developing understanding of the Trinity. As Christians tried to get a clearer grip on God's self-revelation in Christ, disagreements arose. Pastors and bishops would ponder and pray and discuss (and plot and be more than a tad rude about each other—there's nothing new under the sun) and try to reach consensus on authentic Christian understanding. The creeds represent the collective mind of the church on some of these crucial discussions. However, the creeds do not set out to explain the mystery of the Trinity or to state everything that Christians must believe about it. We could think of creeds as being like fences around potholes in a playground that warn us that certain designated areas have been found to be dangerous. The children can play anywhere in the rest of the playground, but if they go past the fences they are liable to fall and get hurt. The creeds mark off certain beliefs as being outside the bounds of Christian faith, but they still leave a lot of questions unanswered and open space for diverse views. The beliefs that were ruled out were ruled out because it was felt that they posed a serious threat to biblical claims about salvation. In this chapter we will briefly outline the key claims central to orthodox Christian faith in the Trinity, the key claims that orthodox Christians reject, and why it matters.

The Main Elements of Trinitarian Belief

"We believe in one God ..." (Nicene Creed)

The *ekklēsia* began life as a Jewish sect and inherited from Judaism a strong belief that there is *only one true God*, Yhwh, and that he alone is to be worshipped. To worship any other deity was idolatry and flatly forbidden. For the Christians to acknowledge more than one god would have been a clear rejection of the faith of Israel, and yet throughout the New Testament we see that the early *ekklēsia* held as firmly to the monotheism of Israel as all other Jewish sects did. As the church spread out into the Gentile world and fast became a predominantly Gentile movement, this commitment to monotheism did not waver.

Many people are confused by Christian faith and suppose that Christians believe in three gods: Father, Son, and Spirit. But whatever Trinitarianism is, it is certainly *not* the belief that Jesus and the Spirit are two other gods existing alongside the God of Israel. The Athanasian Creed puts it as follows: "There are not three Gods but one God . . . not three Lords but one Lord." Christian affirmation of monotheism matters because if the church had elevated Jesus and the Spirit to being gods alongside Yhwh, making a total of three gods, then Christians would have been rejecting the emphatic insistence in the Hebrew Scriptures (the Old Testament) that Yhwh alone is God of gods and that no other gods must be worshipped. If they had done that they would have been rejecting the revelation of God through the prophets. They would have been rejecting the very Scriptures that Jesus came to fulfill.

"Neither confusing the persons . . ." (Athanasian Creed)

Christians believe that the one God exists as *three persons*. The Father is not the Son, nor is he the Spirit. The Son is neither the Father nor the Spirit. The Spirit is not identical with Son or Father. Trinitarian faith says that there are some things that are true of one person of the Trinity that are not true of the others. For instance, the Son was crucified but the Father and Spirit were not. The Father sent the Son; the Spirit did not. And so on.

It was important for the church to emphasize this point because not everyone agreed with it. There was a teacher in Rome in the third century by the name of Sabellius who taught that the Father, Son, and Spirit are merely different manifestations of the one God. Imagine an actor who puts on different costumes and assumes different roles in a play. He plays the parts of a father, a mother, and daughter in a family. Each time he appears on stage he takes on the appearance and character of one of the three and manifests himself to the audience as the daughter or the mother or the father. Sabellius argued that the Trinity was something like this—it helped him understand how God could be three without compromising his oneness. Just as the one actor appears as three characters, so the one God appeared in three modes (thus the view is known as *modalism*).

Although Sabellius was well intentioned, the church rejected his views for good reason. Modalism does not do justice to the way that God has revealed himself, because although it is strong on the oneness of God it does not do justice to the *real distinctions* between the persons. The three persons cease to be the ultimate reality about God and become merely three ways that the one person (concealed behind the appearances of three "persons") presents himself to us. But this makes the "relations" between the persons of the Trinity something of a charade. If there is just one person behind the Father, Son, and Spirit, then to whom did Jesus pray? Himself? When the Father sent the Son, did he send himself? When the Son says to his disciples that he is going away but that he will send the Spirit in his place, was he simply sending himself? Confusing the persons in this way creates havoc with the biblical story of creation and redemption and makes God akin to a deceiver—because although God *appears* to us as three "persons," in actual fact he is *only one person.* This view replaces the relational God at the heart of reality with a fraud.

Sometimes Christians can slide into modalism unintentionally. We may carelessly pray things like "Thank you, Father, for dying for us" or "Thank you, Father, for your wonderful name, the wonderful name of Jesus." Now, of course, God knows what we mean when we make errors like this in our prayers. God is not sitting there waiting for us to make theological slips so he can send lightning bolts to teach us a lesson! God will accept our prayers even if they are often a tad off the mark. Nevertheless, this is no excuse not to learn to speak to God more biblically. Sometimes when we give illustrations of the Trinity to try to explain how God can be three-in-one we actually end up illustrating modalism. For instance, I have sometimes heard people explain the Trinity in terms of H_2O, which is one substance and yet can be ice, water, or steam. The same H_2O is sometimes ice, sometimes water, and sometimes steam, but the problem is that this may suggest that God is *sometimes* the Father, *sometimes* the Son, and *sometimes* the Spirit—the same person experienced in three different ways. Of course, when this is pointed out people usually back off and explain that it is not what they meant, but we do need to be careful in the illustrations we use lest we mislead others and ourselves.

"Their glory equal, their majesty co-eternal" (Athanasian Creed)

Father, Son, and Spirit are all *equally divine*. It is not that the Father is more divine than the Son, nor that the Son is more divine than the Spirit. Each is fully and equally God. The Nicene Creed (AD 325) spells out Jesus' divinity as follows:

> We believe in one Lord, Jesus Christ, the only Son of God,
>> eternally begotten of the Father, God from God, Light from
> Light, True God from true God,
> Begotten, not made,
> Of one Being with the Father.
> Through him all things were made.

The Niceno-Constantinopolitan Creed (AD 381) spells out the Spirit's equality as follows:

> We believe in the Holy Spirit,
> The Lord, the Giver of life,
> Who proceeds from the Father;
> Who with the Father and the Son together is worshipped and
>> glorified.

The Athanasian Creed, which was probably composed in the fifth or sixth century (and not by Athanasius), is emphatic about the co-equality of the persons: *all* are uncreated, *all* are infinite, *all* are eternal, *all* are almighty, *all* are God, and *all* are Lord.

This clarity developed out of a fierce debate. In the fourth century in Alexandria, Egypt, a sincere but misled theologian named Arius (c. 250–336) tried to get his mind around the tricky issue of the nature of the Son. Arius concluded that the Son is not divine and that "there was a time when he did not exist." The Father, he said, is the one God while *the Son is a created being*—the very first and most exalted of created beings and the one through whom God created the rest of the universe. Jehovah's Witnesses teach the same thing today. There are three significant problems with Arius' belief:

First, if Arius is right then God becomes distant and remote, having no *direct* involvement with creation. God creates his Word/Son but nothing else. God does not create the universe but leaves that task to a creature (the Word). God does not redeem the universe either—one of his creatures does. God has no direct involvement *at all* with creation. However, on a Trinitarian view, when the Word creates it is *God himself* who is creating.

When the Word became flesh and dwelt amongst us it was *God himself* who was in our midst. When Christ acts as our savior it is *God himself* saving us.

Second, if Arius is right it would make the Christian worship of Jesus idolatry (the worship of creation rather than God), yet such worship is clearly biblical. Arius himself did worship Jesus, but it is hard to see how he could justify such activity if Jesus was merely an exalted creature.

Third, only God can save us, because sin is primarily a crime against God. No mere creature has the right or the ability to deliver humanity from sin. This is why Paul argues that God took the initiative and was "in Christ reconciling the world to himself" (2 Cor 5:19). If Jesus was not divine he could not *rescue* us.

The Nicene Creed we quoted above was written to rule out Arianism as a Christian option. After the debate on the deity of Christ settled down, attention finally shifted to the deity of the Spirit. Some argued that although Father and Son are divine, the Spirit is not a divine person who can be the object of Christian worship (they were in effect "binitarians" rather than Trinitarians). It was theologians such as Athanasius (c. 296–373), Gregory of Nazianzus (c. 330–390), and Basil of Caesarea (330–379) who demonstrated the deity of the Spirit from Scripture and won the day.

That the Spirit is not to be seen as identical with the Father and the Son is very clear in the New Testament. The case for the full deity of the Spirit is also very strong, in spite of the fact that we have no proof text that says, "The Spirit is God." Especially important for those like Basil of Caesarea was the baptismal formula of Matt 28:19: "Therefore go and make disciples of all nations, baptizing them in the name of the Father and of the Son and of the Holy Spirit." Baptism is intimately connected with our entrance into the Christian community, and very quickly the Trinitarian wording became standard in the churches. Every Christian is a Christian by virtue of his or her faith, sealed in baptism in the name of the Three-in-One. And what do the baptismal words mean?

They declare that the relation of the Spirit to the Son equals that of the Son with the Father. If the Spirit is ranked with the Son, and the Son with the Father, then the Spirit is obviously ranked with the Father.[2]

2. Basil the Great, *On the Holy Spirit*, ch. 17, 70.

Further Reflection

The Deity of the Spirit and the Bible

Is the Trinitarian understanding of the Spirit biblical? I'll mention just a few pieces of evidence here that, taken together, strongly suggest that the idea of the Spirit as a divine person—distinct yet inseparable from Father and Son—is grounded in biblical revelation.

First, it seems very clear that in the Old Testament the Spirit, although not understood then as a person of the Trinity, was conceived of as *the presence and power of Yhwh* at work in the world. There is never any suggestion that the Spirit is a creature, but always and only the empowering presence of Yhwh. This understanding continues in the New Testament. The Spirit is *God's* Spirit and was understood as existing in the closest possible relation with the Father. Paul's analogy of the relationship is that of a person's spirit with their own inner consciousness (1 Cor 2:10–12). Nobody knows your deepest thoughts except your own spirit, says Paul. In the same way, nobody knows the Father's mind except his Spirit, who searches the depths of God. This is no created being.

Second, one particularly telling text in which a high view of the Spirit's deity is expressed is 2 Corinthians 3:17–18. In the process of a complex argument Paul says in verse 16: "But whenever anyone turns to the Lord, the veil is taken away." He then continues: "Now the Lord is the Spirit, and where the Spirit of the Lord is, there is freedom. And we, who with unveiled faces all reflect the Lord's glory, are being transformed into his likeness with ever-increasing glory, which comes from the Lord, who is the Spirit." The details of the argument need not concern us here. What is interesting, however, is that immediately after speaking of people turning to the Lord, the Yhwh of the exodus story, he explains, "now the Lord" he has just spoken about (i.e., Yhwh), "is the Spirit." That is to say, Paul sees Yhwh (in the Old Testament story from Exodus that he is referring to) as the Holy Spirit. In the next breath he *distinguishes* Yhwh and the Spirit by speaking of "the Spirit of the Lord." It is precisely such explosive, whirlwind-like theology-on-the-run that the doctrine of the Trinity seeks to make sense of.

Third, it is important to note that the presence of the Spirit within the Christian community is understood by New Testament writers as fulfilling Old Testament promises of the indwelling of God in believers (1 Cor 14:24–25; 2 Cor 6:16). This is just one of many examples in which *the Spirit is functioning as God*. But there are also examples explaining that the way one treats the Spirit is how one treats God. Thus, for instance, when Ananias deceived the apostles about selling his field he had lied not merely to them, but he had also "lied to the Holy Spirit" (Acts 5:3), which Peter declares to be equivalent to having "lied to God" (Acts 5:4).

Fourth, there are many texts that link Father, Son, and Spirit together as a triad, or trinity. For instance: "There are different kinds of gifts, but the same *Spirit*. There are different kinds of service, but the same *Lord*. There are different kinds of working, but the same *God* works all of them in all men" (1 Cor 12:4–6); "There is one body and one *Spirit*—just as you were called to one hope when you were called—one *Lord*, one faith, one baptism; one *God and Father* of all, who is over all and through all and in all" (Eph 4:4–6); "May the grace of the *Lord Jesus Christ*, and the love of *God*, and the fellowship of the *Holy Spirit* be with you all" (2 Cor 13:14); "Therefore go and make disciples of all nations, baptizing them in the name of the *Father* and of the *Son* and of the *Holy Spirit*" (Matt 28:19). This connecting of Father, Son, and Spirit is very common in Paul (see also 1 Thess 1:4–6; 2 Thess 2:13; 1 Cor 1:4–7; 2:4–5; 6:11, 19–20; 2 Cor 1:21–22; Gal 3:1–5; Rom 8:3–4, 15–17; Col 3:16; Eph 1:17; 2:18, 20–22; Phil 3:3). Paul may never have sat down and worked out a fully-fledged theology of the Trinity, but there is no doubt that his theology arises from primal and deeply Trinitarian presuppositions.

The deity of the Spirit is a significant issue for the story of salvation. In the New Testament it is clear that sin blinds the human mind to the extent that we simply cannot perceive the truth of the gospel and believe. It is only the Spirit that opens the blind eyes to see, opens the dull minds to understand, and softens the sin-hardened hearts to believe. The fact that God came, incarnate in the person of Jesus, to save us would have made no difference whatsoever if the Spirit did not enable us to perceive God in

Christ—God may as well have become incarnate as a filing cabinet for all the good it would have done! Without the Spirit's work, Christ's work is ineffective. However, *what enables the Spirit to reveal God to us reliably is that the Spirit is himself divine.* The Spirit knows the deep things of God in the same way that the spirit of a person knows their deepest parts (1 Cor 2:10–12). God the Father reveals himself in God the Son-made-flesh, and God the Spirit enables us to perceive that divine glory in the words and actions of Jesus.

There is a serious question we shall need to ponder in chapter 6 regarding whether our modern worship is often "binitarian" in its focus rather than Trinitarian. The Holy Spirit is usually pushed to the margins of our prayer and worship and often falls out of sight entirely, even in charismatic and Pentecostal churches. Careful reflection on the place of the Spirit within the Godhead is needed, and the appropriate kinds of responses that are called for will need some attention. But for now we will continue to consider the important elements of Trinitarian belief.

Three Persons

The persons of the Trinity are, in some meaningful sense, "persons" who exist in an eternal relationship of love and self-giving. Richard St Victor (d. 1172) thought that it is only possible for God to be perfect love if he is a Trinity.[3] This is because if God were simply Father his love would be merely *self*-love, so there needs to be an object of the Father's love—a beloved (the Son)—within God, enabling God's love to include love for "the other." However, even this is less than the highest love, for the love of two can become introverted. It is only when this mutual love is joyously shared with a third person, loved equally by both, that their own love is perfected. The Spirit, who is *co-beloved*, is the one who brings God's love to perfection. Whether Richard is correct in his speculations or not, the view that the persons of God love each other means that God does not have to create a universe in order to fulfill some deep "psychological" need to love others. God would be love even if he had never created a universe, because the persons of the Trinity are always and forever loving each other. So God is *free* to choose whether or not to create the universe—although, once he has created it, he will be true to himself and bind himself to it in covenant love.

3. See Richard of Saint Victor, *On the Trinity.*

The weakness of some illustrations of the Trinity is that they make the three persons into "things" or "forces." Consider the egg analogy. A single egg is composed of a shell, a yoke, and an egg white. But shells, yokes, and egg whites do not exist in loving interpersonal relationships like the Father, Son, and Spirit do. Or consider the analogy of the cube: However you cut through a single cube it has three dimensions. In a similar way, however you look at the one God he is three persons. Here, too, there is no hint of any interpersonal relationships between the length, breadth, and height of the cube!

The Christian relates to the Father as a person, and not as a thing or force. Of course, God will always be beyond human language and our words and concepts will never capture or exhaust the reality of God that, like a bar of soap, will always slip from our grasp.[4] In the New Testament, the Christian's relationship with "Abba" is very intimate and familial. This Father loves his children and we cry out from our innermost being in devotion to him: "Abba! Father!" The Son, too, is personal. This is easy for us to grasp because Jesus was a human person just as we ourselves are, even if he was not merely human. He is the personal Lord we worship and to whom we pray.

The Spirit is also personal, and this is much harder for Christians to grasp. I once heard the Trinity described as "a grey beard, a white beard, and a mist." This feeling is quite understandable, for not only is "spirit/wind/breath" not a personal image, but the other symbols used of the Spirit in Scripture are also mostly impersonal—fire, water, oil, and so on. You don't immediately think of a person when you think of the Spirit as a river. Such images are, of course, not intended to capture the personhood of the Spirit, and we must remember that the emphasis in the Bible is on *the experience of the Spirit as transforming power*—his own personhood is somewhat cloaked and reflecting this in our own spirituality is fine. However, in the Bible we do see the eyes of the Spirit looking through from behind the veil and we come to realize that no understanding of the Spirit as a mere divine force field will do. Given that Christians have such trouble thinking of the Spirit as personal, let's unpack this concept a bit.

The Bible presents a variety of indicators that the Spirit has his own self-consciousness and personhood. As we have seen, the Spirit *knows* the

---

4. The Christian tradition has always emphasized the mystery of God and the inability of human language to grasp him. The most radical mode of this appreciation of mystery is found in the work of Pseudo-Dionysius (which is helpfully developed and qualified in the magnificent work of Thomas Aquinas).

mind of the Father (1 Cor 2:10) and the Father knows the *mind* of the Spirit (Rom 8:26–27). Clearly the Spirit has a mind that is distinct from the Father's, and yet both know each other utterly. The Spirit *teaches* believers the gospel (1 Cor 2:13), *desires* godly virtues in the saints (Gal 5:17), and is *grieved* by our sin (Eph 4:30). He *cries out* with our spirits to the Father (Rom 8:15–16), *groans* within us for the redemption of creation (Rom 8:26), and *prays* for us (Rom 8:26–27). The Spirit often *speaks* in Scripture. For instance, he joins with the *ekklēsia* and calls out to the thirsty, "Come" (Rev 22:17). In John's Gospel, Jesus says that he will go but will send the Spirit as his replacement. He describes the Spirit as "another Counsellor" *of the same kind* that Jesus himself had been, and the language clearly implies a personal Spirit (John 14:16). The Spirit will continue the mission of Jesus through the church. He is, in the words of Gordon Fee, "God's empowering presence." A. W. Tozer said,

> Spell this out in capital letters: THE HOLY SPIRIT IS A PERSON. He is not enthusiasm. He is not courage. He is not energy. He is not the personification of all good qualities, like Jack Frost is the personification of cold weather. Actually, the Holy Spirit is not the personification of anything . . . He has individuality. He is one being and not another. He has will and intelligence. He has hearing. He has knowledge and sympathy and ability to love and see and think. He can hear, speak, desire, grieve, and rejoice. He is a Person.[5]

The Spirit is indeed often experienced as life-transforming power, but the one who so transforms us is personal—and we honor him by recognizing this "shy" member of the Trinity as a personal power through whom we also experience the presence of Father and Son.

Indwelling (*perichorēsis*)

An important aspect of faith in the Trinity for many Christians (although not one found in the creeds) is that all the members of the Trinity "indwell" each other. This notion is rooted in the Bible, even though its meaning is not entirely clear. Jesus said that he was "in the Father" and that the Father was "in him," so that to see the Son was to see the Father (John 14:8–10). Both the Son and the Father are present "in the Spirit," so that although the Father and Son are in heaven they are present now in creation through the

5. Tozer, *The Counselor: Straight Talk about the Holy Spirit.* Online: no page number.

Spirit. So it was that Jesus spoke of the Father and the Son taking up residence within the believer, and it is clear that this is a presence experienced through the indwelling of the Spirit (John 14:23). Because the members of the Trinity so interpenetrate and indwell each other, when one is present the other two are present also. It is impossible to encounter one person without also encountering the others. To meet the biblical Jesus is to encounter the Father and the Spirit through him. To meet the biblical Spirit is to encounter the Father and Son in him. This perichoretic unity shared by the divine persons goes beyond any kind of unity found within creation. It is deeper and more profound than anything experienced between the closest human persons. It is only in their dynamic, mutual indwelling that any of the persons of the Trinity exist at all. God is "being in communion." At the heart of reality is the Trinity, and at the heart of the Trinity is living, flowing, eternal relationship. The Christian vision of God is one that places relationship and love at the most fundamental level of reality.

All of this has important implications for Christian spirituality. We need to realize that we cannot even think of any one person of the Trinity without at the same moment thinking of the other two. We cannot think of the Three without thinking of their unity—their oneness. We cannot think of the One without thinking of the Three. Gregory of Nazianzus said that, "No sooner do I conceive of the One than I am illumined by the splendor of the Three; no sooner do I distinguish them than I am carried back to the One."[6] Eastern Orthodox thinker Vladimir Lossky writes that, "our thoughts must be in continuous motion, pursuing now the One, now the Three, and returning again to unity; it must swing ceaselessly between the poles of the [Three and the One]."[7] Christian worship needs to enable the congregation to learn this way of relating to the Three-in-One and to appreciate again the awesome mystery of the God we adore.

Co-workers

This idea leads us to another important point. A few recent feminist theologians have suggested that we replace the words "Father, Son, and Spirit" with the gender neutral "Creator, Redeemer, and Life-Giver." Although the motivation for this suggestion is understandable, it creates a *potential* problem. As we saw in chapters 2 and 3, every action of God is an action of

---

6. Gregory of Nazianzus, *Theological Oration* 40:412.

7. Lossky, *The Mystical Theology of the Eastern Church*, 46.

the whole Trinity. We should not suppose that creation is what the Father does, redemption is what the Son does, and giving life is what the Spirit does. Every member of the Godhead is involved in creation and in salvation. Whenever God acts, the Trinity acts. This is not to say that every person is doing the same thing in the story of salvation. The Father sends the Son. The Son dies. The Spirit makes sinners come alive to God spiritually. However, the Son and the Spirit function together as the two hands of the Father, working as one to bring about the purposes of God.[8]

ILLUSTRATIONS OF THE TRINITY

So how are we going to make sense of the claim that God is three persons yet one God? It is confusing, and Christians speak quite appropriately of the "mystery of the Trinity." Nevertheless it is helpful to try to find ways of thinking coherently.[9] The clearer our thinking, the easier we will find it to pray and worship in appropriately Trinitarian ways. Two families of illustration have proved helpful in the history of theology. Each has its strengths and weaknesses and neither claims to be anything more than analogy. Christians disagree over which is the most helpful, but since such disagreement falls within the bounds of orthodox Christian faith I have no intention of taking sides in this context. Perhaps one or both will appeal to you.

Psychological Analogies

It has been especially common in the Catholic and Protestant churches to look for illustrations of the Trinity in the human mind. The roots of this kind of analogy lie in Scripture, where God's wisdom/thought/reason/word

8. I hasten to add that I have no problem with "Creator, Redeemer, and Life Giver" as a complement to "Father, Son, and Spirit" so long as the caveats expressed in the main text are taken into account. It is the case that the different persons of the Trinity are more in focus in the different acts of God. The first person is more in focus in creating, the second person in redemption, the third person in life giving. So I do not oppose naming the Trinity in this way so long as it is understood aright.

9. A really good introduction to some of the philosophical problems as well as a proposed solution can be found in Michael Rae's article, "The Trinity," in *Oxford Handbook of Philosophical Theology*. The article can be found online here: http://www.nd.edu/~mrea/. It will require a bit of concentration, but for those interested in such issues, the effort is worth it.

are first of all personified (Prov 8) and then understood to be a distinct person—God the Word. Similarly, God's Spirit is seen as a distinct person within the unity of God. Here are a couple of psychological analogies that may help us to understand the biblical reality.

St. Augustine (AD 354–430) argued that, as humans are in God's image, it may be helpful to look within our own human minds to find an analogy of the Trinity.[10] He suggested that we think about memory, understanding, and the will. Although these are three distinct aspects of a single mind, none could be expressed without the operation of the other two. For example, the memory retains information, but only through the operation of the understanding and the will to do so. In a similar way, God is three distinguishable persons who only exist in their co-operative relationships within the single being of God. Augustine was well aware that this was no exact comparison with God, and he never tried to equate the three aspects of the mind with specific persons of the Trinity.[11]

Philosopher Trenton Merricks gives us a modern psychological analogy. In some cases in which people have had the nerves that communicate between the two hemispheres of their brain cut (a procedure sometimes used to treat epilepsy) it appears from their behavior that they have, in some situations at least, two centers of consciousness—one in each half of the brain. If a single human being can have two centers of consciousness, then could not a single God have three? This analogy has the advantage over the previous one of highlighting the personhood of the members of the Godhead. One obvious disadvantage is that it could suggest to some that God is the Three-in-One because something has gone wrong with him!

Social Analogies

The image of the Trinity as a society of three people living in intimate personal and loving communion is a popular image. One may often hear the expression "God is a community." The analogy is often associated with the Eastern Orthodox churches, although many Catholics and Protestants

---

10. See Augustine, *The Trinity*, books IX–XI.

11. We should also note, against the critics of Augustine, that the psychological analogies were intended as no more than analogies. They may not focus on the notion of persons-in-relation, but Augustine did develop a very *relational* doctrine of the Trinity with love at its heart (with the three persons understood as Lover, Beloved, and the Spirit of Love).

favor it also. Some modern theologians speak of the Trinity as being like three dancers moving in complex, interlocking movements. The dancers work as one and spin so fast and perfectly around each other that it is sometimes hard to tell one from the other. Listen to Eugene Peterson:

> Imagine a folk dance, a round dance with three partners in each set. The music plays and the partners start moving in a circle holding hands. On a signal from the caller, they release hands, changing partners, weaving in and out, swinging first one and then the other. The tempo increases, the partners move more swiftly with and between and among one another, swinging and twirling, embracing and releasing, holding and letting go. There is no confusion, every movement is cleanly coordinated in precise rhythms, but each person maintains his or her own identity. To the onlooker, the movements are so swift it is impossible at times to distinguish one person from another, and the steps so intricate that it is difficult to anticipate the actual configurations as they appear. *Perichorēsis* (*peri* = around; *chorēsis* = dance). The essence of the Trinity, arguably the centerpiece of Christian theology, and sometimes considered the most subtle and abstruse of all doctrines, is captured here in a picture anyone can observe in a . . . barn dance or an Irish ceilidh.[12]

Of course, this picture has problems too. The oneness of the dancers is not exactly like that of the persons of the Trinity (the unity of the dancers is only temporary and can hardly be said to be the unity of a single being). The picture also fails to bring out the initiative of the first person (the Father) in the actions of the Trinity. However, the image does communicate powerfully the way in which the persons of the Godhead work together in wonderful harmony in all that they do.

The strength of social analogies is their focus on the three-ness of God and the personhood and interrelationships of Father, Son, and Spirit. Their obvious weakness is that, if taken too literally, they could suggest *tritheism*—the belief in three gods. Clearly three persons are not one in any essential sense. To guard against this danger, those who make use of the social analogy usually add that, unlike a community of three humans, the three persons of the Godhead so indwell and interpenetrate each other (see the "Indwelling (*perichorēsis*)" section, above) that they are indivisible. No

---

12. Peterson, "Evangelical Spirituality," 241–42. William Young's novel, *The Shack*, majors on this social analogy of the Trinity. For a levelheaded analysis of the theology of *The Shack*, see especially Rauser, *Finding God in "The Shack."*

member of the Trinity could exist without the other two and, although their "consciousnesses" may be distinct, they only exist in the interrelationship between the three. This notion of *perichorēsis* is rather mysterious, but it does go some way to rescue the dancers analogy from danger, even if it does not explain the mystery of the Trinity.

I hope that I have shown that the Trinity is at the very heart of Christian belief and practice, and that I have given a reasonably clear explanation of the central elements in Christian belief about the Trinity. I hope, too, that you can see why getting our Trinity talk right does matter. We are now in a position to turn to our central question—worship—and to consider how these explorations into Trinitarian faith cash out.

five

Worshipping with the Trinity

WHAT IS WORSHIP AND, more particularly, what is *Christian* worship? Let's start by looking very broadly and then narrow things down a little. The English word "worship" is derived from the Anglo-Saxon word *weorth-scipe*, which has to do with worthiness, or honor. To worship someone is to pay respect to that person by recognizing their worth. The word used to have a broad application so that one could speak of offering "worship" to fellow human beings without suggesting that the "worshipper" was attributing divine value to the person "worshipped." Of course, the worship that was offered to *God* was the recognition of his infinite value, and clearly only God is worthy of *that* kind of worship. To attribute ultimate value to any creature or aspect of creation is idolatry and strictly forbidden in Scripture.

Armed with this broad understanding of "worship" it seems clear to me that we must see worship as originating *within Godself*. Within the Trinity there is eternal love and a joyous, mutual recognition of ultimate value. Let me speculate a little here. The Father looks at his Son and recognizes him as being God from God, light from light, true God from true God. The Father recognizes the true and unsurpassable worth of his beloved Son. As his thoughts rest upon his Spirit he again rejoices: "Spirit of God, how worthy of honor you are! How lovely! How pure! How holy!" This love and recognition is reciprocated by the Son and the Spirit, who embrace the Father as their eternal source, the fount of the divinity within the Godhead. "He is holy! He is good! He is love!" The Son is eternally being generated by the Father through and for the Spirit and the Spirit is forever proceeding from the Father through and to the Son. They are both forever gifted to the other by the Father, and together they gift themselves back to the Giver.

As they contemplate each other and give themselves to each other there is a spontaneous and willing mutual eruption of praise and love as they hold each other in an everlasting embrace. God is a worshipper because the persons of God love each other and acknowledge the worth-ship of one another.

The human worship of God is not exactly like the worship within God. When the Spirit worships the Father he acknowledges him in all his difference and yet as an equal, but when a human worships the Father she or he acknowledges him as the unique Lord, the creator of all, who alone is worthy of all honor and all praise. God is most certainly *not* our equal, and his worth exceeds ours as the infinite exceeds the finite. However, in the story of salvation it is worship within the life of the Trinity that provides the foundation for our own worship. This chapter will explain what I mean by that.

Let me begin by saying that our own worship is based on a different aspect of the worship within the Trinity than what we have spoken of so far. We do not take our cue from the worship offered by the Father or by the Spirit. Indeed, it is not, strictly speaking, even the worship offered by the divine Word (as divine Word) that enables us to worship acceptably. It is the worship of *Jesus*, the Word-*made-flesh*. Jesus, the perfect human, offers perfect human praise to the Father—and it is *that* worship that we need to appreciate if we are to have a Christian understanding of what it is that is happening when we worship.[1]

The place to begin is with the ancient Christian doxology "Glory be to the Father, *through* the Son, *in* the Holy Spirit." The roots of this doxology are found in the deep structures of New Testament thought that bubble up in Ephesians 2:18: "*Through* him [the Son] we both have access *to* the Father *by* one Spirit." There it is in black and white. As Christians, we come first and foremost *to* the Father, the first person of the Trinity. We come to him *through* the work of the Son, *enabled by* the Holy Spirit. This insight is the key to a Christian understanding of worship. In the next chapter we shall explore the idea of the Father as the object of Christian worship and the implications of this truth for worship today. In this chapter we will consider what it means to worship, "*through* the Son, *in* the Holy Spirit." What I

---

1. However, I would want to add that as humans are created in the image of the divine Son, human worship of the Father is a dim echo of the divine worship eternally offered to the Father by the Son. Human worship is, in other words, like the worship of the Father by the Son but "contracted to a span." In Jesus, the worship of the Father by humanity and by the divine Word are united into a single offering.

want to say can be summed up in the words of a Matt Redman song, "Gifted Response":

> This is a gifted response;
> Father we cannot come to You by our own merit;
> We will come in the name of Your Son
> As He glorifies You,
> And in the power of Your Spirit.
>
> —MATT REDMAN © 2004 THANKYOU MUSIC

"WORSHIP THROUGH THE SON"

What does it mean to say that we offer our worship to God "through the Son"? To understand this aright we need to turn to the book of Hebrews and get our heads around the concept of Jesus as our High Priest. Although this concept played a significant role in the Christian thought of days gone by, modern Western Christians virtually ignore it. That is hardly surprising, since the notions of sacrifices, ancient rites, holy temples, and priests seem about as relevant as a cauldron of magic potion in a hospital. However, it is vital that we make the effort to reconnect with this alien past because amazingly contemporary benefits stand to be gained.

Let's begin on a vast canvas by considering the place of the worship of God within creation. Worship of the true God is, in the words of the Westminster Catechism, "the chief end of man"—the key reason we were created. James B. Torrance expresses the role of human worship brilliantly:

> God has made all creatures for his glory. Without knowing it, the lilies of the field in their beauty, glorify God with a glory greater than that of Solomon, the sparrow on the rooftop glorifies God, and the universe in its vastness and remoteness is the theatre of God's glory. But God made men and women in his own image to be the priests of creation and to express on behalf of all creatures the praises of God, so that through human lips the heavens might declare the glory of God. When we, who know we are God's creatures, worship God together, we gather up the worship of all creation. Our chief end is to glorify God, and creation realizes its own creaturely glory in glorifying God through human lips.[2]

---

2. J. B. Torrance, *Worship*, 1.

However, there is a problem with worship, which Bishop Chris Cocksworth calls "the liturgical dilemma." He writes,

> God [created] the world in order to find a response to his love in time. Humanity, especially in its prayer of trust and song of praise, is to voice that response. However, we know the biblical story faces the fact that we are flawed, unable by ourselves to enter into the perfection of his presence and incapable in ourselves of worshipping with the pureness of life required by the purity of God. This is the liturgical dilemma that runs through the pages of the Old Testament. Created to glorify God we have been corrupted by sin.[3]

Sin corrupts our worship and makes it unacceptable to God. So how can humans fulfill their vocation of "voicing creation's praise"? In the religion of ancient Israel, the priestly system dealt with this problem. The temple in Jerusalem symbolized the reality of God's presence with his people. At the heart of the temple was a chamber called the "Most Holy Place" where the glory of God dwelt. The Israelites could not enter God's presence directly lest they be consumed by his holiness, so various "perimeter fences" were set up around that chamber to keep people away. Only one man, the High Priest, was allowed into the central chamber where God's glory resided, and this was just once a year on the great Day of Atonement. The "Holy Place" was the antechamber to the "Most Holy Place," and every day priests appointed by Yhwh would come and offer sacrificial worship. These ordinary priests got closer to God's presence than other Israelites did, but they were forbidden to enter the heart of the temple. Outside the "Holy Place" was the main court, where the covenant people could come and worship. Yhwh set up the sacrificial system administered by the priests to deal with the "liturgical problem"—this was a temporary solution that allowed sins to be atoned for so that Israel could offer praise and worship. Priests, then, were mediators representing the people before God and God before the people. They drew closer to Yhwh to offer worship, confession, make atonement, and to intercede on behalf of the people. They would also teach the people on behalf of Yhwh.

It is important for us to try to understand the great Day of Atonement (Leviticus 16) a little if we are to grasp a Trinitarian approach to worship. The High Priest had to prepare himself before entering the divine presence by ritual washing before putting on his special garments (Lev 16:4). He had to slaughter a bull for his own sins and those of his household (Lev 16:6).

---

3. Cocksworth, *Holy, Holy, Holy*, 151 (emphasis original).

Two young goats were taken from Israel's flocks. One was to be sacrificed as a purification offering, while the sins of the people were later "downloaded" onto the other goat and it was sent off into the desert to carry the sin away (Lev 16:5, 8–10, 20–22). When the High Priest entered the "Most Holy Place" he took incense to hide the mercy seat from his view, lest he see it and die (Lev 16:13–14). He sprinkled the mercy seat with the blood of the bull slain for his sins and the goat slain for the people's sins, thus purging the "Most Holy Place" from the impurity built up by the sin of the community—sin that would have threatened the ongoing dwelling of God with Israel if it was not dealt with (16:14–16). He then proceeded to cleanse the entire sanctuary (Lev 16:17–20) before various ritual decontamination procedures were followed to wind things down (Lev 16:23–28).

Now consider the following things about the role of the High Priest. First of all, he is the man who represents the entire nation when he enters the inner sanctum. Part of the special clothing he had to wear was a breastplate that had twelve stones on it, symbolizing the twelve tribes of Israel whom he had been chosen to represent. He stands before Yhwh not simply on behalf of himself, but also on behalf of all the people of God. Second, in order to function as the symbolic representative of the nation he also had to be an Israelite—one of those whom he "summed up" in his own role. He was thus a brother, a fellow Israelite who stood in solidarity with the nation. Third, he offers sacrifice for his own sins and those of the people in order to make atonement.[4] Fourth, he enters the very presence of God himself to present the sacrificial, cleansing blood and to intercede on behalf of Israel. The High Priest would worship Yhwh, make atonement, and pray to Yhwh on behalf of the people. He was the one who enabled the "liturgical problem" to be held in check.

However, the Book of Hebrews in the New Testament sees various inadequacies in this system. Firstly, the High Priest himself was *a sinner* who had to make atonement for his own sins, making him less than ideal for the job (Heb 5:3). He also suffered from being *mortal*—meaning that his representation before God was only ever temporary (Heb 7:23). Second, the sanctuary the High Priest entered was the earthly Jerusalem sanctuary that was only ever a pale copy of heaven itself (Heb 8:5). To really solve the liturgical problem he would need to enter into the heart of heaven,

4. For clarification, I should point out that in both the Old Testament and in Hebrews—and contrary to popular opinion—the sacrifice was not the ritual slaughter of the animal (or the Messiah) but the presentation of its blood (representing its life) before God. See Eberhart, *The Sacrifice of Jesus*; Moffitt, "Blood, Life, and Atonement."

and clearly he was in no position to do so. Third, the sacrifices offered did not deal *permanently* with the problem of sin, as is clear from the fact that they had to be offered year on year (Heb 10:1–4). These sacrifices did offer temporary, external cleansing but not permanent or deep cleansing (Heb 9:9–10). Yet God—who in the Old Testament had already spoken of the need for another High Priest who was different from the order of Levitical priests (Heb 7:11ff.; Ps 110:4; Gen 14:17–20)—deliberately built all of these inadequacies into the system. The inbuilt inadequacies of the old covenant priesthood were there so that when the Messiah came as the perfect High Priest we would be able to see how superior his perfect priesthood is.

Jesus, says the book of Hebrews, is our High Priest. However, unlike Levitical priests, Christ did not sin and so does not need to atone for himself (Heb 4:15; 7:26). And, because he has been raised to everlasting life, his intercession for the people before the Father is eternal (Heb 7:24). Christ has not entered the Jerusalem temple like a Levitical High Priest on the Day of Atonement; rather, he has entered the very presence of God in heaven itself (Heb 8:1–2; 9:11).[5] In addition, the sacrifice he offered was not a mere lamb or bull but his own life (Heb 7:27; 9:12, 26). The purifying lifeblood he offers to God is his own lifeblood (Heb 9:11ff.). The superiority of this sacrifice is shown by the fact that it only had to be offered *once* (Heb 9:25–28), as well as by the fact that it cleanses permanently and deep down to our conscience (Heb 9:14). Indeed Christ cleanses heaven itself (Heb 9:23) and brings "eternal salvation" to those who obey him (Heb 5:9). The Levitical High Priest's work was never done because it was imperfect, and so he never sat down in the "Most Holy Place." However, Jesus has *completed* his atoning work and so has "*sat down* at the right hand of the throne of the Majesty in heaven" (Heb 8:1; cf. 1:3; 10:11–12).

It is crucial to grasp the idea that Christ our High Priest is in the presence of the Father *as our representative*. Because he was our representative, it was essential that he stood in solidarity with humanity. He was of "the same family" as those he makes holy and calls them "brothers" (Heb 2:11). "Since the children have flesh and blood, he too shared in their humanity" (Heb 2:14). It was essential that this sharing in our humanity included sharing in our temptations and sufferings so that, like the Aaronic High

---

5. In fact, as the Law of Moses makes clear, because Jesus was not a descendant from Levi he would not have been qualified to act as a priest in the *Jerusalem* temple. And there was *no need* for him to do so as that temple already had legitimate priests (Heb 8:3–4). But Jesus is a priest (in fact, the High Priest) *in the order of Melchizedek*—a *heavenly* order of priests that serve in the *heavenly* sanctuary.

Priest, he could empathize with our weaknesses (Heb 5:2): "[Christ] had to be made like his brothers in every way, in order that he might become a merciful and faithful High Priest in service to God, and that he might make atonement for the sins of the people. Because he himself suffered when he was tempted, he is able to help those who are being tempted" (Heb 2:17–18). This is why Hebrews often speaks of the Son being made "perfect" or "complete" through sufferings (e.g., Heb 2:10). It is not that the Messiah had to be made morally complete, but that he had to share human suffering and temptation in order to be qualified to function as our High Priest. Jesus has walked where we walk and stands in solidarity with us as our representative.

"Therefore, since we have such a great High Priest who has gone through the heavens, Jesus the Son of God, let us hold firmly to the faith we profess. For we do not have a High Priest who is unable to sympathize with our weaknesses, but we have one who has been tempted in every way, just as we are—yet was without sin. Let us then approach the throne of grace with confidence, so that we may receive mercy and find grace to help us in our time of need" (Heb 4:14–16).

He is there right now "before the throne of God above." He stands in the presence of the Father worshipping (Heb 2:12; 8:3) and interceding for us (Heb 7:25). This insight is the foundation of a Christian understanding of worship. James Torrance, the main source of my inspiration on this issue, says that "Christian worship is . . . our participation through the Spirit in the Son's communion with the Father, in his vicarious life of worship and intercession."[6] The problem was that God has required worship from us but we, because of our sin, are unable to offer it. The solution is that God provides for us, in our High Priest Jesus, the very worship that we could not offer. *The response that God required from us has already been made by Christ, our representative.* Christ worships God on our behalf, making God not simply the one who is worshipped but also *the one who worships.*

The Christian life, as we have seen in chapters 2 and 3, is about being united with Christ and identifying with him. In baptism and by faith we are initiated into a relationship in which we are identified with Christ or, in Paul's language, placed "in Christ." In the ongoing journey of the Christian life, Christ is formed in us by the Spirit as our lives become gradually conformed to what we already are in the Messiah. When the Lord returns, the transformation will be completed in the twinkling of an eye and we

6. J. B. Torrance, *Worship*, 3.

shall be like him, for we shall see him as he is. But every aspect of Christian living is about being transformed into the image of God's Son. This is the case with worship as with everything else. Thus worship is not, first and foremost, something that *we* do. *Our worship is no more and no less than a participation in the Messiah's own perfect worship of God.* Our worship is joined to his and is made acceptable. We share in his own relationship of open communion with the Father, and thus it is that we even share in Jesus' own son-ship and are ourselves adopted as children of God. We are accepted by the Father "in Christ," the beloved, and "in Christ" we are "holy and blameless in his sight" (Eph 1:4). In this way we can draw near before heaven's throne of grace with confidence. We know that our worship will be acceptable *because Christ's worship is acceptable,* and it is his worship in which we are sharing. Christ is the chief worshipper and is our worship leader. He proclaims the praises of God in the midst of the Christian congregation (Heb 2:12).[7] As Calvin says, "Christ leads our songs, and is the chief composer of our hymns."[8] Chris Cocksworth summarizes very well: "Our worship is with Christ our brother, in Christ our priest but always through Christ our sacrifice, whose death for us is the means of our cleansing, renewing and perfecting."[9]

Exactly the same thing holds true for prayer. Christ is the one who prays to the Father, and our prayer is simply a participation in Christ's own prayer. He lives forever interceding for us (Heb 6:20; 7:25–28; 8:1–6) and our petition is simply, as Karl Barth puts it, a "repetition of his petition."[10] Thus we pray to the Father "in the name of Jesus" and not in our own names. We join our prayers with his prayer, and this is how we can have confidence that God hears us. Graham Buxton provides a helpful analogy of all that we have said about prayer and worship offered to the Father through the Son.

> There is a delightful story of a little girl who was learning to play the piano, and whose musical skills were still very limited. One day she was playing some notes on the keyboard whilst staying with her family in a hotel in Norway. There was little to appreciate in her playing, and several guests found her "plink . . . plonk . . . plink . . . plonk" intensely annoying. After a while, a man came

---

7. For a great discussion of the implications of this verse for worship see Ron Man, *Proclamation and Praise.*

8. Quoted in Cocksworth, *Holy, Holy, Holy,* 159.

9. Ibid., 162 (emphasis original).

10. Barth, *Church Dogmatics* III/3, 277.

and sat beside the girl, and started to play alongside her. The result was astounding—wonderful music from the two of them, the little girl playing as before, with the man supplying all the other notes. The man was the girl's father, the nineteenth-century Russian composer Alexander Borodin . . .

In the same way that the great composer welcomed the playing of his little girl, embracing it and transforming it into something beautiful, so Christ receives all that we offer to God, in thanksgiving, in worship, and in service, converts it in himself, and presents it as something perfect and wholly acceptable to his Father, who is our Father.[11]

"Worship in the Spirit"

We must not stop our reflection at this point, because Christ's worship of the Father avails us nothing without the work of the Spirit. All genuine Christian worship and prayer is enabled by the Holy Spirit (Phil 3:3). As Jesus said to the woman at the well, those who would worship the Father acceptably must do so "in Spirit and in truth" (John 4:23–24).

Worship is not an attempt to impress God, or to massage God's ego so we can get our own way, or to earn credit and get into God's good books. Worship is first and last a response to God's unconditional love for us and grace towards us. God's love does not follow on from our worship like a reward follows a good deed. On the contrary, his love precedes our worship. God is not gracious to us because we honor him; we honor him because he is gracious to us. Worship is the joyful response of God's people to the salvation freely given in the Messiah. It is something we do, but it is something we do in *response* to love and not something that we do to *gain* love. But even this is only half the story. Although worship is our response to God's love, it is actually better thought of as *the Spirit's gift to us of a response to God* or, in Matt Redman's words, "a gifted response." We can only respond to God in praise because the Holy Spirit causes love for God to arise in our hearts (Rom 5:5), enabling us to cry "Abba, Father!" (Gal 4:6). Without the Spirit we could not even sincerely say, "Jesus is Lord" (1 Cor 12:3). And, as we have seen, even that is not the full story because the response the Spirit enables us to make to the Father is actually simply a sharing in Christ's own response to the Father. The Spirit, in other words, is the one who baptizes us

11. Buxton, *Dancing in the Dark*, 117.

into Christ (1 Cor 12:13) and enables us to share with Christ in his worship of the Father.

The Spirit is the one who places us in Christ at conversion, but he is also the one who slowly transforms our lives so that they conform to what we already are in Christ. It's exactly like this in our actual lived prayer and worship. In Christ our worship and prayer are already perfect, but only the Spirit can transform our actual offerings and motives so that they gradually reflect Christ's own obedience, love, and thanksgiving. The Spirit can still rebuke us in our worship, as in our ethical lives, if we are falling short of who we already are "in Christ." God may point out that our worship is according to the flesh rather than according to the Spirit. So the teaching in this chapter does not mean that we do not need to examine our worship and reflect on how acceptable it is. What it does mean is that we need to ask how much our worship is prideful and self-satisfied rather than humble and God-dependent. The call is not to pull our own worshipping socks up but to surrender to the Spirit and allow him to conform our worship to Christ's.

Spirit-led worship is thus not the special reserve of Pentecostals and charismatics; rather, it is the heritage of all genuine Christian worshippers. "Spirit-led" worship is not a theological synonym for "loud" worship or "bouncy" worship or "worship-led-by-a-rock-band." Spirit-led worship can be very loud and energetic, but it can equally be meditative and candle-lit. Spirit-led worship may be found where incense rises and liturgy is sung just as much as it may be found where flags are waved and the singing is in tongues. And the converse is true—all that glitters is not gold, all that shouts and shakes or glows and rises before the Lord is not worship.

Spirit-led worship is worship that is sincere and honest. It acknowledges our need of God's assistance and sees that only in Christ are any offerings we make acceptable. Acceptable worshippers come to God in weakness and humility and receive grace in a time of need. Spirit-led worship is not insecure worship, ever-anxious of rejection by God, but confident worship that delights that everything necessary has already been done. It is not arrogant self-promotion (thinly disguised as humility) but humble confidence in the one in whom we have been brought to trust. God requires worship and God has offered that worship on our behalf in Christ—and by the Spirit God enables us to offer ourselves to him through Christ. Our response to God is a participation (enabled by God) in God's own response to God. That phrase is a bit of a gobstopper! Try this one: worship is "a gifted response" for which we can claim no credit.

The Spirit's guiding role in worship is one that Pentecostals and charismatics often recognize. The Spirit is the worship leader who enables us to be led by Christ in worship. In the charismatic traditions there is a very deep appreciation of the Spirit as the worship leader who orchestrates gatherings of the community. Spirit-led worship will exalt Jesus and the Father. It will have an intercessory edge, for we will be led to share in the Messiah's prayers for the world. Several commentators have observed how often intercession is marginalized in charismatic worship. This does appear to be the case, and it should not be so—if the Spirit is uniting us with Christ's High Priestly prayer, then how could intercession not be an essential ingredient of our meeting together? The Spirit will also create communities in which everyone is empowered to offer worship through Christ in the Spirit. This may be through liturgy which, contrary to the views of some in my own charismatic free church tradition, can (and should) be very uplifting, egalitarian, and participatory. And/or it may be through spontaneous prayers, readings, prophesy, pictures, testimonies, tongues and interpretation offered by different members of the anointed community. The Spirit generates fellowship, unity, and community between Christian and Christian as well as between Christians and Christ when we worship. He does not make us all the same but enables us to love and embrace each other in all our diversity (1 Corinthians 12). If our communal worship is not like this—if it excludes people from participating or simply draws people as individuals towards God but not towards each other—then we need to start asking hard questions about whether it is as Spirit-led as we may like to imagine. Spirit-led worship will also have an appropriate openness to the new and unplanned. The Spirit blows where he wills and gives gifts to whomever he wishes to (John 3:8; 1 Cor 12:11). Here is where liturgy can sometimes actually shut us down rather than open us up to the work of the Spirit.

And things are much the same with prayer. We are to "pray in the Spirit" (Eph 6:18). Such prayer includes obvious Spirit-inspired praying such as speaking in tongues, but it is far more than that. We are praying in the Spirit whenever we are enabled to pray according to God's will with Christ. Paul writes that, "The Spirit helps us in our weakness. We do not know what we ought to pray for, but the Spirit himself intercedes for us with groans that words cannot express. And he who searches our hearts knows the mind of the Spirit, because the Spirit intercedes for the saints in accordance with God's will" (Rom 8:26–28).

A concluding reflection: some people think that worship and prayer is something we offer to God in order to earn some merit with him and perhaps even to build up a surplus of credit to earn salvation. This is not a Christian view of worship and it is a terrible burden to bear—indeed, it is an impossible one. Other people think that although God has offered us salvation free of charge through grace, worship is still primarily our response. This DIY view of worship is common among Christians, but it is also rather hard work. "Although it stresses the God-humanward movement in Christ, the human-Godward movement is still ours! It emphasizes *our* faith, *our* decision, *our* response in an event theology which short-circuits the vicarious humanity of Christ and belittles union with Christ . . . [It implies] that God throws us back on ourselves to make our response."[12]

Week after week we have to stir ourselves up and offer God his due and, over a period of time, this can exhaust even the most enthusiastic worshipper. If we think, as I have done and as many charismatics still do, that the value of our worship depends on our feeling all warm and fuzzy as we sing and pray, then we have things back to front. The Trinitarian view of worship presented by the Bible and fleshed out in this chapter does not call people to whip themselves up into a worship frenzy but simply points people to the worship that Christ is currently offering and invites them to join him in it. And even our response to God's grace is a response that God has provided us with as a gift.

12. J. B. Torrance, *Worship*, 17–18.

six

Worshipping the Trinity

On the floor of the nave of a glorious little Northumbrian church in the village of Alnham lies a tombstone that has a quite legible, if rather rough, inscription on it dating, as does the tomb itself, from the seventeenth century. The inscription goes halfway down the tomb, describing whom it is that is commemorated and how she died. Surprisingly, this inscription comes to an abrupt halt in the middle of a line. The concluding sentence, to which one's eye is drawn, reads, "Glory be to the Father *and to the rest*"[1]!

WE HAVE SEEN THAT Christian worship is always offered *through* the Son, *in* the Spirit. However, the early Christian doxology, "Glory to the Father, through the Son, in the Holy Spirit" was supplemented with another, equally important doxology, "Glory to the Father *with* the Son, *together with* the Holy Spirit" or, as some later versions have it, "Glory be to the Father *and* to the Son *and* to the Holy Spirit." The difference is clear. The earlier doxology only proclaims the Father as the object of worship, while the later doxology sets up all the members of the Trinity as recipients of worship. This later doxology was reflected in the creed that came out of the Council of Constantinople in 381, which says of the Holy Spirit: "We believe in the Holy Spirit, the Lord, the Giver of Life, who proceeds from the Father; who with the Father and the Son together is worshipped and glorified." That creed has been accepted as accurately expressing biblical teaching by all streams

---

1. The quotation is from a sermon by Bishop John Inge (italics added).

of the orthodox Christian churches: Eastern Orthodox, Roman Catholic, and Protestant. What is clear is that Christians are to worship the Father, the Son, and the Spirit.

What are we to make of the differences between the two doxologies? Well, it is quite clear that although the earlier doxology only identifies the Father as the one who is worshipped, we should not think that the early Christians worshipped only the Father. The evidence for the worship of Jesus within the early Jesus movement is simply overwhelming.[2] From as far back as we are able to trace early Christian sources, Jesus was being worshipped alongside the Father. So when the earlier doxology says that worship was offered "*through* the Son," that clearly did not exclude worship also being offered "*to* the Son." In the fourth century, Basil of Caesarea offered an insight that helps us make sense of the differences. At the time he was writing the earlier doxology was well established in all the churches, but the later one was still very controversial in some churches. Basil's church employed both doxologies, and he explained the difference as follows: When we say "Glory to the Father, through the Son, in the Holy Spirit" we are describing the way in which God deals with creation. The Father comes to creation through the Son, in the Spirit (see chapter 2) and creation comes to the Father through the Son and in the Spirit (see chapter 5). The doxology beautifully captures what Chris Cocksworth calls the "Trinitarian geography" of God's interaction with creation, describing the route by which our worship ascends to God. However, when we say "Glory to the Father with the Son, together with the Holy Spirit," our focus is on God *as God*—God as God is *in Godself* rather than how God relates to creation. It is therefore right and proper that glory is offered to Father, Son, and Spirit. In this chapter we will focus on the need to offer worship to each person of the Godhead.

GLORY BE TO THE FATHER

When you look at prayer and worship in the New Testament, one thing that may strike you is that the prayer and worship of the early believers in Jesus were mostly directed to God the Father. One does, of course, find some prayers to Jesus, and especially some worship of Jesus, but in volume these

---

2. For a very detailed analysis of the evidence see Larry Hurtado, *Lord Jesus Christ: Devotion to Jesus in Earliest Christianity*; Bauckham, *Jesus and the God of Israel*.

are outnumbered by the attention given to the Father (e.g., Eph 1:3; 2 Cor 1:3; 1 Pet 1:3). Here is a small, random sample of such prayers:

> Our Father in heaven, hallowed be your name, your kingdom come, your will be done on earth as it is in heaven. Give us today our daily bread. Forgive us our debts, as we also have forgiven our debtors. And lead us not into temptation, but deliver us from the evil one. (Matt 6:9b–13)

> Praise be to the God and Father of our Lord Jesus Christ, who has blessed us in the heavenly realms with every spiritual blessing in Christ. (Eph 1:3)

> Praise be to the God and Father of our Lord Jesus Christ, the Father of compassion and the God of all comfort . . . (2 Cor 1:3)

> Praise be to the God and Father of our Lord Jesus Christ! In his great mercy he has given us new birth into a living hope through the resurrection of Jesus Christ from the dead . . . (1 Pet 1:3)

When prayer is urged upon the people, it is usually the first person of the Trinity who is the object:

> [Through] Jesus, therefore, let us continually offer to God a sacrifice of praise—the fruit of lips that confess his name. (Heb 13:15)

> . . . always giving thanks to God the Father for everything, in the name of our Lord Jesus Christ. (Eph 5:20)

Notice how every prayer above (apart from the prayer that Jesus taught) makes explicit mention of Jesus. These are clearly prayers offered through the Son. But we must also note that they are offered *to* the Father. This makes it clear that when Christ-followers worship the Father they don't do so at the expense of Christ or by somehow sidelining Christ in the process. Christian prayer to the Father is always conscious of Christ. In fact, worship of the Father is necessarily and always a fully Trinitarian event: "Because you are sons, God sent the Spirit of his Son into our hearts, the Spirit who calls out, 'Abba, Father'" (Gal 4:6). We also call out to God— "Abba, Father"—with the worshipping Spirit (Rom 8:15). So worship of the Father is the product of the Spirit of Jesus given to us by God.

It seems to me that in contemporary Christian worship one can detect clear trends in certain sections of the church in which the first person of the Trinity is increasingly neglected. There have been occasions when we shy away from using the "F-word" (Father) in worship. Sometimes the Father is not so much as mentioned, and at other times he gets in only by a passing reference. Susan White, looking beyond the charismatic movement, notices the same shift:

> As I look around the contemporary scene I see several things happening. I see liturgical attention to the Triune God decreasing as liturgical attention to Jesus increases . . . And I see liturgical attention to God the Father being gradually abandoned. In some churches the person of Jesus has become virtually the sole object of congregational worship, the name of God the Father is almost never invoked. At the same time Jesus has taken on all of the key theological attributes of the Triune God.[3]

This neglect of the Father in worship is a very serious distortion of a fully Christian offering of worship and can only serve to distort the shape of our Christian faith and living. In Revelation there is a wonderful vision of worship offered "to him who sits on the throne and to the Lamb" (Rev 5:13), but I sometimes worry that we are in danger of losing interest in the one sitting upon the throne and of devoting all our attention to the Lamb.[4] Jesus came as the way to the Father (John 14:6), and the tragic irony of focusing on Jesus at the expense of the Father is that when we do this we actually fail to honor Jesus himself. Jesus comes to us and invites us to join him in his worship of the Father—so *to bypass the Father is to dishonor Jesus.*

Why is the Father being eclipsed? Perhaps Jesus seems more "like us" and therefore more approachable. Susan White again:

> In many instances, Jesus of Nazareth is portrayed in worship as the "softer side of God"; if God the Father is the remote and angry judge of human misdeeds, and the ruler of the universe then the human Jesus is the confidant, the one who understands our woes, shares in our misfortunes and feels compassion for our various human predicaments. We need to focus on Jesus in worship because

---

3. White, *Whatever Happened to the Father?*, 9–10.

4. That this is no new phenomenon was brought home to me a few years back in a local Anglican church. The central stained-glass window (which I would guess is from the nineteenth century) is of the scene from Revelation in which all creation worships God. The text around the window said, "Blessing and honour, and glory and power, be unto him that sitteth upon the throne." The words "and unto the Lamb" were omitted. Yet there, seated on the throne, I saw not the Father but Jesus! The window edited the biblical text and made Jesus into "him that sitteth upon the throne"—effectively usurping his Father!

> God the Father is unapproachable. For Jesus' care we are grateful, we are indebted, we are adoring. In short, Jesus becomes the object of worship in his own right, resulting in a kind of Jesus-centered Unitarianism, shading over occasionally into what Sallie McFague first described as 'Jesusolatry.'"[5]

If this analysis is correct, it reveals just how distorted our perceptions of God our Father can be. The Father may be a transcendent authority figure before whom we bow, but he is never any less than the one who loves us with the very deepest passions of his heart. The New Testament emphasizes both the *transcendent mystery* of the Father and his *great love* for the world.[6] Worship of this Father can spiral to the same heights of intimacy and passion as any worship of his Son. We can sing to our Abba and ask that he would let us be his and his alone, never letting us go.[7] We can wonder how we even managed to exist without knowing his parenthood and loving care.[8] We draw near without guilt or fear, knowing acceptance and forgiveness and the fatherhood of the true and living God.[9] How could we ever think of such a God as "remote and angry"?

GLORY BE TO THE SON

As we have already seen, prayer in the New Testament was usually addressed to the Father. But we do see Paul asking the Lord Jesus to remove the thorn from his flesh (2 Cor 12:8–9) and Stephen, as he dies, praying, "Lord Jesus, receive my spirit" (Acts 7:59). The prayer *maranatha* (1 Cor 16:22), meaning "Our Lord, come!" seems to go back to the very earliest days of the Jesus movement and reflects an early instinct to address Jesus in prayer. The worship of Jesus was a revolutionary step that the early *ekklēsia* took right from the start. In the New Testament, the Book of Revelation powerfully portrays the ultimate vision of worshipping the Son: the Lamb sits down *on the very throne of God himself*, alongside the Father, and receives the worship of all creation (Rev 5:11–14).

5. White, *Whatever Happened to the Father?*, 14.

6. Kendall Soulen argues that the first person of the Trinity is especially associated with the divine mystery, particularly as focused in the name Yhwh. See Soulen, *The Divine Name(s) and the Holy Trinity*.

7. Dave Bilbrough, "Abba, Father, Let Me Be" (Kingsway's Thankyou Music, 1977).

8. Ian Smale, "Father God, I Wonder" (Kingsway's Thankyou Music, 1984).

9. Rob Hayward, "I'm Accepted" (Kingsway Thankyou Music, 1985).

Then I looked and heard the voice of many angels, numbering thousands upon thousands, and ten thousand times ten thousand. They encircled the throne and the living creatures and the elders. In a loud voice they sang: "Worthy is the Lamb, who was slain, to receive power and wealth and wisdom and strength and honor and glory and praise!" Then I heard every creature in heaven and on earth and under the earth and on the sea, and all that is in them, singing: "To him who sits on the throne and to the Lamb be praise and honor and glory and power, for ever and ever!" The four living creatures said, "Amen," and the elders fell down and worshipped.

In a similar way, Philippians 2:6–11 shows Jesus receiving the worship of every creature in the universe. They bow the knee and confess him as "Lord." The worship offered to Jesus in that passage is very clearly presented as worship offered to Yhwh in the person of Jesus.

Worship offered to Jesus is a fully Trinitarian event. It is clearly honoring to the Father because of the close relationship between them. In John's Gospel Jesus suggests that whoever honors the Son honors the Father who sent him (John 5:23; 12:26), and Paul looks to the great day when all creatures will bow before Jesus in worship and confess his name "to the glory of God the Father" (Phil 2:10–11). Worship of Jesus also honors the Spirit, because the Spirit delights to draw attention to the Son. It is he who opens our eyes to see the glory of Christ (2 Corinthians 3). It is he who takes what belongs to Christ and makes it known to the disciples (John 16:12–15). It is he who loves to work through the disciples to proclaim Christ to the world (John 15:26–27; 20:21–23). The Spirit delights when people fall in love with Jesus. One could extend these thoughts perhaps in the light of our discussion of *perichorēsis* in chapter 4. Because the persons of the Trinity exist in deeply interpenetrating, loving relationship, to honor one is to honor all and to worship one is, indirectly at least, to worship all. Likewise to dishonor one is to dishonor all.

It would be true to say that contemporary Christian worship of Jesus is "to the glory of God the Father," and it is true that wherever Jesus is present the Father is present also. But that is not an excuse for the neglect of the Father (and Spirit) discussed above. There are a couple of relatively recent songs that proclaim, "it's all about you, Jesus."[10] There is a sense in which this claim is true and, if it is understood clearly by those singing, then these

10. "Jesus, Lover of My Soul" (Paul Oakley, 1995) and "When the Music Fades" (Matt Redman, 1997).

songs can be wonderful instruments of worship (I must confess to liking both of them). However, taken in a fairly straightforward sense the claim is simply false. It is *not* all about Jesus. It is all about God—Father, Son, and Holy Spirit. My concern about songs like that is that the ordinary person in the congregation may well not interpret the song in a suitably qualified way and may simply run with the straightforward (false) meaning, perhaps undermining, little by little, the place of the Father and Spirit in their own spirituality. I want to suggest that worship of Jesus is central to Christian faith, and that it is honoring to both Father and Spirit, but that it must not move towards an exclusive focus on worshipping Jesus that denies the reality of the Trinity by pushing the Father and the Spirit to the margins. Trinitarian spirituality requires a balance that *some* are in danger of losing.

However, there is another danger present that must also be resisted— and that is to neglect the worship of Jesus by singing songs exclusively to "God" and "Lord" and "Father." I know of one denomination in the UK in which one member of a liturgical reform committee seriously suggested that all references to Jesus should be removed from the church's liturgy because they were liable to cause offence! Thank God the suggestion was gunned down, but that it could even be *suggested* beggars belief! Such worship would fail to be Christian at all. Christian worship will focus on the person and narrative of Jesus.

Some have expressed concern that my desire to restore the place of the Father and Spirit could lead to the undermining of the core Christian narrative in worship—the story of Jesus. I appreciate the concern, and so let me say that Jesus' story is, and must remain, at the heart of Christian worship. However, it is precisely in the story of Jesus that the Father and the Spirit are revealed, and so worship that pivots around this narrative and yet is not fully Trinitarian has actually failed to understand the very tale it claims to make central. Sensitive worship that is Jesus-centered will be the worship of a Jesus who cannot be understood apart from his relationship with the Father and the Spirit—it will be Trinitarian worship.

This reflection on the centrality of the Jesus story for worship brings up another concern I have with some contemporary Jesus-songs. It seems to me that there is a trend towards singing songs addressed to a Jesus who has been stripped of any references to the narrative that makes him who he is. Such songs speak of a "Lord" called "Jesus" who makes the singers feel loved and accepted, but often there is no reference to his incarnation, his teaching, his miracles, his life, his death-resurrection-ascension, or his coming return. It is not that there is anything necessarily wrong with a song that does this. If in a meeting some of the other songs, Scripture readings, prayers, and sermon fill in the details, then the congregation understands that the Jesus in these minimalist songs is the same Jesus painted elsewhere in such rich colors. The problem is that if such songs become dominant, we gradually lose sight of the biblical Christ and replace him with "Jesus-my-personal-therapist" or "Jesus-my-mystic-boyfriend." Jesus-the-personal-therapist and Jesus-the-mystic-boyfriend are vague characters who give worshippers warm fuzzy feelings of acceptance, but I think one has to seriously ask whether such messiahs are the real Messiah at all. If such songs dominate worship meetings one has to ask at what point worship ceases to be *Christian* worship and degenerates into some mutant offspring.

This leads to one final issue: the place of the humanity of Christ and his actual life on earth in our worship. The strong tendency in Christian worship is to focus on the deity of Christ. James Steven points out that if this focus obscures his humanity then it imbalances what the creeds were so careful to balance—the deity and humanity. He comments that in a number of Anglican worship services that he observed every single song addressed to Jesus was about Jesus as risen and exalted king. "Thus instead of singing to a Jesus who in his humanity faced temptation, conflict and suffering, we sang to a triumphant Christ who in his majesty and power defeats the powers of evil."[11] Perhaps the problem can be put a little differently. Perhaps it is not so much that we focus on the deity of Christ at the expense of his humanity but that we focus on one part of the story (the victorious God-man in his resurrection and ascension) to the exclusion of the rest. Steven is certainly correct that we need to draw the full narrative of Jesus into our worship. Christian worship will always be addressed to the risen and ascended Lord and will celebrate his victory but we must not forget that, as the Gospels and the Book of Hebrews remind us, this risen Lord stood in total solidarity with his people.

> He walked where I walk, (echo)
> He stood where I stand, (echo)
> He felt what I feel, (echo)
> He understands. (echo)
> He knows my frailty, (echo)
> Shared my humanity, (echo)
> Tempted in every way, (echo)

11. Steven, *Worship in the Spirit*, 189. Bruce Hulme has made a similar observation in his study of the Christology of 184 Hillsong lyrics (Hulme, "Hillsong Christology," unpublished, 2004).

Yet without sin. (echo)

God with us, so close to us. God with us, Immanuel! (all)
(Repeat)

One of a hated race, (echo)
Stung by the prejudice, (echo)
Suffering injustice, (echo)
Yet He forgives. (echo)
Wept for my wasted years, (echo)
Paid for my wickedness, (echo)
He died in my place (echo)
That I might live. (echo)

—G. KENDRICK © 1988 MAKE WAY MUSIC

GLORY BE TO THE HOLY SPIRIT

Things get more complicated when it comes to the Holy Spirit. The church was not quick to clarify exactly what it thought about the status of the Spirit because it was so preoccupied with debates over the person of Jesus. It was not until the fourth century, as controversy over the person of Christ began to die down, that eyes turned to the Spirit and the need for clarity became pressing. The question was intimately connected with worship—whether Christians should offer glory to the Spirit along with the Father and the Son. Some felt that to worship the Spirit was an alien departure from the faith, while others maintained that it was the only way of remaining faithful to the heart of the Christian tradition.

One can understand the fears of those who felt that it would be wrong to worship and pray to the Spirit because there are no examples of anyone praying to or worshipping the Spirit in the New Testament. The earliest churches directed their worship to God and to Christ, having a "binitarian" object rather than a Trinitarian object. Now, shocking as some readers may find this, I want to suggest that contemporary Christian worship needs to move beyond the exact balance found within the New Testament documents. I think that a biblical view of the Spirit has implications for worship that were not fully realized in the earliest communities of Jesus-followers and took some time to come to maturity. To some this will sound like I am departing from the sufficiency and authority of Scripture, but that is not so. It is the very teaching of this authoritative and sufficient Scripture that compels us, or so the Christian tradition has maintained, to move beyond the practices of the first-century *ekklēsia* and to transform their binitarian focus in worship into a Trinitarian focus. We need to understand that the teaching of the New Testament will often have implications that were not developed fully in the early church but that later Christians can draw out and legitimately claim as biblical. For instance, although neither the Old Testament nor the New Testament say that slavery should be abolished, and although both Testaments actually seem to go along with it in places, many Christians feel that the main themes of creation and redemption actually undermine the institution, making slavery unbiblical.[12] This is indeed so, and the situation with the Spirit is not dissimilar. Basically, I want to defend the odd-sounding claim that worshipping and praying to the Spirit are completely biblical, *even though they are never done in the Bible!*

The argument for this claim is very simple in outline and somewhat more complex in its detailed defense. It proceeds as follows:

1. The Bible teaches that the Spirit is fully divine without being identical with the Father and the Son.

2. The Bible teaches that worship and prayer are among the appropriate human responses to one who is fully divine.

3. Therefore, from what the Bible teaches we can deduce that worship and prayer are among the appropriate responses to the Holy Spirit.

That's it, really. The logic is impeccable, and the conclusion *must* be correct *if* premise 1 and premise 2 are true. Notice that the conclusion avoids saying that the Bible teaches that worship and prayer are among the appropriate responses to the Spirit, because the Bible does not actually say this. There is no proof text that one can point to and say, "Look! Here is the verse where we are told to worship the Spirit!" The conclusion says, instead, that taking the biblical teachings contained in premises 1 and 2 seriously logically entails the appropriateness of worship and prayer being directed to the Spirit. That's what I meant when I said that the argument was very simple in outline. The more complex part of the case is building up an argument for premises 1 and 2, and I have no intention of doing that here.[13]

So the logic of the biblical revelation of God makes the worship of the Spirit alongside the Father and the Son an appropriate human response to this "Lord," this "Giver of Life." The creed issued from the Council at Constantinople was quite correct to say that the Spirit "with the Father and

12. E.g., Webb, *Slaves, Women, and Homosexuals.*

13. See chapter 4.

the Son together is worshipped and glorified," and the church was right to accept this statement as being faithful to biblical revelation. Thus it is that one finds prayers and hymns in developing Christian spirituality directed to the Holy Spirit.

> Spirit of holiness,
> Let all Thy saints adore
> Thy sacred energy, and bless Thy heart-renewing power.
> Not angel-tongues can tell
> Thy love's ecstatic height,
> Thy glorious joy unspeakable,
> The beatific sight.
>
> —Charles Wesley (1707–88)

> Breathe on me, Breath of God,
> Fill me with life anew;
> That I may love what Thou dost love
> And do what Thou wouldst do.
>
> Breathe on me, breath of God,
> Until my heart is pure,
> Until my will is one with Thine
> To do and to endure.
>
> Breathe on me, breath of God,
> Till I am wholly Thine;
> Until this earthly part of me
> Glows with Thy fire divine.
>
> Breathe on me, breath of God,
> So shall I never die,
> But live with Thee the perfect life
> Of Thine eternity.
>
> —Edwin Hatch (1835–1889)

> Spirit of the living God,
> Fall afresh on me.
> Spirit of the living God,
> Fall afresh on me.
> Melt me, mould me, fill me, use me.
> Spirit of the living God,
> Fall afresh on me.
>
> —Daniel Iverson
> © 1963 Birdwing Music/Universal Songs

It has to be said, though, that the Holy Spirit is the member of the Trinity who has been most short-changed in the honor that is due to him. If you look through any book of Christian hymns and choruses you will find that the percentage of songs that include any direct address to the Spirit in prayer or worship is tiny (we will explore this further in chapter 7). It is also the case that you may well have to attend many Christian meetings before ever encountering a prayer or song directed to the Spirit. I quite often hear non-charismatics lament the overemphasis on the Spirit in charismatic and Pentecostal worship. As a charismatic, I have to report that this is emphatically *not* the case. When it comes to giving glory to the Spirit, charismatics and Pentecostals are almost as bad as those we may refer to in our less charitable moments as "the frozen chosen." When we remember to include the Father, our worship is more or less binitarian as far as its focus is concerned, because although we worship "in the Spirit" we very rarely give worship "to the Spirit." And this is not just true of charismatics. James Steven writes:

> The texts of the Western liturgical tradition are symptomatic of this weakness with their hesitant acknowledgement of the economy of the Spirit. Take for instance, the Holy Communion rite of the *Book of Common Prayer*, a foundational liturgy for Anglicanism. Apart from the Nicene Creed, the only clear mention of the economy of the Spirit is in the Collect for Purity, with its petition to Almighty God to "cleanse the thoughts of our hearts by the inspiration of thy Holy Spirit." The other references to the Spirit are in concluding doxologies to the immanent Trinity, such as . . . "through Jesus Christ our Lord; by whom, and with whom, in the unity of the Holy Ghost, all honour and glory be to thee, O Father Almighty, world without end." The eucharistic prayer . . . is strictly binitarian in form, addressing the Father and celebrating the death of Christ.[14]

The revisions to the *Book of Common Prayer* found in the *Alternative Service Book* (1980) and *Common Worship* (2000) are most certainly moving in the right direction on the Trinitarian front, giving more attention to the Spirit's presence in the gathering and even including direct prayers to the Spirit

The reason for the neglect of the Spirit is fairly clear. On the one hand, it reflects the trouble that Christians, especially Catholic and Protestant

14. Steven, *Worship in the Spirit*, 181.

Christians (as opposed to Orthodox Christians), have had in coming to terms with the "personhood" of the Spirit. Psychologically, the Spirit is simply not as easy to relate to as the Father and the Son. He seems so much more mysterious, ever eluding our grasp and perhaps, as a consequence, our attention. On the other hand, our worship songs and prayers often employ words taken directly from the Bible's prayers and, as I've already said, there is no worship of the Spirit in the Bible. So, almost by accident, the Spirit gets neglected. On the third hand (I'm assuming a readership including some spiders at this point!), there is the theological concern that the Spirit is self-effacing and prefers to draw attention to Christ rather than to himself (John 14:26; 15:26; 16:14). Some Christians feel that to worship the Spirit is actually to *dishonor* him. I remember well some of the fuss made about John Wimber's habit of praying "Come, Holy Spirit" at the start of ministry times. This is not a biblical prayer, we were told, and the Spirit himself does not want us to pray in this way.

Let's briefly deal with these issues one at a time. First, I grant that the Spirit is deeply mysterious—but we should not let ourselves think that this amounts to a good reason to neglect him. We need to seek to recover the personhood of the Spirit and communicate that in our prayers, songs, and teaching. I'm not suggesting that we lose sight of the biblical emphasis on the life-transforming power of the Spirit's presence or that we somehow dilute the biblical images of fire, water, oil, and so on. I am arguing that we understand that this life-transforming power is a *personal* power. We also need to grasp hold of the mystery of the Spirit as an inspiration to worship. People are fed up with the neat "God in a box" that churches have sometimes served up, and the recovery of the transcendent and mysterious in worship is a positive imperative. So, rather than seeing the mysteriousness of the Spirit as a hindrance to worship, let's use it as an opportunity to refresh worship.

Second, it is a very good thing that biblical language infuses our prayers and songs, for there is power in singing Scripture.[15] But there is

---

15. Here is where I differ in emphasis from Nick Page's excellent book *And Now Let's Move into a Time of Nonsense: Why Worship Songs Are Failing the Church*. Page argues that we need to find contemporary language for our songs rather than falling back in a lazy way on culturally unintelligible biblical language. While I am in considerable sympathy with this proposal, I would still argue that we need to find ways of blending contemporary images with biblical ones so that we open up the biblical language for contemporary worshippers. I'm sure Page would agree, but his emphasis is on shifting an imbalance and thus he sounds more extreme than I think it really is.

no reason in the world why songs could not speak about the Spirit or be directed to the Spirit and still be rooted in biblical language. Neither is there any reason in the world why prayers and songs to the Spirit could not employ biblical concepts—even if the language cannot be pinned down to a single text or expression (see "Breathe on me, Breath of God" above). If our songs only use biblical prayers and songs as source material, then the Spirit will be largely neglected because there is no prayer or praise to the Spirit in Scripture. But Christians have always felt free to use the whole of Scripture to resource prayer and worship, and once we do this we can have our cake and eat it too (and what is the point of having cake if you can't eat it?).

Third, the concern that the Spirit would not draw attention to himself but would throw light on Christ instead contains an important insight and raises the crucial question of what *kind* of worship is appropriate to the person of the Spirit.[16] My earlier argument merely established that the worship of the Spirit is proper, but the *shape* of such worship needs to be biblically informed. The Spirit does indeed draw people to Christ, speak of Christ, and glorify Christ. The Spirit's mission is tied up with Christ's mission, and worship focused on the Spirit to the neglect of Christ is dishonoring to the Spirit. The Spirit does want us to understand that we cannot think and speak aright about him if we think or speak of him disconnected from the Father and the Son. However, if we understand the Spirit as the Spirit *of God* and as the Spirit *of Christ* then we can honor him in the way he desires. We can praise him without losing sight of the Messiah to whom he points us. Indeed, we can praise him *precisely because of* the Messiah to whom he points. In this way we honor the Spirit in the way most fitting to both his divine honor and his love of the Father and the Son. If I could make one complaint about many of the Spirit-songs, both ancient and modern, it is that they tend not to emphasize the Spirit's connections with Christ and the Father. In contrast, consider this prayer from St Gregory of Narek (AD 951–1003), an Armenian Orthodox Christian.

> Almighty, beneficent, loving God of all . . .
> O mighty Spirit of the Father,
> We entreat you with open arms,
> And pray with sighs and cries,

16. However, it is misleading to suggest that the Spirit never says anything about himself. After all, it was the Spirit who inspired all those biblical texts that talk about the Spirit. Also, although *the Spirit* draws attention to the Son and the Father rather than to himself, that does not mean that *the church* cannot draw attention to him in worship. The key is that our worship of him must always be connected to the Father and the Son.

> Standing before your awe-inspiring presence.
> We draw near with great trembling and utmost fear
> To offer first this reasonable sacrifice to your unsearchable power,
> As to the sharer of the inalienable honor of the Father . . .
> the Father of Emmanuel who sends you and who is our Savior, the
> giver of life and Creator of all.
> Through you, the three persons of the one God were made known
> to us.[17]

The prayer goes on, linking the Spirit with the story of Israel and then with the story of Christ and finally with the new creation. Throughout, Gregory is linking the Spirit he worships with the Father and the Son. That is the kind of Spirit-worship I consider to be truly Christian.

As we have seen with both Father and Son, worship of any one person of the Godhead is necessarily a Trinitarian event with the other persons implicated in our devotion. So it is with the Spirit—when we worship him, we must worship him as the Spirit sent *by* the Father *through* the Son. The Spirit enables us to call out to God, "Abba! Father!" (Rom 8:15) and to say, "Jesus is Lord" (1 Cor 12:3). It is precisely as the one who draws us into a living relationship with the Father and the Son that we love him and honor him. Such honoring is not out of place: "Understanding all this [the meaning of His name, and the greatness of His deeds, and the multitude of blessings He has showered on us and on all creation], how can we be afraid of giving the Spirit too much honor? We should instead fear that even though we ascribe to Him the highest titles we can devise or our tongues pronounce, our ideas about him might still fall short."[18]

Christian churches need a new injection of worship of the Spirit. We need to pray to him and sing to him more if we are to move into a more rounded Trinitarian spirituality. It will not be the case that worship directed to the Spirit ever holds the same central place within the church as worship directed to the Son and the Father and that is as it should be.[19] Nevertheless

---

17. Marsh, *Prayers from the East*, 13–14.

18. Basil, *On the Holy Spirit*, chap. 19, 78.

19. Readers may suspect that I am backtracking somewhat here, given my preceding arguments. To be honest, I'm still thinking this one through. I wish to give credence to the self-effacing nature of the Spirit and I want to honor the place that the Spirit carves out for himself—namely, pointing to Christ and the Father. I am not quite clear about my thinking on this, but I want to say that the imbalance of the church in the past is not without some theological warrant. I want to readjust the balance but not to deny some real insight in the neglect of the Spirit.

there should be honor where honor is due and, in the case of the blessed Spirit—"the kiss of the Father and the Son," as St. Bernard of Clairvaux (1090–1153) called him—honor is most certainly overdue.

seven

Singing the Trinity

SINGING HAS BEEN PART of Christian worship for as long as there has been Christian worship, and it has been part of the worship of the Jews for a good while longer than that. While one can worship without singing, believers across many ages and diverse cultures have found singing to be of enduring value as a means of expressing and evoking praise. This chapter offers some reflections on how songwriters might go about writing more Trinitarian songs and how worship leaders might think about selecting songs so as to facilitate a greater awareness of the richness of the Trinitarian God.

God has not gifted me as a songwriter. My one attempt at the tender age of five produced a "masterpiece" with a lyrical profundity that would leave many a modern Christian hymn writer drooling with envy:

> If I were an angel
> I would fly high above the sky
> (repeat until bored)
>
> —ROBIN PARRY © 1974 FISHYMUSIC

And if you think that's naff, you should have heard the tune! So, I am not a songwriter. But I do sing. Not very well, I grant you, but the noise I make is (often) joyful even if not . . . pleasant. And I do worship God in song. And, as someone who has a moderately theological inclination, I do think about the words of songs. It is really in that capacity that I offer my reflections. I will leave it to the real live songwriters to supplement my comments with the poetic and musical advice that may remain lacking. The best practical advice on lyric writing of which I am aware is Nick Page's hilarious and provocative book *And Now Let's Move into a Time of Nonsense*. It should be required reading for all songwriters.

What I want to show is that it is possible to write songs with rich Trinitarian lyrics in all sorts of different ways. I want to argue that if Christian songwriters have absorbed the Trinitarian theology expressed in chapters 2 to 5, they can let it loose in as many and diverse ways as their creative imaginations allow. I will give examples of "good practice" not in order that people should seek to copy them but in order to inspire fresh imagination. I use modern songs and a fair few old hymns. The old hymns may not resonate with contemporary audiences as they once did (although it depends who you talk to), but they do provide some wonderful examples of sound theology worshipping.

SUBSTANTIALLY TRINITARIAN SONGS

The most obvious kinds of Trinitarian songs are those that are *about* the Trinity—songs that take the Trinity itself as the central theme to be celebrated.[1] Here are three verses from *O Pater Sancte*, a tenth-century hymn.

> Father most holy, merciful, and loving,
> Jesus, Redeemer, ever to be worshipped,
> Life-giving Spirit, Comforter most gracious,
> God-everlasting.
>
> Three in a wondrous unity unbroken,
> One perfect Godhead, love that never faileth,
> Light of the angels, succour of the needy,
> Hope of all living.
>
> Lord God Almighty, unto thee be glory,
> One in Three Persons, over all be exalted;
> Thine, as we meet thee, be honor, praise and blessing,
> Now and for ever.

(TR. ALFRED EDWARD ALSTON)

---

1. A terrific modern example is "Dance of Our God" by Geraldine Lattey and Mike Busbee (© 2004 Thankyou Music). It develops the metaphor of the three persons dancing and inviting creation into that dance. Consider too "Father Most Holy" by Nathan Fellingham (© 2005 Thankyou Music), which is based on *O Pater Sancte*, quoted above. There is also "Triune God" by the Vineyard songwriters Brenton Brown and Brian Doerkson (© 2005 Thankyou Music). All of these can be found on the album *Trinity* (Authentic Music, 2006).

Notice how the song draws attention to each person of the Trinity in verse one and then the unity of the Three-in-One in the second and final verses.

One ancient way of structuring strong, "in-your-face" songs about the Trinity is to devote a verse to each member of the Godhead in turn. There may also then be a final verse that pulls the three together and emphasizes their unity. Here is an example by Isaac Watts (1674–1748):

> We give immortal praise
> To God the Father's love,
> For all our comforts here,
> And better hopes above.
> He sent his own eternal Son
> To die for sins that man had done.
>
> To God the Son belongs
> Immortal glory too,
> Who bought us with his blood
> From everlasting woe:
> And now he lives, and now he reigns,
> And sees the fruit of all his pains.
>
> To God the Spirit's name,
> Immortal worship give,
> Whose new-creating power
> Makes the dead sinner live:
> His work completes the great design,
> And fills the soul with joy divine.
>
> Almighty God, to thee
> Be endless honors done,
> The undivided Three,
> And the mysterious One:
> Where reason fails with all her powers,
> There faith prevails, and love adores.

Notice how the hymn balances the honor due to each person of the Trinity. This song takes very seriously the theology expressed in the old creeds. Notice, too, how each verse identifies things specific to each of the persons. The Father "sent his own eternal Son"; the Son "bought us with his blood" and now "lives" and "reigns"; the Spirit "makes the dead sinner live" and "fills the soul with joy divine." And then, just in case any of you were mistakenly thinking that this is all "brain stuff" rather than "heart stuff," the last verse wonderfully expresses how the Trinity can restore the sense of mystery to our worship. How can these three be one? Here reason fails but "faith prevails, and love adores." And how true this is! I have no problem with Christian theologians and philosophers trying to articulate how God can be both three and one, but when the rubber hits the road we cannot avoid the mystery. Our brains may seize up, but we worship all the same. Oh, what a mystery—this is our God. Though he is wrapped in enigma as with a garment, we adore him.

Here is Charles Wesley (1707–88) working to the same pattern:

> Father in whom we live,
> In whom we are, and move
> Glory and power and praise receive
> Of thy creating love.
> Let all the angel throng
> Give thanks to God on high;
> While earth repeats the joyful song,
> And echoes to the sky.
>
> Incarnate Deity,
> Let all the ransomed race
> Render in thanks their lives to thee,
> For thy redeeming grace.
> The grace to sinners showed
> Ye heavenly choirs proclaim,
> And cry: "Salvation to our God,
> Salvation to the Lamb!"
>
> Spirit of holiness,
> Let all thy saints adore
> Thy sacred energy, and bless
> Thy heart-renewing power.
> No angel-tongues can tell
> Thy love's ecstatic height,
> The glorious joy unspeakable,
> The beatific sight.
>
> Eternal triune Lord!
> Let all the hosts above,
> Let all the sons of men, record
> And dwell upon thy love.
> When heaven and earth are fled
> Before thy glorious face,
> Sing all the saints thy love has made
> Thine everlasting praise.

Charles Wesley took worshipping the Trinity seriously. In 1767 he published a whole collection of songs entitled *Hymns on the Trinity* containing 136 hymns to which he later added another fifty-two, making a grand total of 188. Not all these hymns were of the structure shown above, but they were all infused with a deep Trinitarian theology. I suspect that we need something very similar today as a resource for worship.

It is not just the great hymn writers of the past who employed the model. Keith Getty and Kristyn Getty provide an excellent contemporary example:

Come let us sing to the one
To the Father of life
For His light fills the earth like the sun
Come—tell of the wonders He's done
Great is the world He has made
Are the mysteries untold
Is His measureless power of old
Come—come let us sing to our God

Come let us sing to the one
To the Savior of life
Find the fullness of God in the Son
Come—tell of the wonders He's done
Wild is the mercy of Christ
Is the richness of grace
Is the unending life we embrace
Come—come let us sing to our God

Come let us sing to the one
To the Spirit of life
Leading us in the way of the Son
Come—tell of the wonders He's done
Strong is the Spirit within
Is the boldness to speak
Is the power to run when we're weak
Come—come let us sing to our God

To our God who is able
To strengthen us in His grace
Beyond all we imagine
Be all glory and praise
Be all praise

© 2003 THANKYOU MUSIC

What is interesting here is how the hymn expresses the equality of the three persons. The repetition of the first line of each verse ("Come, let us sing to the one") and the last line ("Come—come let us sing to our God"), as each new verse focuses on the Father, Son, and Spirit in turn, communicates that these three are all "the one" and are all "our God." The hymn gives equal attention and equal praise to each person of the Trinity. It is also worth noting how the writers have used some evocative language that sparks the worshipping imagination in ways that more familiar language may fail to. In particular, the words "wild is the mercy of Christ" provoke fresh ways of seeing Christ's mercy, and with that fresh vision can come renewed worship. Finally, for those who have eyes to see, this hymn contains numerous allusions to biblical teachings about the persons. For instance, the reference to the Spirit "leading us in the way of the Son" alludes to the prominent theme of the Spirit as the one who draws us to Christ, teaches us the things of Christ, and transforms us into the image of Christ. The line about the Spirit giving "boldness to speak" reminds us of the early stories in the book of Acts in which the Spirit empowered the believers to speak of Jesus with great courage in the face of hostility. Being steeped in Scripture allows those with a poetic gifting to write with a freedom and creativity that also reflect the purpose and meaning of biblical teaching.

Here is the climax of another overtly Trinitarian song by Keith Getty, co-written with Margaret Becker:

> Oh my soul, come taste and see
> The brilliance of the Trinity;
> Holy Spirit, Father, Son,
> Living waters poured from one.
> In their shadow hide yourself,
> In their company find your help,
> Cleave to them it will be well,
> Oh my soul, come praise your God.

© 2003 Thankyou Music

One final thought on the tripartite pattern of song: the examples we have examined so far are what we could call "fruitcake" songs. I don't mean that they were written by people who were (or are) fruitcakes! I mean that they are very rich in theological content. They are what my hippy friends would call "heavy" songs. While there is an important place for "heavy" songs in the worship of the church, if the charismatic renewal has taught us anything it is that there is also a place for simpler, more intimate songs ("meringue" songs?). There is no reason in the world why very simple songs cannot exhibit the tripartite structure. The following song, for example, is by Donna Adkins:

> Father, we love you,
> We worship and adore you,
> Glorify your name in all the earth.
> Glorify your name, glorify your name,
> Glorify your name in all the earth.
>
> Jesus, we love you . . .
>
> Spirit, we love you . . .

© 1976 MARANATHA! MUSIC

They don't get much simpler than that!

David Tripp did some telling research in the 1980s into some popular collections of worship songs. He looked at the percentage of each book given over to what he called "substantially Trinitarian content."[2] By this he had in mind songs such as those discussed above. His results for these books were as follows:

14.6% *Christian Prayer* (American Catholic, 1976)

9.6% *The Church Hymnary*. 3rd ed. (Anglican, 1973)

9.1% *Hymns and Psalms* (Methodist, 1983)

8.9% *Mission Praise* (The Billy Graham Mission England Hymnal, 1983)

0% *Faith, Folk and Clarity* (an influential private collection, 1967)

David Tripp observes that song collections that were put together by denominational bodies have a noticeably higher percentage of "substantially Trinitarian" songs. Collections put together by interdenominational or charismatic groups tend to have fewer "in-your-face" Trinitarian songs.

There is a great need today, and in every generation, for songwriters to revisit this ancient Trinitarian song pattern and to bring it alive again and again and again. In fact, for those with the gift of word-craft and theological

---

2. Tripp, "Hymnody and Liturgical Theology." I ought to point out that my figures represent the figures Tripp gives when the hymns with a Trinitarian doxology are taken out of the equation.

insight there are an infinite number of variations of this theme. However, such a song type, helpful though it is, is not essential for worship to be richly Trinitarian—as we shall see in the next section.

Songs That Highlight Their Trinitarian Syntax

A concept that is important to grasp when it comes to understanding Trinitarian worship is that of Trinitarian syntax. All Christian songs need to be consistent with a Trinitarian syntax. What do I mean by that? Well, think first of the notion of syntax. All languages have a syntax—a set of rules about how words do and do not fit together meaningfully in that language. All communication in a language must express this syntax correctly—otherwise meaning and communication begin to break down. The stronger the deviation from the syntax, the more unintelligible an utterance becomes. Every time you open your mouth and speak you are manifesting the syntax of whichever language you are using. You may not be speaking *about* syntax—in fact, it is unlikely that you are. You may be talking about the weather, or what you saw on TV last night, or how Granny Weatherspoon from down the road got fined for speeding in her motorized wheelchair. *Whatever* you are speaking about, you are bringing syntax into play. What I want to suggest is that there is an analogy between the role syntax plays in a language and the role the Trinity plays in Christian living and faith. Although it is not an exact analogy, I think it will help us begin to get at how our songs may express the Trinity more fully.

Here is my basic claim: The Trinity functions in Christian God-talk in such a basic and foundational way that it starts to function something like a syntax—a set of rules about how Christian language works. Christian beliefs about God and about the world are so deeply influenced by Trinitarian thought that, whenever Christians open their mouths to speak about God, creation, humanity, ethics, love, salvation, or whatever else, their words should be consistent with a Trinitarian syntax. Rich Christian language will display the vast range of this syntax. I base this claim on the kind of things we discussed in chapters 2 through 5. There we saw how the Trinity is connected to all the different parts of the biblical story and Christian living. This fact has big implications for songwriting. It means that even songs that are not *about* the Trinity can still be deeply Trinitarian.

At the most basic level, no Christian songs should break the rules of the Trinitarian syntax. If they do, they end up becoming the Christian equivalent of gibberish. It seems to me that virtually no Christian songs violate the rules of the syntax. They do not contradict what is taught in the creeds and so can be seen as legitimate Christian speech to and about God. So if there is a problem with contemporary Christian worship it is not at the level of breaking the rules—it is not the problem of singing heresy.

To understand what I perceive the problem to be, perhaps we could use a different analogy. Imagine Adam and Eve in Eden's garden. God says, "You may eat from any tree in the garden except for the tree of the knowledge of good and evil." Suppose that Adam and Eve choose to obey the command and never eat from the tree of the knowledge of good and evil. However, imagine also that they only ever eat from an apple tree just to the left of it. They are surrounded by lemons and oranges, pears and plums, figs and grapes, and every imaginable fruit under the sun, but they never touch them. Clearly they have broken no rules, but it is also clear that they are robbing themselves of some great fruit-eating experiences. In the same way, although our songs do not break the rules of the Trinitarian syntax they often fail to explore the richness and freedom it allows. The songs fail to bring out the Trinitarian dimensions of Christian faith and life for worshippers to enjoy. If there is a problem with Christian worship songs, it is more a failure to bring out the Trinitarian dimensions of the God we worship than a problem of violating Trinitarian faith.

It is both possible and imperative to write songs that highlight the Trinitarian syntax. If we are to enjoy rich Trinitarian worship, it is crucial that we sing songs on all sorts of topics—from creation to new creation, from repentance to lament to celebration, from the cross to the resurrection, from salvation to sanctification, from mission to the love of God—that highlight the place of Father, Son, and Spirit in connection with the topic. Highlighting the syntax is somewhat like designing a building with the pipework on show rather than hidden behind the walls. The following are good examples of songs that are not *about* the Trinity as such but that put the Trinitarian pipework on show.

In 1977 Dave Richards wrote a song about the church that also draws deeply from the Trinitarian streams. Although the first person of the Trinity is not named, the song is clearly a dialogue between him and the congregation.

For I'm building a people of power
And I'm making a people of praise
That will move through this land by my Spirit,
And will glorify my precious name.

Build your church, Lord,
Make us strong, Lord,
Join our hearts, Lord,
through your Son.
Make us one, Lord,
In your body,
In the Kingdom of your Son.

Here is a well-known Graham Kendrick song about renewal and revival that wears its Trinitarian heart upon its sleeve.

Lord, the light of your love is shining,
In the midst of the darkness, shining;
Jesus, Light of the world, shine upon us,
Set us free by the truth You now bring us,
Shine on me, shine on me.

Shine, Jesus, shine,
Fill this land with the Father's glory;
Blaze, Spirit, blaze,
Set our hearts on fire.
Flow, river, flow,
Flood the nations with grace and mercy;
Send forth Your word,
Lord, and let there be light.

Lord, I come to Your awesome presence,
From the shadows into Your radiance;
By the blood I may enter Your brightness,
Search me, try me, consume all my darkness.
Shine on me, shine on me.

As we gaze on Your kingly brightness
So our faces display Your likeness.
Ever changing from glory to glory,
Mirrored here may our lives tell Your story.
Shine on me, shine on me.

This is clearly not a song about the Trinity but about spiritual renewal. Nevertheless, in a very non-contrived way it brings out the Trinitarian syntax of renewal in the all-important chorus. Other renewal songs with overt Trinitarian syntax include Dave Fellingham's "Days of Heaven" (1994) and Andy Park's "Down the Mountain the River Flows" (1994). One could, in theory, go on to add songs about all sorts of topics, but my search for examples has run aground. I have not yet found many illustrations of modern songs about the cross or creation, for instance, which bring out the Trinitarian dimensions discussed in chapter 2 of this book. One example is Nathan Fellingham's song "You are the Lord."[3] It is my belief that such songs could be the most important kinds of songs for fostering a renewal of Trinitarian worship, so their scarcity is both a disappointment and a great opportunity for those who compose new songs. If you are a songwriter and wish to start writing more Trinitarian material then here is a vast land just waiting to be explored.

It is worth noting that such songs often focus on one of the persons of the Trinity but bring out the relationship with the other two. For instance, in "Shine Jesus Shine," above, the Son is the main focus but the Spirit and the Father are present too. We could imagine a photograph of a person standing in focus in the foreground with two other characters slightly out of focus standing some way behind. The photograph picks out the three characters and draws special attention to one without wanting the viewer to lose sight of the others. Many songs with overt Trinitarian syntax do just this. So the song may, as does Melody Green's "There is a Redeemer," address the Father but thank him for giving us his Son and for leaving his Spirit until the completion of the work on earth. Or a song may address Jesus, praising him for his rule in heaven at the Father's side and asking him to pour out his Spirit upon the congregation. The out-of-focus members of the Trinity can be very out of focus and merely mentioned in a single overt reference or they can be moderately prominent. The highlighting of the Trinitarian syntax can be quite subtle or it can be very overt.

It is also worth noting that sometimes one of the persons of the Trinity can be clearly present without being named. For instance, a song may invoke the Lord Jesus to pour rivers of living water down upon his people.

3. © 2004 Nathan Fellingham. Thankyou music/MCPS. It can be found on the Phatfish album *Faithful: The Worship Songs* (Authentic Music, 2004) and on the worship compilation *Trinity* (Authentic Music, 2006). The latter is a worship CD that Nathan Fellingham was inspired to put together after reading the first edition of this book. It includes sixteen Trinitarian worship songs written and performed by a range of contemporary songwriters.

Most Christian congregations are so familiar with the allusion to the Holy Spirit suggested by the water imagery that I imagine few would miss it. Other allusions may be much more subtle, and the subtler they are the less likely it is that people will be aware of them. For instance, the fourth stanza of Wesley's hymn "And Can it Be" alludes very subtly to the Spirit when it says, "Long my imprisoned spirit lay, fast bound in sin and nature's night; thine eye diffused a quickening ray; I woke, the dungeon flamed with light." The words are addressed to Jesus, and the "quickening" (meaning "life-giving") ray must be the Spirit. There is nothing wrong with using subtle references that many may miss, but if we are seeking to draw attention to the Three-in-One in our worship we need to realize that songs with very subtle allusions will only do the job if we explain them or use them in combination with other, clearer songs about the Trinity. However, the potential of various degrees of allusion to the persons opens up endless possibilities for the creative songwriter that are well worth exploring. This leads me to a final reflection on syntax.

The language of songs needs to do at least two things. First, it must accurately reflect the biblical revelation of God. Secondly, it must inspire those singing to offer up their devotion through the song to God. The Spirit will often anoint a skill as a wordsmith to forge new ways of "seeing afresh" old biblical truths. I do not want to suggest that we should abandon biblical language in our songs. Not at all! I am convinced of its power and life. I am simply arguing for the freedom to allow songwriters to sometimes generate new imagery and language that remains true to the revelation of God in Christ. As the hymn writers of old knew, it is not a requirement that all Christian songs should restrict themselves to biblical language. Nick Page's book *And Now Let's Move into a Time of Nonsense* explores at some length the idea of finding contemporary language for worship and, while he goes further than I would, his book is very helpful and thought-provoking. Sometimes, by finding new ways to express the biblical understandings of God, we can open them up again for people who have become jaded in their vision through sheer familiarity with the language. In the Wesley hymn we just looked at, for example, the image of Christ's eye diffusing the Holy Spirit like a life-giving beam that floods the sinner's dark dungeon with flaming light is both imaginative and inspirational.

Songs with a Trinitarian Doxology

A final category of overtly Trinitarian songs include songs which, oddly enough, are not really very Trinitarian at all but which add Trinitarian doxologies at the end. For instance, William Kethe's hymn "All People That on Earth Do Dwell" (1561) simply refers to "God" and "the Lord" in the verses, and then adds the following doxology to the end:

> Praise God from whom all blessings flow,
> Praise him, all creatures here below,
> Praise him above, ye heav'nly hosts:
> Praise Father, Son and Holy Ghost.

Similarly, the English translation of Francis of Assisi's hymn "All Creatures of Our God and King" by William Henry Draper (1855–1933) ends with the following words:

> Let all things their Creator bless,
> And worship him in humbleness.
> O praise him! Alleluia!
> Praise, praise the Father, praise the Son,
> And praise the Spirit, Three in One!

At first sight these appear to be the least satisfactory kinds of Trinitarian songs because the Trinity seems like something of an afterthought, tacked onto the end rather than being integral to the song. Nevertheless, they do offer the Trinitarian equivalent of an adrenalin rush—a short, focused, and intense burst, explicitly highlighting the Three-in-One. These doxologies also draw the singers back to reconsider the "God" and "Lord" that they have just sung to. The doxology makes explicit what may be merely implicit in the rest of the hymn—that this is no mere "unitarian" deity but the triune God and Lord. This could possibly have the beneficial effect of forging a habit whereby congregations learn to consciously construe seemingly "unitarian" songs in Trinitarian ways. Of course, this habit would only be formed if such doxologies were common—sadly they are very rare in songs and seem to find a more ready home in liturgy.

Trinitarian doxologies could serve as endings to Christian choruses that set Psalms to music. Although with the benefit of Christian hindsight we can see that the God addressed in the Psalms is the Trinity, the psalmists were not aware of this fact. The language of the Psalms is consequently not Trinitarian, and yet Christians through all ages have found them a wonderful resource for worship. One classical way of handling this liturgically is to add a Trinitarian doxology to the end of a Psalm recital to provide an explicit context for a Christian understanding of the Psalm. If Christian songwriters used the same practice musically, we would have a simple way of putting a Christian "spin" on the Psalms that we sing. One can also make Trinitarian use of the Psalms by actually modifying the words in the light of God's revelation in Christ.

A Full Typology of the Trinitarian Content of Worship Songs

Having looked at three different kinds of songs that include all the persons of the Trinity, it will be helpful to have a system for categorizing all Christian songs in terms of how they relate to Trinitarian thought. The following categories cover the various possibilities:

1. *Three-person Songs*

    (a) Substantially Trinitarian songs

    (b) Songs with overt Trinitarian syntax

    (c) Songs with a Trinitarian doxology

2. *Two-person Songs*

    (a) Father and Son

        (i) Substantial

        (ii) Overt syntax

    (b) Father and Spirit

        (i) Substantial

        (ii) Overt syntax

    (c) Son and Spirit[4]

        (i) Substantial

        (ii) Overt syntax

---

4. I have actually come across yet another category, which could be called "You Lord and Spirit songs" in which it is not clear whether it is the Father or the Son who is being asked to send the Spirit.

3. *One-person Songs*

   (a) Father Songs

   (b) Son Songs

   (c) Spirit Songs

4. *"You, Lord" Songs*

"You, Lord," songs are ambiguous songs that do not clarify exactly which person the song is about or being addressed to. I sometimes refer to them as "God" songs. Arguably they highlight the unity of God, and there ain't nuffin' wrong with that. Their ambiguity allows for a certain flexibility since they can be used to refer to the whole Godhead or to any of the persons. That flexibility is something that a worship leader can exploit, as we shall discuss later in this chapter.

I want to emphasize that there is nothing wrong with any of these kinds of songs. *None* of them violate Trinitarian syntax, and I can honestly say that I did not find a single song in my research for this book that was anti-Trinitarian. I did find some with naff tunes (you know what I'm talking about!) and some with words that fell short on grounds other than Trinitarian orthodoxy, but we're not interested in such failure here. The point is that any of the above kinds of songs can be legitimate Christian songs.

You may be thinking that I have just undermined my own argument that our worship is often not Trinitarian enough. If, as I have just stated, any of the types of Christian songs are okay, then what is the problem? The problem lies in the selection of songs in the context of individual meetings and over a series of meetings. Suppose that most or all of the songs selected for a meeting are "Son songs." Clearly the worshippers will be brought to focus on Jesus, but what of the other two persons? If this pattern of song selection continues over a period of time, then a Trinitarian imbalance begins to occur in our spiritual lives.

Sometimes, though less often, the imbalance is that everything becomes so Father-focused that the Son and the Spirit fall from view. It is also possible (although I have never heard of it happening) that the Spirit could receive attention at the expense of the Father and Son. It is exactly this kind of unbalanced focus that I contend is all too common—especially in non-liturgical and charismatic worship.

Why does this imbalance occur? It is not because worship leaders intentionally decide to serve up unbalanced devotion. Such thoughts never cross the minds of those who lead communal worship. I suggest that it usually happens by sheer accident. It is rare, in my experience, to find worship leaders thinking about how best to achieve a Trinitarian balance in worship. Why would they? After all, it is not something that is often (or ever) suggested to them. When worship leaders are thinking about song selection they may be thinking about the theme of the service; they may be praying and "listening" to God for ideas; they may be thinking of the songs that have blessed them recently; or they may even be looking for songs with groovy tunes or the right kind of tempo or in the right key so that they can seamlessly flow from tune one to another. They may be thinking about all these things and more besides, but they are probably not also thinking, "How can I help the people focus their devotion on Father, Son, and Holy Spirit?" Trinitarian imbalance, consequently, goes unnoticed. The Trinitarian content of the selection of worship songs, if it is present, is there by happy accident and, if it is absent, is missing unintentionally.

Because Trinitarian concerns do not often govern song selection, any Trinitarian emphasis in worship often results from a leader just happening by happy accident to have chosen songs that do the job. So it is a matter of interest to know how many songs out there in the vast supermarket of worship songs fit into the different categories. For instance, if a high percentage of available songs are "Son songs," then lack of attention to Trinitarian balance is more likely to lead to worship in which the Father and the Spirit drop out of view. Similarly, if the percentage of songs that mention the Spirit is low then it becomes highly likely that the Spirit will accidentally be neglected.

In order to give a taste of the Trinitarian content of some contemporary worship songs, I have analyzed the lyrical content of many of the worship song albums that have come out of the Vineyard movement over a period of four and a half years. Vineyard have exerted an enormous influence on the worship songs used in churches across the world, and so they make an interesting case study.

Categorizing songs is not an exact science. For instance, some of the songs I have classified as "Son Songs" may refer in passing to Jesus as "Lamb of God" or "Son of God." Such references clearly imply Yhwh, even if he is not in focus. Songs such as these could have been classified as "Two-person songs," however, I have classified songs with brief and incidental allusions to the Father or Spirit as "Son songs." Some of the songs that I have classified as "You Lord" songs employ biblical allusions which would enable those who are familiar with the Bible to identify the person of the Godhead implied by the words. However, unless such an allusion was obvious and likely to be recognized by the average Christian in the congregation, I have classed them as "You Lord" songs. With the three "You Lord and Spirit" songs I have taken an educated guess as to whether the "Lord" refers to the Father or the Son. Such blurring of categories could be multiplied but I have found that, on the whole, the songs fit neatly into the different groups.

Vineyard Worship Songs 1999–2004

I have looked through twenty-eight worship albums[5] produced by Vineyard Music between 1999 and 2004, containing 362 songs (though some songs appear more than once).[6]

1. *Three-person songs* (5 songs = 1.4 percent)

    (a) Substantially Trinitarian songs (3 songs [inc. 1 repeat])

    (b) Songs with overt Trinitarian syntax (1 song)

    (c) Songs with a Trinitarian doxology (1 song)

2. *Two-person songs* (substantial "binitarian" songs or with overt "binitarian" syntax) (32 songs = 8.8 percent)

    (a) Father and Son (19 songs)

    (b) Father and Spirit (4 songs)

    (c) Son and Spirit (9 songs)

---

5. The albums are *Hungry* (1999), *Believe* (2000), *Jesus I Believe You* (2000), *Surrender* (2000), *Fruit of the Spirit* (2001), *Breathe* (2001), *Wonderful Mercy* (2001), *Prayer Expressions of Worship* (2001), *All I Need* (2001), *Change Me on the Inside* (2001), *Never Look Back* (2002), *Humble King* (2002), *The Call* (2002), *Beautiful* (2002), *Holy* (2002), *If You Say Go* (2002), *1000 Generations* (2002), *Free to Fly* (2002), *Desire* (2003), *Hungry Live* (2003), *Lord, Reign in Me* (2003), *One Glimpse* (2003), *Just Like Heaven* (2003), *This is Love* (2003), *You and You Alone* (2003), *Set Me Free* (2003), *Hold On* (2004), *Shout to the Earth* (2004).

6. Because of this small number of repeats the results are less than 100-percent precise, although these repeats still reveal the overall emphasis of an album. Also, some songs are borderline. A song may hint strongly that it is about Jesus, for example, but not name him. In such cases I simply had to make a call as to whether it is a Jesus song or a "you, Lord," song.

3. *One-person songs* (140 songs = 38.7 percent)

   (a) Father songs (20 songs = 5.5 percent)

   (b) Son songs (115 songs = 31.8 percent)

   (c) Spirit songs (5 songs = 1.4 percent)

4. *"You, Lord," songs* (185 songs = 51.1 percent)

These can be represented in a pie graph as follows:

The Trinity in Vineyard Lyrics

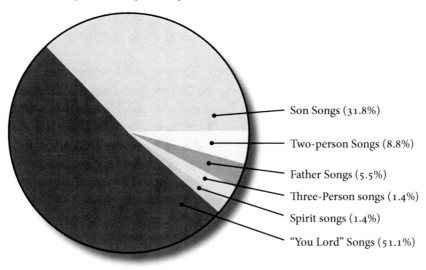

Son Songs (31.8%)

Two-person Songs (8.8%)

Father Songs (5.5%)

Three-Person songs (1.4%)

Spirit songs (1.4%)

"You Lord" Songs (51.1%)

Now I do not wish to suggest that Vineyard are representative of all the diverse streams of contemporary Christian worship music, and it may well be that analyses of other song sources or a different cross-section of Vineyard albums would yield different results. Nevertheless, it does seem that contemporary worship songs from other sources often share with Vineyard a strong twin focus on "You Lord" and "Jesus" (82.9 percent of the Vineyard songs surveyed were Son songs or "You Lord" songs. About 87 percent of the songs did not mention the Father and about 94 percent did not mention the Spirit). For instance, a cursory glance at three worship albums from the influential Hillsong Church in Australia (*Blessed*, 2002, *Hope*, 2003, and *For All You've Done*, 2004) reveals that nineteen of the forty-six songs are "You, Lord," songs, twenty-four are "Son songs" and just three combine Father and Son. So the Father only received three references and the Spirit did not feature at all. The challenge for all worship songwriters (Vineyard, Hillsong, and others) is this: how can you maintain the particular vision for worship that God has given you and at the same time deepen the Trinitarian dimension? I must emphasize that all I am saying about Vineyard and Hillsong (or anyone else) is that whatever God-given emphases they have, they must go hand in hand with an emphasis on the Christian God—the Trinity. I have no intention of criticizing any particular songs nor of undermining the distinctive DNA of any particular song-producing group. If, for instance, the emphasis of Vineyard worship songs is intimacy then so be it—but let it be intimacy *with the Triune God*. My criticism here is not intended as the destructive criticism of an enemy looking for songwriters to devour, but the constructive criticism of a supporter looking to help songwriters to think more theologically.

It seems to me that two practical conclusions follow from this. First, we need our songwriters to write more "Three-person songs" of the substantial Trinitarian variety, as well as those with overt Trinitarian syntax. The more good songs we have with this content, the more likely it is that they will be chosen and, by happy accident, shape a more Trinitarian spirituality. It should be a priority in each age to produce a good number of fresh three-person songs. I would urge Hillsong and Vineyard songwriters and others to do this. There is absolutely no reason why the style of worship they represent could not be deeply Trinitarian.

Second, we do need to train those who lead worship to bear in mind the need for Trinitarian balance as they select songs. If we use "Son songs," let's also use "Father songs" and "Spirit songs." Let's throw in a couple of "Father and Son" songs alongside "Spirit and Father" songs and so on. And let's think up ways of addressing "You Lord" songs to specific persons of the Trinity or to the Godhead as a whole. This could be as simple as the worship leader saying, "Let us worship Jesus" before beginning to sing. Or if a "You Lord" song is set in the midst of various songs addressed to Jesus, that particular song is then colored by that context and functions as a song addressed to Jesus. Alternatively, a prayer afterwards could pick up the language of the song and address it to the whole Godhead, making the song function as a "Three-person song."

Such training and preparation is crucial, but it is not at all easy—so I have a practical suggestion to make. A church could have someone look at their list of songs used in public worship and color-code it according to the typology I gave earlier. Although it would take the person who did the initial coding quite some time, it would enable every person who then selected songs from the list to see exactly what Trinitarian balance they were achieving through their selection in glorious Technicolor. Without this sort of system, worship leaders may start off with the best intentions in the world but find that it is just too much hassle to maintain such a balance week after week. A color-coded list would keep the issue at the forefront of the leader's mind and make the task much easier. Suppose the leader felt that the congregation needed to focus more on the Spirit. The leader would not have to sit and stare blankly at the wall, racking his or her brain to try and recall a good Spirit song. The color-coded list would enable the leader to quickly find all the relevant songs and then pick the one that would work best. If the songs were available on a computer, as is increasingly the case in churches, then they could be coded there in such a way that a worship leader could simply type in a search for "Father-Son" songs, say, and have them all appear before her instantly. Indeed, more detailed computer classification could allow searches for combinations of categories, like songs about the cross that are also "three-person songs" or "songs about creation" that are "Son songs" and so on. Computers offer numerous ways of making such balanced song selections possible and easy.

While this chapter makes no pretence at being the definitive guide to Trinitarian songwriting and selection, we have seen the mandate to correct the imbalance in our worship and have begun to explore the way ahead. God willing, these ideas will begin a mighty avalanche of praise to the Three-in-One as those whom God has gifted to lead worship allow the infinite possibilities to capture their holy imaginations.

eight

Praying the Trinity

IF PRAYER IS THE "Christian's vital breath," then the Trinity is the air we breathe. As we have already seen, our prayer is Trinitarian in its foundation (by the Spirit we participate in the Son's prayer to the Father—chapter 5) and in its destination (we pray to Father, to Son, and to Spirit—chapter 6). This chapter simply seeks to zoom in on how we can develop a more Trinitarian prayer life—both individually and corporately.

EXTEMPORE PRAYER

(Almost?) all Christians will pray extempore prayers at times. For Christians from non-liturgical traditions, most or all of their spoken prayers (as opposed to sung prayers) will be made up on the spot just as their conversation in ordinary life is. But Christians who rely more on set prayers and liturgy will still pray extempore prayers at times. So how can we learn to pray extempore prayers that are Trinitarian?

Most of the things I would want to say about praying the Trinity have already been said. The typology of songs set out in chapter 7 applies equally to prayer. One can find "three-person prayers," "two-person prayers," "one-person prayers" and "God prayers" (along with prayers falling into the various subdivisions outlined in the song typology). As with songs, one seeking a deeper Trinitarian spirituality will try to weave between the Three and the One—between the Father, the Son, and the Spirit in prayer. The dynamic interconnections between the persons of God will be reflected in a dynamic movement in prayer that brings such connections and relations into language and worship. But all this can seem rather daunting to believers—it seems to make their intimate prayer life with God something like an exam they have to pass to make the grade. When I speak to various groups about Trinitarian worship there is often a sense of awkwardness at the point when someone has to pray publicly. You can see them thinking, "Flipping Nora! I'd better get my theology right!" I myself can feel the same awkwardness, because people expect me to cross all my "*t*"s and dot all my "*i*"s when I pray!

We need to remind ourselves, first of all, that God is not sitting in heaven waiting for us to make some theological blunder so he can throw a lightning bolt down on us. God is very gracious and kind and lets us make all sorts of theological mess-ups. God knows our hearts, and it is our *hearts* he is after. While that does not excuse us from seeking to enrich our prayers by making them more Trinitarian, it does alleviate some of the stress.

The second thing that needs to be said is that not all prayers have to get all three persons in! Prayers just to the Father or just to Jesus or just to the Spirit are absolutely fine. Prayers to two persons are not a problem. Not every prayer needs to have overt Trinitarian syntax, nor does every prayer have to be substantially Trinitarian. It would be absolutely ridiculous to suggest that every prayer should bring the whole Godhead into focus (that would rule the Lord's Prayer out, for a start, as well as the Jesus prayer!). This should also take some pressure off. What I am saying, however, is that a Christian with a Trinitarian prayer life will, over a period of time or over several consecutive prayers, weave a prayer-tapestry that is fully and overtly Trinitarian. This tapestry can be stitched together from prayers that cover every type on the typology ("one-person," "two-person," "three-person," etc.). The richness of a Trinitarian prayer life cannot be measured from a single prayer.

Having said all of this, I do think that we should be seeking to learn to pray three-person prayers that are either substantially Trinitarian or that have overt Trinitarian syntax. Such prayers really focus our attention on the Christian God and can bring a Trinitarian prayer life to its greatest heights and most focused expression. How can we learn to pray in this way? The word "learn" is important here for two reasons. First, it is important because such praying does not come naturally to everyone, especially if they have picked up sub-Trinitarian prayer habits from their churches. Second, it is important to think of it as learning because we will need to make a *conscious effort* to pray such prayers. We will need to think carefully about what we are praying.

If prayer is like fire, then theology is an important part of the fuel we burn. Praying "three-person prayers" requires some theological fuel, and this means that we need to learn about the Trinity. Chapters 2, 3, and 4 are included in this book for precisely this reason—they provide the basics of a Trinitarian vocabulary, grammar, and syntax that can come to expression in prayer. If you don't know where to start, reread those chapters and pray them. When you pray about creation, think about the work of the Father, Son, and Spirit and pray it. When you pray about the cross, let the Trinitarian suggestions about Golgotha find their way onto your lips as you speak to the Lord. As you read Scripture with your eyes open to the revelation of the Trinity, let what you read inspire your prayer. This is a learning process and it will probably feel somewhat awkward at the beginning. When you learn to drive you have to think very hard about every single movement you make. Look in the mirror, put on your left indicator, move out, foot on clutch (unless you're in an automatic), change gear, foot off clutch, and so on. After a while you do these things automatically, often not realizing that you are doing them. Praying the Trinity is just like that. The more you do it, the more it becomes the way you relate to God and increasingly you find yourself becoming less conscious of it. That is how it should be. We need to consciously teach ourselves Trinitarian prayer habits and break any sub-Trinitarian habits we have picked up along the way. If that makes us feel a little embarrassed and awkward in the meantime, then it is a price well worth paying.

St. Paul provides some good examples of prayers with overt Trinitarian syntax. He didn't sit down and think how to get the whole Trinity into his prayers, but since his whole theology was so Trinitarian (or perhaps proto-Trinitarian would be more accurate) in structure, when he opened his mouth the Trinity just came out. Consider the following prayer and doxology:

> I keep asking that the God of our Lord Jesus Christ, the glorious Father, may give you the Spirit of wisdom and revelation, so that you may know him better. (Eph 1:17)

> May the grace of the Lord Jesus Christ, and the love of God, and the fellowship of the Holy Spirit be with you all. (2 Cor 13:14)

Here is an example of a real extempore Trinitarian prayer recorded during a time of worship: "O come Holy Spirit, in Jesus's name. Father, as we stand, and as the Spirit comes, we admit to our doubts, deliberately and purposely before you now in heavenly places . . . Lord Jesus, send down the Spirit we pray. Lord Jesus, be with us today." It seems unlikely to me that the person praying this prayer was consciously trying to include the whole Trinity. Rather, the person's relationship with God was naturally Trinitarian, and such prayer just flowed out. Let it be so with us.

If you are leading the worship in a meeting it is important to think carefully about your prayers. You are in a position to guide the way a congregation relates to God by your words, and praying the Trinity will help them to relate to the Trinity. Your prayers can also frame songs in such a way that the content of the song is given a certain interpretation. For instance, suppose that you sing a "God song" that does not identify the person to whom it is sung. You could pray before singing it, using the words of the song and directing them to a particular person of the Godhead or to all three. This prayer then changes the way that many in the congregation will use the song. It is a truism that the person leading worship needs to be someone who models genuine worship—you usually cannot lead the people where you have not gone yourself. In just the same way, worship leaders need to pray the Trinity as a role model for the congregation. You can even invite worshippers to offer prayer to the Father, then to the Son, and then to the Spirit. This semi-guided prayer focuses the minds of the congregation on the Trinity without requiring from them a high level of theological sophistication before they can contribute publicly.

WRITTEN PRAYERS AS A SCHOOL FOR PRAYER

Most Christians find that prayers written down by others can be very helpful in their own spiritual lives. Such prayers have a double function. On the one hand, they can be simply wonderful to pray as our own prayers. On the other, they can teach us patterns of prayer and a prayer vocabulary that we can imbibe and make use of in our own extempore prayers.

Some of us are good with words and some of us are not. There are times when we simply don't have anything to say and our words have run dry. All that comes out is another uninspiring, "Lord, I just really want to say that I really think that . . . ummmm . . . you're really great" (we've all been there). When words run out, it is sometimes helpful to turn to prayers that have been provided by others because the words of such prayers can be like scaffolding that we can use to refocus our hearts on the Lord. Sometimes I will simply pray such prayers, and at other times I will use written prayers to give me a kick-start—I'll start by praying what is written and then launch off in my own direction before returning to the prayer for a bit then launching off in my own words again.

When it comes to learning to pray the Trinity there are some very helpful written prayers that can serve us both as our own prayers and as a school for learning to pray our own Trinitarian prayers. Here are some examples from different Christian traditions. First, an Eastern Orthodox prayer:

> You were transfigured on the mountain, and your disciples beheld your glory, O Christ our God, as far as they were able to do so, so that when they saw you crucified, they might know that your suffering was voluntary, and might proclaim to the world that you are truly the brightness of the Father, the power of the Holy Spirit resides in you, O Triune Lord.
>
> Come, let us enter the inner chamber of our soul, offering prayers to the Lord and crying aloud: Our Father, who art in heaven, remit and forgive our debts, for you alone are compassionate. Giving wings to our soul, in a spirit of compunction, let us weep with joy for the deliverance of our souls and sing the praises of Christ forever! We bless the Lord, Father, Son and Holy Spirit. Consubstantial Trinity, uncreated Unity, the God of all, we exalt you above all forever. (Mattins in Lent)

Here are Roman Catholic prayers from the Catholic Sacramentary, or Roman Missal:

> Let us pray to the one God, Father, Son and Spirit, that our lives may bear witness to our faith: Father, you sent your Word to bring us truth and your Spirit to make us holy.
>
> Through them we come to know the mystery of your life. Help us to worship you, one God in three Persons, by proclaiming and living our faith in you.
>
> Grant this through our Lord Jesus Christ, your Son, who lives and reigns with you and the Holy Spirit, one God, for ever and ever.
>
> Amen.

(Opening Prayer for the Solemnity of the Most Holy Trinity)

Let us pray to our God who is Father, Son, and Holy Spirit: God, we praise you:

Father all-powerful, Christ Lord and Savior, Spirit of love. You reveal yourself in the depths of our being, drawing us to share in your life and your love.

One God, three Persons, be near to the people formed in your image, close to the world your love brings to life.

We ask you this, Father, Son, and Holy Spirit, one God, true and living, for ever and ever.

Amen.

(Alternative Opening Prayer)

Here is a traditional Anglican prayer—the collect for Trinity Sunday:[1]

Almighty and everlasting God you have given us your servants grace by the confession of a true faith to acknowledge the glory of the eternal Trinity and in the power of the divine majesty to worship the Unity:

Keep us steadfast in this faith that we may evermore be defended from all adversities through Jesus Christ your Son our Lord who is alive and reigns with you in the unity of the Holy Spirit one God, now and for ever.

Amen.

Here is a recent Anglican prayer from *Common Worship*.

We come boldly to the throne of grace, praying to the almighty God, Father, Son, and Holy Spirit for mercy and grace.

We plead before your throne in heaven.

Father of heaven, whose love profound a ransom for our souls has found:

We pray for the world, created by your love, For its nations and governments . . .

1. This prayer is from the 1662 *Book of Common Prayer* and was subsequently included in the *Alternative Service Book* and then in *Common Worship*.

Extend to them your peace, pardoning love, mercy, and grace.

We plead before your throne in heaven.

Almighty Son, incarnate Word, our Prophet, Priest, Redeemer, Lord:

We pray for the Church, created for your glory, for its ministry to reflect those works of yours . . .

Extend to us your salvation, growth, mercy, and grace.

We plead before your throne in heaven.

Eternal Spirit, by whose breath the soul is raised from sin and death:

We pray for families and individuals, created in your image, for the lonely, the bereaved, the sick, and the dying . . .

Breathe on them the breath of life and bring them to your mercy and grace.

We plead before your throne in heaven.

Thrice holy! Father, Spirit, Son, Mysterious Godhead, Three in One:

We pray for ourselves, for your Church, for all whom we remember before you . . .

Bring us all to bow before your throne in heaven, to receive life and pardon, mercy and grace for all eternity, as we worship you, saying,

Holy, holy, holy Lord, God of power and might, heaven and earth are full of your glory. Hosanna in the highest. Amen.

Here is a neo-Celtic prayer from the Northumbria Community's Ebba Compline. Even if the postmodern spirituality of so-called Celtic Christianity bears only a remote relation to that of ancient British Christians, many of the prayers are still excellent:[2]

2. *Celtic Daily Prayer*, 40–41. For a helpful critique of the "Celtic Christianity" movement see Meek, *The Quest for Celtic Christianity*. However, even if the "Celtic Christianity" movement is not, in any straightforward sense, recovering a past spirituality, that does not negate the Trinitarian spirituality that it fosters.

Come I this night to the Father, Come I this night to the Son,
Come I to the Holy Spirit powerful:
Come I this night to God.
Come I this night to Christ,
Come I with the Spirit of kindness.
Come I to thee, Jesus.
Jesus, shelter me . . .

The peace of all peace
Be mine this night
In the name of the Father,
And of the Son,
And of the Holy Spirit.
Amen

For a classic, ancient British Christian prayer consider the well-known St. Patrick's breastplate, which concludes:

I bind unto myself the Name,
The strong Name of the Trinity,
By invocation of the same,
The Three in One and One in Three.
By Whom all nature hath creation,
Eternal Father, Spirit, Word:
Praise to the Lord of my salvation,
Salvation is of Christ the Lord.[3]

LITURGY

The discussion of set prayers flows naturally into a discussion of liturgy, for liturgy obviously contains many set prayers. There is, however, far more to liturgy than set prayers. A liturgy provides the structure of a collective act of worship. It includes prayers, Scripture readings from the lectionary, music, creeds, gestures (such as making the sign of the cross), and movements (such as kneeling and standing), the use of various ritual objects (such as bread and wine) and the structuring of the space and time during the act of worship. I love some of the subtle yet profound aspects of liturgy. For instance, when priests say "in the name of the Father, and of the Son, and of the Holy Spirit," they will make the sign of the cross. This unspoken association of the Trinity with the cross is striking and very suggestive.

3. This translation from Gaelic was made by Cecil F. Alexander in 1889.

Most Christian traditions are liturgical, but certainly not all of them are. Although my own charismatic, nonconformist tradition has no set liturgy, inevitably informal liturgies are at work—we humans are creatures of habit. Now although I am not part of a liturgical community, I have little time for the suggestion that liturgy is somehow second-rate worship or mere dead ritual.[4] Of course, liturgy *can* become a dead ritual, but so too can *any* form of worship. The experience of innumerable Christians is that liturgy can provoke very powerful and profound acts of heartfelt worship. It also needs to be emphasized that liturgy is perfectly compatible with the freedom of the Spirit so prized in charismatic worship. Many renewal churches successfully combine liturgical and charismatic dimensions in their corporate worship.[5]

There are many things that commend Spirit-filled, liturgical worship, but I want to focus on just one: good liturgy can foster and preserve a Trinitarian spirituality. Many of the liturgies in use today have grown up over generations and reflect something of the deep Trinitarian faith of our ancestors. And many of the newer liturgies, likewise, have sought to preserve this Trinitarian dimension of Christian worship. What liturgy often does is provide the Trinitarian structure of worship for us and, if we participate in such worship week by week, it can have the effect of getting the Trinity deep under our skin. Churches that have such a liturgy shift much of the burden for shaping the direction and focus of worship off the songs. The benefits of this should be blindingly obvious in light of the last chapter. In a nutshell, liturgical worship that is properly Trinitarian can preserve its Trinitarian integrity *even if* the songs are weak in this regard. Those of us who lack liturgy need the songs to do most of the work, and that is asking a lot from them.

Liturgy also preserves the Trinitarian structure of worship over time. Those of us who lack liturgy have to address a very serious issue here—namely, how can we avoid Trinitarian prayer and worship becoming the latest worship-fashion that is here today and gone tomorrow? We shall reflect on this question in the Epilogue, but liturgy provides one attractive solution to the problem.

4. While many modern charismatics look down on liturgy, we do well to bear in mind that the public worship of almost all Christians in the past was liturgical and that this remains the case for the majority of Christians (Orthodox, Catholic, Anglican, and so forth) still today. To claim that the devotion of all such Christians is "dry" and not "Spirit-led" is a suggestion of breathtaking arrogance and ignorance.

5. See Leach, *Living Liturgy*.

Liturgy can foster Trinitarian prayer simply because it contains Trinitarian prayers, and often the very framing of a prayer in the wider context of the liturgy can express Trinitarian truth. All of this, of course, presupposes good liturgy—and not all liturgy is as Trinitarian as it could be. Liturgy needs to be constantly under review and open to revision. Also, new liturgies need to be written and at the heart of all such renewal should be the Christian vision of the Trinity.

I am not trying to persuade non-liturgical Christians to accept liturgy as the way forward—attempting that is almost as pointless as trying to persuade a lion to be a vegetarian. As we have seen, however, there are inevitably informal liturgies at work in *all* worship contexts. I would encourage leaders to step back and, through a Trinitarian framework, identify those elements of their worship practice that have become *de facto* liturgy. Which elements should you discard, and which ones could you renew with a Trinitarian focus?

While I think that formal liturgy has much to commend it in enabling Christians to walk prayerfully with the Trinity, I certainly do not think that it is essential. It is perfectly possible to enjoy fully Trinitarian praise and prayer in just about any form of worship known in the Christian church, so if your tradition, like my own, is not formally liturgical you need not despair. But we will need to think very carefully and regularly about the structure of our worship and the public prayer within it.

Tongues

Tongues are human utterances in words not understood by the speakers, rising from deep within the psyche (what Paul calls the "spirit") and addressed to God. The Spirit releases this gift within individuals for their own edification. Very occasionally tongues are human languages not learned by the speaker, but on the vast majority of occasions they are not any languages known to humans (*perhaps* the languages of angels, 1 Cor 13:1) and often may not even be languages at all but deep, inarticulate groanings which are more expressive than cognitive.[6] So how can this phenomenon (or range of phenomena) be part of a Trinitarian prayer life? Those who speak to God in tongues do not know what they are saying, so it doesn't make much sense

6. Here I am following Anthony Thiselton's controversial exegesis of 1 Corinthians 14 in Thiselton, *The First Epistle to the Corinthians*, 1081–1130. See also Hilborn, "Glossolalia as Communication."

to suggest that they should get more of the Trinity into their words. Neither do I think that the answer is to suggest that worshippers should think about the Father or the Son or the Spirit as they pray in tongues. Although that is possible, my own experience is that when I pray in tongues "my mind is unfruitful" (1 Cor 14:14). I may be thinking about the Son, but that does not mean that my words are directed to the Son. My own experience of tongues is that I am conscious that the mystery of my words means that I do not know whether I speak to Father, Son, Spirit or all three. Indeed, the benefit of such prayer is that I am utterly dependent on God for what I say, so I am not thinking at all about what I should be saying—I just speak. The meaning or the significance of the words is not determined by my decisions. But perhaps it is here that we can perceive the Trinitarian dimension of such prayer. In tongues I am dependent on the Spirit poured out on me by Christ as I pray to the Father (and perhaps also to Christ and his Spirit), and to appreciate the gift of tongues I ought to be aware of this fact. I may not be able to have any say in the significance of what I am saying or even which divine person I address, but the Christian significance of tongues is given by the Trinitarian nature of the gift itself. In my experience, Pentecostals and charismatics are usually very conscious that when they speak in tongues it is because Christ has poured the Spirit on them and enables them to speak to God. That Trinitarian consciousness is part of the fabric of the gift itself. Simply being conscious of this is all that is needed for tongues to be a conscious expression of Trinitarian prayer—anything further must be left to God.

In summary, then, we need to enrich the way we relate to God by developing a consciously Trinitarian prayer life. Shaping our spirituality in this way is simply a matter of molding the content of our prayers around the shape of the God to whom we pray. It may seem contrived and awkward at first, but as good habits form it becomes second nature and we find ourselves instinctively praying with, and to, the Trinity.

nine

The Trinity and Lament[1]

LAMENTING THE LOSS OF LAMENT

WHEN WAS THE LAST time that you heard a prayer in church that went something like this?

> But I, O Yhwh, cry out to you; in the morning my prayer comes before you. O Yhwh, why do you cast me off? Why do you hide your face from me? Wretched and close to death from my youth up, I suffer terrors; I am desperate. Your wrath has swept over me; your dread assaults destroy me. They surround me like a flood all day long; from all sides they close in on me. You have caused friend and neighbor to shun me; my companions are in darkness. (Ps 88:13–18)

Or this: "How long, O Yhwh? Will you forget me forever? How long will you hide your face from me? How long must I bear pain in my soul, and have sorrow in my heart all day long? How long shall my enemy be exalted over me?" (Ps 13:1–2).

About a third of the Psalms in the Book of Psalms are prayers of lament—both individuals lamenting and the whole community lamenting—and yet somehow many Christians feel distinctly uncomfortable with the idea of such spirituality. How could we pray to God like the Psalmist? "Rouse yourself! Why do you sleep, O Lord?" (Ps 44:23). "Why, O Yhwh,

---

1. A longer version of this chapter appears in Cohen and Parsons, eds., *In Praise of Worship*, 143–61.

do you stand far off? Why do you hide yourself in times of trouble?" (Ps 10:1)

Surely to speak to God in such ways is ungrateful and irreverent! Surely the faithful should be rejoicing in the Spirit, even in affliction, so how can grief be a Christian response? And yet there in the Bible stands this vast collection of prayers—not simply in the Book of Psalms but throughout the OT—that gnaw away at our fixed-grin spirituality. Something is missing in public Christian worship and that something is honesty.

Do not misunderstand me—we Christians often find these "irreverent" prayers very helpful when they are used *in private* but we would not usually wish to be heard speaking in those ways in public. And even though, if asked directly, we may say, "Of course lament is a good thing," we still often feel rather uncomfortable about it. If we are honest we often feel somewhat ambivalent about sadness. Thus some pastors, such as Rick Warren, have a policy of never using songs that reflect sadness.[2] Cheerful worship is compulsory. My point is not that we ought to purge joy from worship. God forbid! It is simply that we need to recall that there is "a *time* to weep and a *time* to laugh, a *time* to mourn and a *time* to dance" (Eccl 3:4).

The loss of lament in Christian spirituality is, or so I want to suggest, a costly loss.[3] Given that public worship plays a significant role in shaping the contours of the relationship with God of individual Christians we are possibly failing to enable each other to handle tragedy and pain with honesty and integrity. The lack of prayers and songs of lament is potentially depriving Christians of a language with which to make sense of, and express, sorrow. There is a danger of modeling only joyful prayer in communal worship—encouraging grieving people to pull themselves together and join in the joyful worship of the community when this sometimes amounts for them to little more than telling lies in musical form.

So let me deal with a couple of common Christian concerns about lament.

Lament is Hope-less

After the resurrection we have solid grounds for hope so how can resurrection hope exist alongside the hopelessness of lament? This is a good question, but biblical lament does *not* lack hope. As Jamie Grant observes:

2. Warren, *The Purpose Driven Church*, 286–87.
3. The phrase is from Brueggemann, "The Costly Loss of Lament."

For the Christian, neither hope in Christ nor certainty of ultimate divine resolution to our problems in any way denies the human need for lament. Lament is not based on the psalmist's lack of future hope; lament is grounded in the psalmist's *present* experience of life with God in the world. Lament is intrinsic to humanity living in relationship with God in his good *but fallen* world . . . The knowledge that everything will be alright does not change the fact that, in our humanity, we need to respond before God to those present realities that are not alright.[4]

The Psalmist asks, "Why?" and "How long?" but neither of those questions need indicate a lack of hope for an ultimate salvation. After the death of his son in a climbing accident, Nicholas Wolterstorff wrote:

Elements of the gospel which I had always thought would console did not. They did something else, something important, but not that. It did not console me to be reminded of the hope of resurrection. If I had forgotten that hope, then it would indeed have brought light into my life to be reminded of it. But I did not think of death as a bottomless pit. I did not grieve as one who has no hope. Yet Eric is gone, *here* and *now* he is gone; *now* I cannot talk with him, *now* I cannot see him, *now* I cannot hug him, *now* I cannot hear of his plans for the future. *That* is my sorrow. A friend said, "Remember, he's in good hands." I was deeply moved. But that reality does not put Eric back in my hands. That's my grief. For that grief, what consolation can there be other than having him back?[5]

So Christian hope for the future can co-exist with lament *precisely because* deliverance and consolation lie in the future and our present experience can be dark.

Lament is Irreverent

At times those praying come out and directly complain about God and this, we fear, is irreverent. But in the book of Job it was the friends—those who spoke all the theologically sound words—that God rebuked. And it was Job, the man who had spent a long time criticizing God very openly, that God said had spoken rightly about him or *to* him (the Hebrew in Job 42:7 could

---

4. Grant, "Psalm 44 and a Christian Spirituality of Lament," 10–11.

5. Wolterstorff, *Lament for a Son*, 31.

be translated either way). Job feared God and the fear of God is compatible with honest lament. God was saying that when Job brought his pain in prayer *he spoke rightly*. There will be times in which psalms of individual and communal lament will be the appropriate way of relating to the Lord honestly.

While we may see lament as an act of unbelief this is not the case. Lament is not a severing of relationship with God but takes places precisely *within* that relationship.

> The lament is the response of one who cares enough to take the meaningless before God. This is an act of faith. To take our honest questions to God is not an act of defamation towards the character of God, but an act of affirmation. Why are there wrongs in this in-between time? Why are they so severe? How long must we endure? These are the cries within the context of faith-struggle in this in-between time. And if Christians can muster at least as much faith as the Old Testament Psalmist and Prophets, then the release of such questions finds its form in the lament.[6]

Lament gives voice to our sorrow, our pain, our grief, our anger. The sense of powerlessness and the loss of one's voice are intrinsic to many kinds of suffering and lament counters that. It gives the powerless and broken ones their speech back.

Lament, however, is not simply the voicing of sorrow but is also a prayer for salvation—a yearning for a future different from the present that rises up within the depths of our being. Lament is simultaneously sorrow, yearning, and intercession.

So lament is one important biblical mode of engaging with God when the lights go out. It is not a rejection of God but an act of clinging to God for dear life when there is nowhere else to go. However, it is my contention that a *Christian* understanding of the place and practice of lament will be enhanced once it is incorporated within a full-orbed Trinitarian theological vision of God.

LAMENT AND THE TRINITY

As we have already shown, one of the great insights of Trinitarian theology is that all worship and prayer is not merely a human response to God but

6. Resner, "Lament: Faith's Response to Loss," 131.

is a "gifted response."[7] That is to say, the response that we make to God in worship is a response that is enabled by God.[8] This has implications for how we think about the human activity of lamenting. We should conceive of our lamentation as being offered *to the Father, through and with Jesus, in the power of the Holy Spirit.*

It is clear in all biblical laments that the one to whom the lament is offered is Yhwh, the God of Israel. And Yhwh, in *this* context, is the God and Father of our Lord Jesus Christ. Lament is not merely the *expression* of pain but is first and foremost a *plea* directed towards God the Father.

The Sorrow of the Father

How is God related to our pain? An interesting place to begin thinking about *that* is the book of Jeremiah. The book is mostly given over to warnings of coming judgment from God. But how does God "feel" about the suffering that such punishment would bring? There are three passages in the book (Jer 4:19–21; 8:18–9:2; 14:17–18) in which the line between Jeremiah's words and God's words blur. The prophet speaks his own sentiments but also speaks God's. Here is one such passage:

> My joy is gone; grief is upon me; my heart is sick within me. Behold, the cry of the daughter of my people from the length and breadth of the land: "Is the LORD not in Zion? Is her King not in her?"
>
> Why have they provoked me to anger with their carved images and with their foreign idols?
>
> "The harvest is past, the summer is ended, and we are not saved."
>
> For the wound of the daughter of my people is my heart wounded; I mourn, and dismay has taken hold on me. Is there no balm in Gilead? Is there no physician there? Why then has the health of the daughter of my people not been restored? Oh that my head were waters, and my eyes a fountain of tears, that I might weep day and night for the slain of the daughter of my people! (Jer 8:18—9:1)

7. Matt Redman, "Gifted Response," ©Thankyou Music, 2004.

8. See now Ngien, *Gifted Response.*

Who speaks here? Jeremiah? Yes. God? Yes.[9] I believe that God does "suffer," in his divine being, when his people suffer.[10] He is "grieved" to see them in pain, even if he himself has inflicted it. This is reflected in Rabbinic Jewish writing on Lamentations. *Lamentations Rabbah* pictures the following scene in heaven:

> At that moment the Holy One, blessed be he, wept, saying, "Woe is me! What have I done! I have brought my Presence to dwell below on account of the Israelites, and now that they have sinned, I have gone back to my earlier dwelling. Heaven forfend that I now become a joke to the nations and an object of ridicule among the people" . . . When the Holy One, blessed be he, saw the house of the sanctuary, he said, "This is certainly my house, and this is my resting place, and the enemies have come and done whatever they pleased with it!" At that moment the Holy One, blessed be he, wept, saying, "Woe is me for my house! O children of mine— where are you? O priests of mine—where are you? O you that love me—where are you? What shall I do for you? I warned you but you did not repent."[11]

Such is the love of the Father. However, a full-blown Christian theology must go further. Trinitarian theology would lead us to see a double movement in lament. First, a movement *from* the Father *towards* creation, through the Son and in the Spirit. Second, a movement *from* creation *towards* the Father, through the Son and in the Spirit. In Christ, God moves downwards towards humanity and humanity moves upwards towards God.

Perhaps we see the downwards movement in the lamenting of Jesus over Jerusalem. As he approached and saw the city he wept over it and lamented the spiritual blindness that would lead to its inevitable destruction (Luke 19:41–44. cf. Matt 23:37–39; Luke 13:34–35). Is this not the lament of the Father expressed to his creatures through the Son, in the Spirit? Do we not see something of the "passion" of the Father here in the passion of the Son? Of course, we must beware of imagining that God is just like us and should remain reverently agnostic about what it is like for *God* to "suffer" in his divinity. Nevertheless we should not shy away from using

9. See Fretheim, *The Suffering of God*, 156–59; McConville, *Judgment and Promise*, 65–67.

10. See Fretheim, *The Suffering of God*; Alan Torrance, "Does God Suffer? Incarnation and Impassibility."

11. *Lamentations Rabbah* XXIV.ii.1.I–2.C–D. The reference system is that of Jacob Neusner.

the bold language of emotion, which the biblical writers had no hesitations about using of God.[12]

Lamenting through the Son

But, whatever it means for God to "suffer" in sympathetic love, in Christ something radically different happens: God suffered *in the flesh.* That is to say that *the Logos was the divine subject of the human suffering of Jesus.* In Christ, *God* experienced human suffering, not simply as a divine sympathizer who stands beside us but *as a human* who suffers *with, as,* and *for* us. This is beyond mere divine sympathy and places God in shocking proximity to our broken condition.

When considering lament in terms of Christ's role as the-creature-before-the-Creator—the upward movement of lament from creation to the Father, through the Son and in the Spirit—the focus for our reflections must be Golgotha. At the place of the skull we find a complaint psalm on the lips of Christ—"My God, my God, why have you forsaken me?" (Ps 22:1). It is important to appreciate that this Psalm was not incidental to the crucifixion narratives but was fundamental—in Matthew, Mark, and John at least—in shaping them.[13] We must also bear in mind that Mark's passion narrative alludes not merely to Psalm 22 but to various other lament psalms.[14] Richard Bauckham explores the implications of this:

12. Arguably the church fathers did not teach *absolute* impassibility, see Gavrilyuk, *The Suffering of the Impassible God* and Castello, *The Apathetic God.* The primary concern of the fathers was to maintain that God was not subject to *irrational* and *sinful* passions and also to defend *divine transcendence* against those who presume that God's love or anger, say, are simply a magnified version of what humans experience.

13. Evidenced by the fact that there are numerous allusions to Psalm 22 in the passion narratives and not merely the quotation of 22:1 found on Jesus' lips. (See also Heb 2:12; 5:7.)

14. Bauckham lists the following allusions to lament psalms:

Mark	Psalm
14:18	41:10
14:34	42:5, 11; 43:5
14:55	37:32?
14:57	27:12; 35:11; 69:4
15:24	22:18
15:29	22:7

> Through allusions to other psalms of lament Mark places Jesus'
> dying words in the context not only of Psalm 22 as a whole but
> also of the psalms of lament in general . . . In relating the passion
> and death of Jesus to the psalms of lament in general, Mark relates
> the passion and death of Jesus to the situation of all who wrote and
> used those psalms, those who cried out to God from the desperate
> situations those psalms describe . . . [T]he experience of the Mes-
> siah gathers up into itself the experiences of all whose sufferings
> find expression in those psalms.[15]

In his messianic role Jesus partakes in the covenant curses that a
disobedient Israel has brought upon itself. Compare the exilic sufferings
of Daughter Zion (a personification of Jerusalem) in Lamentations 1 with
those of Christ. Jesus' suffering runs in parallel to Jerusalem's in numerous
ways as he plays out his role as her representative. Like Jerusalem tears were
upon his cheeks as he prayed alone in the garden (Lam 1:2a); like Jerusalem
he knew betrayal by his "friends" who left him to suffer alone (Lam 1:2b);
like Jerusalem Jesus was beaten, stripped naked, publicly humiliated, and
afflicted (Lam 1:8–10); like Jerusalem he was reduced from a high and noble
status to dust (Lam 1:1, 7); like Jerusalem he bore the divine curse for covenant disobedience (Lam 1:3, 5; Gal 3:13); like Jerusalem he was violently
attacked by a pagan occupying force (Lam 1:10, 15); like Jerusalem he felt
abandoned by Yhwh in the face of these pagan military oppressors (Lam
1:9b, 11b, 20); like Jerusalem he was mocked and despised by those who
looked on at his destruction (Lam 1:7d, 21). The suffering Christ embodies
the sufferings of his city and his people depicted in the moving lament of
Lamentations 1.

We should note that Jesus' experience of alienation from God was
not simply an inner feeling of despair but the *concrete reality* of suffering
injustice, betrayal, torture, and defeat at the hands of those who worship
false gods. "It is somewhat misleading to say—of the psalmist or of Jesus

Mark	Psalm
15:30–31	22:8?
15:32	22:6; 69:9
15:34	22:1
15:36	69:21
15:40	38:11

Bauckham, "God's Self-Identification with the Godforsaken in the Gospel of Mark," 255.

15. Ibid., 256.

echoing his words—that he *feels* forsaken by God as though this were an understandable mistake. What Jesus experiences is the concrete fact that he has been left to suffer and die. God has, in this sense, abandoned him, not merely in psychological experience but in the form of the concrete situation that Jesus experiences."[16]

And he yells out to Yhwh from the depths of his being. Christ lamenting in our place! Here *our* alienation from God is taken up within the very humanity of God himself. This is God "abandoned" by God; our human experience of God-forsakenness relocated within the being of God. God does not simply suffer in sympathy with us; *in Christ* God the Son suffers in our place *as one of us*. God knows what it is like to be a powerless human victim.

Returning to Jesus' use of Psalm 22, we need to note the "contradiction" between Psalm 22:1–2 and 22:24. Contrast "My God, my God, why have you forsaken me? Why are you so far from saving me, so far from the words of my groaning? O my God, I cry out by day, but you do not answer, by night, and am not silent" (Ps 22:1–2) with "For he has not despised or disdained the suffering of the afflicted one; he has not hidden his face from him but has listened to his cry for help" (Ps 22:24).

This suggests that the Psalmist's perception of the situation has changed. He is in terrible suffering having been abandoned by God (22:1–8, 12–18). He calls to Yhwh for salvation (22:9–11, 19–21) and *then*, perhaps after receiving some salvation oracle from the priest, takes on an attitude of confidence that God has heard him and will deliver him (22:22–31). The same pattern is seen in the story of Jesus on the cross. Mark 15:25 sees Jesus on the cross from the third hour (about 9AM). From the sixth hour (12PM) until the ninth hour (3PM) an ominous darkness descends over the land (Mark 15:33; Matt 27:45; Luke 23:44). During this period of six hours Jesus has been experiencing the suffering of the righteous individual in the psalms. At about 3PM Jesus cried out in a loud voice, "My God, my God! Why have you forsaken me?" When groping around for words to express the feelings of grief at his "abandonment" by the God whom he had worshipped from birth it is no surprise that these words came to mind. Jesus was saturated in the Scriptures of Israel and cannot have missed the parallels between his predicament and that of the psalmist.

It is interesting that the cry of dereliction comes not long before Jesus dies. This is not a period of doubt he went through near the beginning of

16. Ibid., 257.

his time on the cross and quickly got over. This was a simmering, growing grief held back in dignified silence until he can hold in no longer. For Matthew and Mark it is the last thing they record Jesus saying before his crying out in a loud voice and dying.

Luke and John record more positive last words ("Father, into your hands I commit my spirit," Luke 23:46; "It is finished," John 19:30). While we need to respect the different emphases of the different Gospels, it is perfectly possible to imagine Jesus drawing hope and inspiration in the midst of his despair from the ultimate deliverance experienced by the psalmist that he has so identified himself with. But even if we use Psalm 22 to hold together the dark words of Jesus recorded in Matthew and Mark with the positive, final words in Luke and John we must emphasize that (i) the darkness of his suffering expressed in the cry of dereliction was not a momentary doubt but a growing and prolonged anguish, (ii) the darkness experienced was not some Scripture-quoting ritual done for show but a genuine expression of how Jesus felt, (iii) Jesus was not *abandoning* God in this prayer (for the psalmist, as for Jesus, God is still "*my* God." This is grief expressed *within* a covenant relationship with God) and (iv) that the positive change in Jesus' final moments may well have been influenced by the end of Psalm 22.

Now where does this story place the Christian vis-à-vis the laments of Israel? Jesus himself takes the prayer tradition of complaint against Yhwh upon his own lips. Jesus prays the lament *as his own prayer.* He stood as Israel's messianic representative suffering *and lamenting* with his people Israel. He stood as the Adamic representative of the whole of humanity suffering *and lamenting* with those broken upon the wheel of life. This must, for the Christian, legitimate Israel's worship tradition of lament.

Lament serves as a complaint against God but also as a turning towards and clinging to the divine promise thus reconfiguring praise as a revival of hope in the midst of darkness. In a similar way, Barth suggestively claims that the act of hope in Christ is a "comforted despair," something that stands in contrast to non-Christian forms of optimism and pessimism (*CD*, IV.1, 633, 636).

But, I suggest, Christ does not simply mediate our lament in his suffering upon the cross. As the Book of Hebrews explains, Jesus stands now as our High Priest, as man-for-God in the presence of the Father. In this priestly role he intercedes for us as our representative. He fulfils this role as one who understands our pain and sorrows—our brother made like us in every way. It seems to me theologically plausible to suggest that Christ's ongoing prayers to his Father include laments and as such he can mediate our own laments to the Father. In this way we know that God hears our cries *because we know that he hears Jesus' cries.*

But I spoke of the lament in the Trinity so what of the Spirit?

Lament in the Spirit

Romans 8:18–30 helps us to get some insight into the Spirit and a certain mode of lament. I offer the two diagrams reproduced at the end of this chapter as a way to clarify the logic of the text. Paul draws a parallel between Jesus' suffering, the suffering of Christians, and the suffering of the whole created order (8:17–25). Indeed, Paul's underlying theology is one that sees an intimate relationship between humanity, Israel, Christ, and the *ekklēsia*.

First of all notice that the stories of Christ, church, and creation run in parallel: suffering then glory; death then life. Jesus was crucified, died, was buried and *then* was raised from the dead by God through the Spirit (Rom 8:11). Paul is saying that the story of believers will be like Christ's. Currently we are in our mortal bodies and we suffer with Jesus. We shall die. But *then* we shall be raised by God through the same Spirit that he raised Christ. Paul speaks of this future as one in which the very glory of God himself is revealed in us. It is a resurrection to immortality, it is our adoption as sons—that is, children and heirs of God.

In the same way the story of the whole created order is one of frustration and slavery to death and decay followed by liberation and participating in the freedom of the children of God. In other words, when God resurrects his people he will then resurrect the whole creation. And Paul pictures both the creation and the church (and, by implication, Jesus himself on the cross) as currently "groaning." We'll come back to that.

So the story of the church and of creation is *darkness now* but *light to come*—a story *already* played out in the life of Jesus. So Paul can write that, "our present sufferings are not worth comparing with the glory that will be revealed in us" (8:18). And Paul knew some serious sufferings and times of real despair (2 Cor 1:8–9; 11). It is *this* man who says that "our present sufferings are not worth comparing with the glory that will be revealed in us." That future is what enabled him to face the present darkness. Paul who, for the joy set before him, endured the shame and suffering. But we need to see that, for Paul, this eager expectation of God's new days existed alongside the present experience of grief and sorrow. This is where the groaning comes in. The groaning is three things at once.

First, it is *an expression of sorrow, pain, and frustration at the current state of affairs.* In this respect it is something like a lament. It is like moan from the depths of our being—a painful awareness that all is not as it should be.

Second, it is simultaneously *a groan of expectation for a better future.* Paul describes it as "groaning as in the pains of childbirth"—notice how that image blends pain with an expectation of, and longing for, new life. He speaks of us "groaning eagerly as we wait eagerly for our adoption as sons" (cf. 2 Cor 5:2–4).

The idea of lament as an expression of grief and expectation is well put by Nicholas Wolterstorff in his comments on Matthew 5:4—"Blessed are those who mourn, for they will be comforted." Who are the mourners? "The Mourners are those who have caught a glimpse of God's new day, who ache with all their being for that day's coming, and who break out into tears when confronted by its absence . . . The mourners," he writes, "are aching visionaries."[17] Aching visionaries who simply refuse to accept the current state of affairs. Here we also glimpse something of the way in which the Spirit moves the people of God into action, even rage, *against* injustice and *for* love in his gathering up of the people of God into the responsive and creative action of lament. It is what John Swinton refers to as "raging with compassion."[18]

Third, it is *intercession.* We have already spoken of how the OT laments serve as expressions of sorrow and also as prayers for salvation. Well, this deep primal moaning that Paul speaks of is also an expression of grief and simultaneously a prayer to God for new creation. It is at this point that Paul introduces the Holy Spirit. The Spirit himself groans. In *sorrow* for the present darkness? Yes. In *hope* for a better future? Yes. But most critically, in *intercession* for that new future. The Holy Spirit is praying for the church. The Holy Spirit knows the Father's will and purposes fully. We do not. So when the Spirit prays for us he is praying in perfect accord with God's cosmic purposes—his ultimate purposes for the whole created order.

Earlier we reflected christologically on the sufferings of Jerusalem in Lamentations 1. I would now like to reflect on them pneumatologically. In the light of Romans 8 I suggest that the Spirit of God participates in

17. Wolterstorff, *Lament for a Son*, 85–86.

18. Swinton, *Raging with Compassion.*

Jerusalem's sorrows. The Spirit groans with all those who groan as they yearn for liberation. Jerusalem groans at her humiliation and turns away her face from onlookers (Lam 1:8c), just as her priests groan at the cessation of temple festivals (Lam 1:4b) and her people groan as they search for food (Lam 1:11a). This groaning in Lamentations 1 is motivated by the mourners looking *back* (mourning what is lost), looking *around* (expressing despair at the current situation), and looking *forward* (yearning for a reversal of the calamity). So also the Spirit, participating in the groaning of creation, groans as he looks *back* and looks *around* seeing a shattered world but he also groans like a woman in childbirth looking *forward*, bringing to birth a new creation. The Spirit's groaning, while a participation in creation's groaning, also transforms it. It is a hope-infused groaning that looks to the future with confidence. The Spirit can enable our groaning to become a participation in his groaning and in Christ's groaning. That is to say, Spirit-transformed groaning is still an expression of pain at the current situation but it is not an expression of hopelessness.

So the Spirit is groaning *with* and *for* us as he seeks to bring us through to resurrection. The Spirit is praying creation into glory. And here is the amazing thing—the Spirit does not simply pray for us: he prays for us *through us*. He makes our own groanings a vehicle for his groanings. And that's good because so often we don't know what we should pray for or how we should pray for it. But the Spirit does and he helps us in our weakness.

How? Many people have struggled to know what phenomenon Paul refers to here. Nowhere else does he speak of the Spirit praying in groans. Is this some odd phenomenon not mentioned elsewhere? Or is it tongues? Or is it something else? I suggest that we not try to pin it down too tightly as I think it can manifest itself in a range of ways. Sometimes speaking in tongues is a manifestation of the Spirit praying in groans too deep for words through us. Now this is an unusual and fascinating perspective on tongues. Charismatics usually think of it as a language of joyful praise but why can't it sometimes be the language of lament? Speaking in tongues as lamenting in the Spirit. Finding a language for pain is one of the needs for those afflicted. Here is a pneumatic gift of lament that can play a role parallel to more conventional modes of lament.

Sometimes, I think the Spirit's groaning can manifest itself in a deep primal scream that rises up from the depths of our being. Sometimes the Spirit can pray through us in simple tears. The old spiritual masters used to speak of the "gift of tears"—something one rarely hears of these days. Also, while this is not Paul's main focus, I do think that the Spirit can inspire and pray through our conventional laments spoken in normal human languages—"My God, my God, why have you forsaken me?" We are to pray in the Spirit at all times and praying in the Spirit is far more than simply speaking in tongues. Praying in the Spirit is *all* Spirit-inspired prayer *whatever form* it takes.

SHOULD WE INCLUDE LAMENT IN PUBLIC WORSHIP?[19]

But should we include lament within our public worship? And if we should, how can we do so with *authenticity*? The problem is that the chances are that on any particular Sunday gathering in which worshippers are invited to participate in some way in laments many of those present may very well not *feel* like lamenting. Within the worship culture of many modern evangelical churches this is enough to preclude its use. After all, who wants to have disengaged congregants speaking words that they do not mean? Is such worship not inauthentic at best?

What are we to say about this concern? Well, one is tempted to reply that this problem is simply the reverse of the "problem" that one finds week after week in such churches already. Modern evangelical worship is uncompromisingly happy and those present engage weekly in declaring how thankful and joyful they feel about God. If the concern is not to have people sing songs that do not reflect where they are at then what are we to say about the culture of unremitting joy? Is *this* inauthentic?

But I will set aside this simplistic "tit for tat" response because the songs that Christians sing are not always used in a declarative mode (I *am currently* rejoicing in God) but are often appropriated in aspirational mode (I *desire* to rejoice in God). The singing of the song can cultivate Christian desires and aspirations. But in a very similar way one can use laments as part of a process of aspirational spiritual formation even if one is not currently sad.

Now the most obvious objection to this proposal is that while we might understandably aspire to rejoice in the Lord, who on earth would want to encourage people to lament? Is an aspiration to *misery* a Christian aspiration? Let us consider that issue. Is there "a time to weep" (cf. Rom 12:15) in Christian worship or have we moved into an era of unceasing

---

19. This section is based on a section of Parry, "Wrestling with Lamentations in Christian Worship."

rejoicing since the resurrection? I would like to speak about the role that laments can play in spiritual formation, if used well within public worship.

Christian theologian Stanley Hauerwas very helpfully discusses the importance of engaging in practices as a way of learning the habits essential to become a skilled practitioner in a trade. Hauerwas considers the way in which one learns to become as master bricklayer or a master stonemason.[20] To become such one must learn from the acquired wisdom of those who have practiced the trade before by inhabiting the history and traditions of the trade and by being apprenticed to a master. Part of this learning is learning the language of the trade and one must practice, practice, practice, and practice again the basic skills until they become second nature. Only then is one able to innovate with any skill. This is not cerebral learning but an engaged *learning by doing*. Now Hauerwas insists that a life of Christian virtue is acquired in the same way. Not by the impartation of information but by a participation of the prayerful and worshipful life of a Christian community. We learn to pray, "Our Father, in heaven," we partake in the Eucharist, we hear the Scriptures, and we intercede for others. We are inducted into the language of the Christian life through engaging in the prayers of the community even before we understand exactly what they mean and we practice, practice, practice, and practice again until the language and habits are part of the warp and weft of who we are. Engaging in the stories of the community in communal worship and Christian practice shapes us into a certain kind of people—people of Christian character. Clearly on this understanding of being formed into a Christian disciple there is an important place for engaging communally in practices that we might not fully understand and that might not express how we currently feel. But the ongoing participation in such practices is essential for rounded spiritual formation. So liturgical engagement with laments can, in principle, play a role in the training of Christian emotions—not simply expressing how we currently feel but training us to see and to feel in certain kinds of ways. They are, in theological terms, vehicles for the Spirit to shape us into the image of Christ.

Take Lamentations 1 and 2. The poetry presents the wretched figure of Lady Zion in her broken state—beaten, raped, and deprived of her beloved children. The narrator presents her tragic plight to the audience and we also hear her own impassioned voice. The poetry is unrelenting and refuses to allow the audience to glance away for relief but forces them to keep looking.

---

20. See Hauerwas, "How We Lay Bricks"; Hauerwas, "Carving Stone."

The constant focus on the theme of Zion's lack of a comforter serves to invite the readers themselves to take on such a role—to weep with those who weep. To inhabit this poetry is to learn to become sensitized to pain, to pay attention to the suffering of others, to eschew the option to walk by on the other side. And as we proceed into chapter 2 we see that the narrator himself moves from his sympathetic but somewhat distant engagement with Zion's grief to a deep, gut wrenching sorrow. Readers are invited to make the same journey. To engage such literature in worship can play a role in the emotional formation of a community of disciples.

What the public use of laments will also do is to provide a language of lament. If the only prayer language into which believers are inducted through communal worship is that of thanksgiving, praise, and adoration then we are depriving believers of a language for dealing with the dark periods of life. We are also communicating the message that to speak to God with words of complaint and lament is somehow inappropriate, irreverent, and unfaithful. In this way we are in danger of failing to train disciples to walk with God through the valley of the shadow of death. It is important that the Christian community acknowledges and affirms the legitimacy of articulating honestly both the awkward and the uncomfortable—the fact that "things are not as they should be." Learning how to speak to and of God in such situations is important and it can only be done through inhabiting the narratives and worship practices reflected in the biblical story and in the Jewish and Christian traditions.

CONCLUSION

All this puts lament in whole new light. The Holy Spirit enables us to participate in Christ's lament to the Father. This lament is not the voice of faithless, hopeless, rebels who have given up on God and blaspheme him to his face. It is not the morbid moaning of miserable and weak Christians who need to pull themselves together. It can be a faithful, Spirit-inspired way of engaging with our covenant Lord and in his own feelings towards the world. It allows us to engage God honestly. It enables us to express our pain and to find a voice when we feel weak and powerless. It embodies an aching and a yearning for a different future and a refusal to accept things as they are. It is prayer that God's kingdom comes and his will be done *on earth* as it is in heaven. Perhaps Jesus was right after all—Blessed are those who mourn for they shall be comforted. God says yes to those who mourn, yes to those with the courage to admit that things are not all right, yes to those who have given up pretending that they know why God has allowed disaster to fall, yes to the weak and smashed, yes to those who sing a broken hallelujah, yes to those raging with compassion, and yes to the aching visionaries, for they shall see God.

Diagram 1

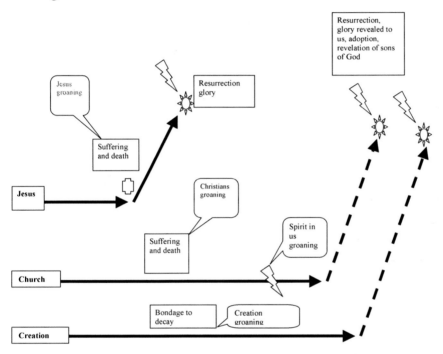

Diagram 2

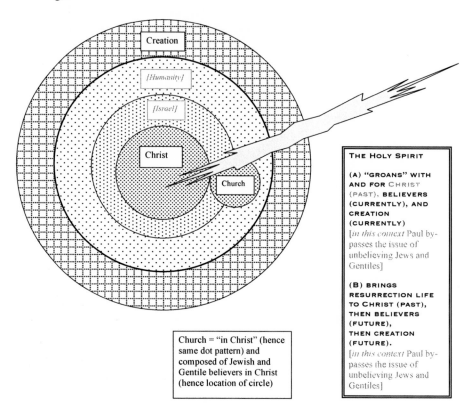

Creation

[Humanity]

[Israel]

Christ

Church

THE HOLY SPIRIT

(A) "GROANS" WITH
AND FOR CHRIST
(PAST), BELIEVERS
(CURRENTLY), AND
CREATION
(CURRENTLY)
[*in this context* Paul by-
passes the issue of
unbelieving Jews and
Gentiles]

(B) BRINGS
RESURRECTION LIFE
TO CHRIST (PAST),
THEN BELIEVERS
(FUTURE),
THEN CREATION
(FUTURE).
[*in this context* Paul by-
passes the issue of
unbelieving Jews and
Gentiles]

Church = "in Christ" (hence
same dot pattern) and
composed of Jewish and
Gentile believers in Christ
(hence location of circle)

ten

A Herd of Other Ideas
for Trinitarian Worship

IT IS EASY FOR those of us in charismatic churches to get stuck in the mind-set that preparing worship is simply, or at least primarily, choosing which songs to include in the "worship set." But there is so much more to worship than singing. Most obviously, the other elements of worship include praying, Holy Communion, the exercise of spiritual gifts, and listening to the word of God proclaimed in Scripture readings and sermons. In these common practices lie rich resources for accentuating Trinitarian worship. But why stop there? Perhaps we need to explore and experiment a little bit more and learn to "worship outside the box." If used well, the arts can also play a very positive role in worship, and so in this chapter we will begin to explore not only possible ways of accentuating the Trinitarian dimensions of the Eucharist and preaching, but we will also look at how dance, poetry, music, and the visual arts could hold potential for shaping a more Trinitarian spirituality.

THE LORD'S SUPPER, HOLY COMMUNION, OR EUCHARIST

Almost every Christian in the history of the world has seen the Lord's Supper as an important aspect of worship. For the majority of Christians, past and present, it is the *central* act in worship. Of course, there are some very different views on exactly what it means, what it should be called, how it should be done, by whom, where, when, and how often. However, in spite of the diverse traditions there is a clear common core to the practice—the differences are clearly variations on a single practice.

The question I wish to pose is this, how can we bring out the Trinitarian dimensions of the Eucharist? The place of Christ in the Eucharist is obvious, and it is right that Christ is the focus of the celebration, but sadly the Spirit and the Father are often neglected. Communion is a Christ-*centered* rite, but it is not a Christ-*only* rite. How can we heighten awareness of the place of all three persons in the practice? The place to begin is to understand the Trinitarian theology presupposed by the practice of Holy Communion (at least, in some of its forms).

Communion is a remembrance of Christ's death (Luke 22:19), but not the kind of remembrance that simply involves us recalling a historical event that occurred a long time ago. Rather, we remember his death in such a way that we see that *we* are those for whom Christ died. He bore *our* sins out of love for us. As we eat and drink there is a sense in which we share in Christ's death 2,000 years ago, participating in the benefits that it brings (1 Cor 10:16–17). The Spirit is the one who helps us remember in this participatory way. It is not the mere act of Communion that has value, as if it worked by some kind of magic. Rather, by faith, the Spirit uses the act to be a channel of God's grace to us.

Communion holds in tension the two crucial truths: the *absence* and the *presence* of Christ. Christians celebrate the Lord's Supper looking to the past death but also to the future return of the Lord. We proclaim in this meal "the Lord's death until he comes" (1 Cor 11:26). This reminds us, as we eat, that Christ is currently *absent*. Christ will not drink the cup with his disciples again until he drinks it in his Father's kingdom (Matt 26:29). We still await this full communion with Christ in the kingdom. And yet the Eucharist is also a celebration of our current relationship with Christ, for Christ is *present* with us in the act of Communion through his Spirit. There is a sense in which, after the resurrection and ascension, Christ is now in his Father's kingdom and is sharing the Communion meal with us. Christ is *really present*—spiritually present—as we eat the bread and drink the wine. This is not to suggest that the physical substance of the bread and wine changes, but it is to suggest that its *significance* is transformed by the Spirit and through receptive faith. In Holy Communion we experience both the "now" and the "not yet" of Christ's fellowship with us.

We have spoken of the centrality of Christ and the Spirit in the Eucharist, but what of the Father? When Christ took the Passover bread at the

Last Supper he gave thanks to the Father for it, as a good Jew should (Matt 26:26) and as the *ekklēsia* has ever since. Christ himself is the bread of life given by the Father to the world (John 6:32–33). The Father draws people (through the Spirit) to Christ, the bread of life (John 6:35–37). The new covenant that Christ establishes in his blood is a new covenant between humanity and the Father (Matt 26:28). Once we understand the Trinitarian theology underlying the Eucharist, the way is open to consider how to bring that to the surface in our practice. One common and helpful way is in prayer. Numerous modern communion prayers and post-communion prayers bring in the different persons of the Trinity. The most ancient eucharistic prayers are addressed to the Father, thanking him for sending Christ and feeding us on his body and blood. While the Eastern Orthodox churches always had a fully Trinitarian eucharistic liturgy,[1] Western eucharistic prayers often ignored the Spirit until recent years, when he has been acknowledged in both Roman Catholic and Anglican liturgies.[2] This is encouraging, and non-liturgical churches should follow suit in making extempore or set communion prayers more Trinitarian. A fully Trinitarian understanding of the cross, the church, and the new creation, all of which are central to communion, will provide the theological fuel for such prayers. Here is an example of an extempore Trinitarian postcommunion prayer:

> Holy Father, we thank you for sending your Son to die for us and for making a new covenant in his blood. In this act we remember and celebrate your great love for the world shown in Christ.
>
> Precious Jesus, we thank you that by your Spirit you have enabled us to fellowship with you at this table by faith. You are here in our midst by your Spirit.
>
> Lord, we thank you that your body was broken and your blood was poured out for the forgiveness of our sins. With joy we partake in the benefits of your body given and your blood shed. Lord, we proclaim the wonders of your gracious love and look forward to the time we will see you as you are and fellowship with you in the kingdom of your Father.
> Amen[3]

1. See, for instance, *The Divine Liturgy of Our Father among the Saints John Chrysostom.*

2. See Ephraim, "The Trinity in Contemporary Eucharistic Liturgy."

3. This prayer has even been turned into a song: "Holy Father" by Nathan Fellingham and Robin Parry. © 2005 Thankyou Music. It can be found on the album *Trinity* (Authentic Music, 2006).

And here is part of an overtly Trinitarian Syrian Orthodox Epiclesis—a prayer calling for the Spirit to be sent down and sanctify the bread and wine offered on the altar.

> Have mercy on us, O God the Father, and send upon these offerings your Holy Spirit, the Lord who is equal to you and to the Son in dominion, reign, and eternal substance . . . So that by his indwelling, he may make this bread the life-giving body, the redeeming body and the body of Christ our God . . . And may he perfect this cup into the blood of the new covenant, the redeeming blood and the blood of Christ our God.[4]

Some of the other ideas in this chapter and throughout this book will provide inspiration for making the rest of a service in which the Lord's Supper is celebrated more Trinitarian. How a picture is framed and placed in a gallery makes a huge difference to how it is appreciated. In the same way, how the Eucharist is framed in a meeting makes all the difference to the way it functions. Here is a Roman Catholic prayer used in eucharistic services that forms part of such a frame:

> Father, all-powerful and ever-living God,
>   we do well always and everywhere to give you thanks.
> We joyfully proclaim our faith
>   in the mystery of your Godhead.
> You have revealed your glory as the glory also of your Son
>   and of the Holy Spirit:
>   three Persons equal in majesty,
>   undivided in splendor, yet one Lord, one God,
>   ever to be adored in your everlasting glory.
> And so, with all the choirs of angels in heaven
>   we proclaim your glory
>   and join in their unending hymn of praise:
> Holy, holy, holy Lord . . .
> (Preface to the Eucharistic Prayer for the Solemnity of the Most Holy Trinity)

The frame need not be as formal as this, but worship leaders do need to think very carefully about Trinitarian framing for the Eucharist.

---

4. Marsh, *Prayers from the East*, 104.

SCRIPTURE READING

Reading from the Scriptures is a part of both public and private Christian worship, so I will offer some reflections on how we can better see and appreciate the Trinitarian God as we read different parts of the Bible. When we read the Bible devotionally—on our own, in small groups, or in a larger congregation—how can we do so in such a way that we see the Trinity?

First, and most obviously, we can pray before we read. Such prayer can focus on the Scriptures as the Father's gift, inspired and opened up to us by the Spirit and testifying to Christ. Prayers with such grammar heighten our awareness of the Trinitarian nature of Bible reading and also bring glory to God, who will answer them by helping us to see him revealed in his fullness through the word.

Second, we can simply keep our eyes peeled for references to the three persons and to the relations between them. Many Christians can testify that, once they were alerted to this issue and were on the lookout for the Trinity in the Bible, suddenly they saw it everywhere! Old texts that had washed over them were opened up in new ways, throwing wonderful light on the Godhead. We might also select key Trinitarian texts, such as John's Gospel (especially chapters 14–17), or Romans, for special study. Sermons with a Trinitarian focus also highlight the Trinity in the texts used in public worship, training congregations to look for such things. For instance, I spoke at one church on the theme of having confidence in God's grace. I outlined the shape of God's grace and in so doing drew attention to the work of all the persons of the Trinity in God's gracious activity.

Third, as we gain a greater knowledge of the Scriptures, we will be able to fill in Trinitarian blanks in biblical passages when reading scriptural texts that have no overt Trinitarian syntax. Let me give an example of what I mean. John 6 speaks of the Father drawing people to Christ. On the surface this seems to be a "binitarian" theology, but it is not. A reader familiar with the teaching of the rest of the Gospel and the rest of the New Testament will be able to "see" that the Father draws people to Christ *through his Spirit* even though this is not stated in John 6. It is a Trinitarian blank that a reader can fill. Building up a familiarity with the Trinitarian geography of Scripture allows readers to fill in such blanks in a responsible way. Preachers can help congregations learn such skills by filling in such blanks.

Perhaps the most difficult area for Trinitarian Scripture reading is the Old Testament, because this literature only hinted at the Trinity and never made it explicit. There are some who would argue that, since the Old Testament writers did not have a belief in the Trinity, we should not read such a doctrine in their work. I disagree. While the God referred to in the Old Testament was not understood in his Trinitarian fullness, he was still the Trinity. That is to say that the God of Abraham, Isaac, and Jacob *is* the Trinity.[5] The God worshipped in ancient Israel and worshipped by Jews today *is* triune, even though most of them did/do not realize this. Once we recognize this truth, the legitimate question becomes how we might perceive the work of the Trinity in the Old Testament in light of the fuller revelation we have in the New Testament. This is a difficult area that requires a more careful and thorough treatment than I am yet able to give it. However, it is clear in the New Testament that the Father never works in creation except through his Word or Wisdom (the Son) and his Spirit. So the activity of Yhwh in the Old Testament must also be mediated via his Wisdom and his Spirit. Sometimes the Old Testament texts speaks as though the Father acts directly in Israel and in creation generally, but at other times we see that such activity is mediated by his Word/Wisdom and Spirit/Arm/Hand (even if they were not understood at the time as the divine persons that we now know them to be). In the light of the New Testament we can fill in the Trinitarian blanks and see the dim shadows of the pre-incarnate Son and the Spirit in the story of Israel.[6] Such a reading practice clearly sees more in the text than the original author and audience did, but that does not make the interpretations illegitimate. We have a fuller revelation of the God of Israel in Christ than Old Testament Israel had. Not to seek to see the shadow of the Trinity in the Old Testament is to abdicate our responsibility as Christian Bible readers. Bible teachers and preachers will play an important role in helping Christians see the Trinity in the Old Testament, because a considerable degree of biblical sensitivity and knowledge is required to do it well. Dogmatism will usually be out of place in such interpretations, especially when locating the presence of the pre-incarnate Christ, because often we cannot be certain. The New Testament interpretation of the Old Testament will play a crucial role in learning how to find the Spirit, and

5. See Marshall, "Israel: Do Christians Worship the God of Israel?"; Soulen, *The Divine Name(s) and the Holy Trinity*.

6. It is important to note that seeking to find the presence of the Son in the Old Testament is not the same as the practice of finding types of Christ in the Old Testament. For instance, Israel's High Priest functioned, in some senses, as a type prefiguring the work and ministry of Christ, but he was not the pre-incarnate Son at work in Israel's story—he was just a man.

especially the Messiah, in the Old Testament. My hope is that, by drawing attention to this issue, I can encourage others to take upon themselves the task of offering some fuller reflections.

PREACHING

While some Christians see the sermon as the centre of the act of worship, there are others who view it as obsolete in a postmodern, post-monologue, visual, and dialogical culture. I find myself reacting against both extremes. On the one hand, I think that preaching is only one of many ways in which education happens in the church and its importance needs to be relativized. We need to think about Christian education more broadly, not limiting it to sermons. On the other hand, I think that preaching and teaching are important sacramental ministries in the church and I have yet to meet a Christian to whom God has never spoken through a sermon. Listening to the message of Scripture proclaimed week after week is an important part of worship. In fact, in some parts of the church there is a need to recover the sense that the sermon is actually a part of our worship. There is a tendency in some quarters to see "the worship" as the part of the meeting that (usually) happens *before* the sermon. This way of speaking unhelpfully sets the preaching outside of "the worship," implying that listening to the proclamation of God's word is somehow not worship! I know of some worship leaders who now refer to the whole meeting as "the worship" and insist on calling the first part "the singing"—not in order to distinguish the music from worship but in order to identify it as only *part* of the worship.

So the question we need to ask is this, how can we make sermons more Trinitarian? The answer is, I think, simple. First, and most obviously, preachers can tackle the issue of the Trinity occasionally. The idea of a Trinity Sunday is not a bad idea, so long as it is not seen as an excuse for only "doing the Trinity" once a year. It is good to have a regular Trinitarian adrenalin rush in our churches. After all, preaching about the Trinity is simply saying to the Lord's people, "Behold your God!" and declaring the wonders of the Lord of creation and salvation. Should we expect anything less of our preachers? Of course, a Trinity Sunday is not the only way of doing this, but regular sermons on the Trinity are a good idea.

Secondly, and much more importantly, there is a need to train teachers and preachers to give talks and sermons with an overt Trinitarian syntax. We explored the idea of Trinitarian syntax in chapter 7 and outlined such a syntax in chapters 2 and 3, so I will not repeat myself. My point is simply that sermons and talks, whether on topics or specific biblical texts, need to seek to bring out the roles of the different persons of the Trinity. They need to make explicit the dynamic connections between the persons of the Trinity and move back and forth between the Three and the One. This can be done in an evangelistic sermon as well as in a talk on ecology, the cross, caring for our neighbor, walking worthy of the Lord, Christian hope, or whatever. My contention is that regular exposure to such an overt Trinitarian syntax will shape Christians who learn to think in a Trinitarian way, relate to God in a Trinitarian way, and read Scripture in a Trinitarian way. Trinitarian sermons working hand in hand with Trinitarian praying and singing will, over time, reinforce each other and shape Trinitarian Christians.

Exercising Spiritual Gifts

Not all Christians are charismatics, but for those churches that stand directly or indirectly in the spiritual stream that flows from the early Pentecostal movement (and there is no doubt that such churches are now a major force in global Christianity), the question of how we can realize the Trinitarian potential in the use of spiritual gifts is an important one.

The place to start is to appreciate the Trinitarian theology that undergirds the charismatic gifts. Clearly such gifts come from the Spirit, but they also serve as the medium through which Father and Son speak to the church and through which the church speaks to Father and Son. In prophecy, the Father or Christ speaks through Spirit-inspired words or visions in order to build up Christ's body. So it is that the words of a prophet can be both the words of *Christ* and what the *Spirit* says to the churches (Rev 2:18–29). Through the gifts of healing the Father and Son work through the Spirit to mend the brokenness in the church, and so on. Thus Paul, in 1 Corinthians 12:4–6, speaks of the gifts as coming from all three persons of the Trinity even though they are usually associated most directly with the Spirit. All of this is well understood by charismatics who attribute their words, pictures, and visions to the Spirit as well as to the Son or Father. They understand the words of a prophecy to be the words of Father or Son (and the content will often make clear which they are) given through the Spirit. They clearly understand their tongues as Spirit-inspired words directed to Father and/or

Son and/or the Godhead. In this way spiritual gifts almost inevitably bring about some subtle Trinitarian awareness.

Many charismatic churches have "ministry times," when people can be prayed for and ministered to "in the Spirit." There is a natural fluidity in such contexts in which the pray-er alternates between Father, Son, and Spirit. "Father, pour your Spirit upon your child here" flows into "Jesus, send your power and healing" flows into "Come Holy Spirit, rain down on this precious child of God." The natural flow in prayer from Father to Son to Spirit in an almost unthinking way emerges from the deeply Trinitarian nature of the gifts and the spirituality they generate. The Pentecostal and charismatic movements have great potential for being deeply Trinitarian, and it is something of a sadness that they have not seen this potential fully realized. Pentecostal-charismatic experience is essentially Trinitarian and often wears its triune heart upon its sleeve.

The Arts

Human beings are multidimensional creatures who respond to the world and to God in all sorts of ways. It seems to me that there is a very positive place for the arts in worship, as the history of Christianity testifies and many Christians today experience. What follows are some examples of the different arts and how I have seen them used (or how they could be used) to sharpen an awareness of the triune God.

Dance

One of the metaphors for the Trinity that has gained some prominence in recent years is that of the Godhead as three dancers. This metaphor offers potential for the use of dance to celebrate God through "theology in motion." Clearly this needs to be done with pastoral sensitivity, since there may be some people present who feel that using humans to represent the persons of the Trinity may be close to idolatry. It may need to be stated loud and clear that the dance only gestures in the direction of the Trinity and does not seek to show exactly what the Trinity is like, that the dancers are not exactly like God and the congregation is not worshipping the dancers. Having to say such things may seem like stating the obvious, but some Christians will understandably feel very sensitive about this and it may even be that for some people such a dance is positively unhelpful. The theological justification for a Trinitarian dance is that God has shaped human beings in his own image and thus, while we would never collapse the distance between God and humanity, it does seem appropriate that humans can serve as a picture of Yhwh.

For some people, "dance is doxology, embodied prayer, a beautiful blend of body, spirit, community and gift."[7] I must confess to being the kind of person who thinks that the use of "performance" dance in worship is great in theory, but in practice I don't tend to find it helpful—some people love it, but it is just not my cup of tea. However, I did observe one dance that swept me up in worship of God in a way that no other dance has ever done before. This was an interpretation of "the dance of the Trinity" in which the three main dancers worked together as one in a graceful movement of synchronized difference, and everyone present was absolutely "blown away" by it. Ruth Norris was one of the creative minds behind this dance:

> We decided to create a "Dance of the Trinity" as part of our worship to express the picture of God as three persons intertwining with each other and flowing with each other as though in a dance: distinct yet in perfect harmony.
>
> We began with the reading of some prose[8] before three dancers began circling, then interweaving, against the background of three melodic instruments that mirrored their movement. Using an arrangement of the tune "Lord of the Dance" as our basis, the music and dance varied from gentle and lyrical to fast and exciting. At times the dancers moved in unison; at times one took the lead and the others followed; sometimes one was lifted up, or one was out in front with the others lining up behind. Whichever dancer you were more aware of at any one time you never lost sight of that dancer's relationship to the other two as their movements flowed from one to the other.
>
> And we were invited to join this dance of God. So the congregation, having been primed beforehand, joined the dancers in a rhythmic clap as three children began jumping and interweaving with the "Trinity," then were encircled by them before joining the circle themselves and being lifted off the ground by the "Trinity" as the circling continued. Finally the congregation stood and joined the dancers in a simple movement, linking arms and

7. Thomas, *Paper Boys*, 36.

8. The prose is quoted in full in the creative writing section at the end of this chapter.

stepping from side to side, continuing this as the "Trinity" broke out into more dance, ending close together, their arms reaching out on three different levels in a gesture of invitation.

A mother told me later how her fifteen-year-old daughter had asked her, and then her grandfather, to explain the Trinity. After seeing this dance she phoned her mum saying: "Mum, I've just seen a dance on the Trinity and NOW I understand."[9]

The Visual Arts

Celebrating the Trinity through the visual arts is well established in Christian history, although the presence of these arts varies greatly from one tradition to another. Amongst the vast amount of visual representation of the Christian God, one thinks of some of the many abstract symbols of the Trinity, of the icons, and of the classical paintings. From altar cloths to stained glass windows, from banners to architecture, from statues to priestly clothing, the Three-in-One has been represented in many different ways. Artists have worked with paint, glass, metal, wood, clay, stone, plastic, and fabrics in their creative explorations of Trinity. Following are a few of the various ways in which such arts can play a role today in worship.

Decoration

First, and most obviously, one could decorate the building used by a church with Trinitarian art. The aim is simply to immerse people in an environment that makes the Trinity prominent. Such an environment contributes towards the experience of worship. Perhaps the architecture itself or the stained glass windows already reflect the Trinity, but if this is not so then there is probably not much that can be done on that front without major expense. The use of colorful banners and pictures is a less expensive way to saturate the environment with Trinitarian art. Another advantage to this option is that it can be changed every once in a while so that the stimulating effect is refreshed.

---

9. Personal correspondence (15 April 2004).

Meditation on Art in Worship

Secondly, a guided meditation on some Trinitarian artwork can, for many people, be a helpful entry into God's presence. Again some pastoral sensitivity is needed here—there is a concern among quite a few Christians that such reflection is tantamount to idolatry. (I refer to some Protestants here. Catholics and the Orthodox have long been at home with images.) It looks on the surface like the worshippers are worshipping an image of God instead of the real God, and this brings to many minds all sorts of biblical texts about the sin of idolatry. Anyone who leads such a meditation needs to do it in such a way that people are clearly aware that the image is not seen as being God and is not being worshipped. Instead the image is providing a focus for reflection on God in a way not dissimilar to a verbal image such as "the Lord is my shepherd." Of course, the Lord is not literally identified with a shepherd, nor are we literally identified with sheep (baa)! The words are being used metaphorically to point beyond themselves to the Lord who refuses to be bound by any image, whether verbal or visual. So the group of worshippers needs to be clear that the image is not God but functions as a window through which our reflections on God may pass.[10] The worshippers must be guided to treat every image, whether verbal or visual, with care, because every image will reveal but will also conceal. People also need the freedom not to find particular images helpful. For instance, I find some of the classical images of the Father with a long white beard and what seems to be a scowl to be positively unhelpful.[11] It is also important, if such

10. Which is how the Orthodox understand icons to function. Indeed, representing Christ in icons was seen as *theologically critical* because it affirmed that the invisible God had chosen to become visible in the flesh of Jesus. To refuse to have icons of Christ was seen by the Orthodox as tantamount to denying the incarnation.

11. There is an issue of theological import here—namely, whether one should represent the Father visually at all in painting and sculpture. Here one sees the difference between Catholic art, in which one often sees the bearded Father, and Orthodox icons, in which the Son but never the Father (except, on some interpretations of the icon, as a hand coming down from the sky) is portrayed. In the icon it is thought to be appropriate to represent the incarnate body of the Christ, but to represent the Father in this way would be to violate the biblical command to make no images of God. Protestants typically share the Orthodox instinct here and shy away from Father-art. Personally, I *do* have theological reservations with representing the *Father* in images. Images of Christ are fine—the Word *became flesh* and can be represented in this way—but the Father remains "in light inaccessible hid from our eyes." This should give us pause for thought before representing the Father in an image and such images should, at very least, be handled with caution.

guided meditation is used, that it not be imposed on people in such a way that those who object cannot opt out. Forcing people to act against their conscience is not Christian behavior.

One kind of guided meditation involves providing everyone with the same piece of artwork (either projected on a large screen or handed out on individual copies such as postcards) and then slowly walking them through a reflection on it. Pictures for meditation need not be overtly Trinitarian. Overtly Trinitarian art is the obvious place to start. For instance, a popular candidate is Rublev's famous icon of the Trinity (c.1410) or a modern re-working of it.

Here is an image that has inspired many Christians and has proved its value over hundreds of years. The picture shows the three angels that visited Abraham and Sarah sitting down together for a meal. The Eastern Orthodox do not allow pictures of the Father, but Rublev cleverly gets around this by having angels indirectly represent the persons of the divine Trinity. In a meditation on this piece, for instance, the image would be set before the people and the "guide" would slowly draw their attention to different features so that people could have the space to respond to the art in their own ways. Look at the expressions on the angels' faces. Consider their body language. How do they relate to one another? In what way are they like each other? How do they differ? What do the colors of their garments suggest to you? Do you find the background images suggestive? Such questions are open and do not close down interpretation by giving "the right meaning." Worshippers are invited to actively engage with the artwork, both interrogating it and being interrogated by it. For those who want some slightly more directed guidance there is a helpful interactive, guided meditation on the icon at the Wellspring website.[12]

Another kind of meditation is less guided and more open-ended. The worshippers could be provided with an image (or images) and simply invited to look at it carefully and respond to it.

Let me tell you about three artistic Trinitarian meditations in worship in which I have taken part. In the first, a separate room from the one in which most of the worship occurred was set out and the congregation left in groups at different times to spend twenty to thirty minutes in this room. The room was darkened, and around it were placed many diverse images of the Father, of the Son, and of the Spirit from the history of Christian art across different cultures. Each image was illuminated by a small, scented candle placed in front of it. Most of the images were picture postcards, but there were also some statues and some of the images were copied onto transparent material and illuminated from behind by candles. Quiet Gregorian chants played in the background, creating a mystical atmosphere. People were encouraged not to speak but to find one or two images to carefully reflect on. General guidance on such reflection was provided in advance, but those who found themselves at a loss could use cards placed facedown in front of each image as prompts. The cards provided some basic information about the image and gave some questions to guide reflection.

12. Online: http://www.wellsprings.org.uk/rublevs_icon/rublev.htm.

In the second meditation, there were three rooms set up—one for each person of the Trinity. People were encouraged to spend their time in the room corresponding to the person of the Trinity they tended to most neglect in their prayer and worship.[13] The Son room was very visual. At its centre was a large table dominated by bread and wine. Around the table were lots of fruit and chocolate to take and eat. The walls were covered in images of the Son that related to the "I am" sayings in John's Gospel alongside biblical texts and poetry. There was a wooden cross set against red and purple fabrics and quiet music playing in the background. The responses of those who took part in these activities were very positive.

A third example of the use of creative arts would not easily work in a large gathering but is an example of something that individuals could benefit from if such an artwork was installed in a church building permanently or semi-permanently. Christian artist Susan Hicks produced a powerful triptych composed of three large panels placed at ninety degrees to each other, creating a semi-enclosed space into which the viewer would enter. The installation was placed in a room of its own that had been darkened and was lit only by a dim uplighter in the far corner. Each of the three panels was a painting of one of the persons of the Trinity. Approaching the triptych, one was immediately confronted by the middle panel of Christ on the cross. Christ was painted upon a semitransparent material behind which was a wooden cross, and real nails were driven through the hands and feet into the wood. Behind the cross was some red backlighting. In Christ's chest was a large wound in which was placed a mirror so the viewer could see his or her own reflection. This spoke to me of my identifying with Christ in his death—of dying with Christ and being placed in Christ. The panel on the right was a large backlit sheet of glass (partially mirrored) upon which were painted large flames and a black background. When you looked into the flames you saw your reflection surrounded by the fire of the Spirit. This produced a different effect on me than the Christ-mirror had. Instead of the identification that the Christ-mirror inspired, this Spirit-mirror made me feel like I was empowered by the Holy Flame and surrounded by

---

13. The Spirit room (it was actually a corridor) and the Father room (which I did not visit) were actually imageless. After the model of the Stations of the Cross, there were twelve "Stations of the Holy Spirit" set out, tracing the Spirit's involvement in creation from Genesis 1 to Revelation 22 through Scripture texts. People were encouraged to walk and pray through the stations of the Spirit. Now I have read all these texts many times before, but seeing them all set out around the room and reading them together gave me a profound sense of the deep interconnections between the Spirit and the Father and Son.

its presence. To the left of the Christ-panel was the Father panel. Here, in pale tones, was painted a beautiful, backlit image of the Father, eyes closed, with a smile on his face of pure joy and contentment. He was seated with his hand cupped on his knee, holding a mirror in which I could see myself reflected. This time the mirror had a different impact again. Instead of the "identification" of the Christ-mirror and the "surrounding presence" of the Spirit-mirror, the Father-mirror made me feel that I was gently held in the hands of the Father and that he derived deep and peaceful bliss from this. But it was not simply the impact of the panels considered individually but also the way that they interrelated that made the triptych so powerful. One could not view it from the outside but had to step right into the midst of it to view it. Once in a position to view the installation, the observer was surrounded by Father, Son, and Spirit and felt the invitation to participate in the inner triune life. The Father and Jesus both have their heads slightly angled towards each other, eyes closed, in a subtle acknowledgement of the other. Jesus' hands on the cross reach out not only to invite the viewer in but also stretch out towards the Spirit and the Father perichoretically. The feel of *perichorēsis* was accentuated if one stepped back slightly to see the Spirit panel reflected in the Father's mirror and the Father in the Spirit's. Moving from left to right, one felt the movement in salvation and worship from the Spirit drawing us through Christ's cross towards home with the Father. All of these reflections were evoked in me by a wordless piece of art.

Artistic Worship

In addition to decoration and meditation, the whole act of worship can be integrated with the visual arts. Let me tell you about an experiment I took part in called "Journey with the Trinity." The aim of the "journey" was to generate a sense of coming to the Father, through the Son and in the Spirit. Worshippers had to follow a trail marked out that ran through several rooms and corridors. Room 1 contained a red box. We were invited to write down any ways that we felt our earthly father was not like God. We then posted these in the box, which was later burned, unopened. We also wrote down any ways in which our human father was like God and kept these pieces of paper with us as we moved on. Next we were invited to take a piece of white cloth representing the righteousness of Christ and wear it as a garment of some sort before moving through a torn curtain onto which was projected a large red cross. This led us into room 2—the Spirit room. Here was a fountain. We were invited to listen to the sound of the waters and commit our tiredness and strain to God. We then drank from the fountain and moved to a box from which a large flame issued. We took a candle and lit it from the flame receiving, in faith, the power of God for the ministry he has called us to. Finally we took our candles in to a hall. It was completely blacked out, and at the centre was a large wooden, gold-painted model of the Ark of the Covenant. We placed our candles at the feet of the cherubim whose wings were made of gold netting. We were invited to pin our positive thoughts about our earthly father onto the wings and then join in worship of the Trinity. The room was dark except for the candle lighting and some ultraviolet lighting that made all the white garments stand out dramatically. The worship was profoundly moving and deeply Trinitarian. The sense of standing in God's grace was intense and the prayer, prophesy, testimony, and song was awesome.[14]

Doing Art as Worship

We've considered just a few of the ways in which art can be used in worship. All of them, however, involve worshippers participating in the art that others have created. Another possibility for using the arts in Trinitarian worship is to invite the worshippers to create art for themselves in worship. I have been part of worship workshops in which people have tried to represent something of the Trinity and express something of their response to the Trinity through clay, through paint, through fabrics, and through printing. The results were, for the most part, really impressive. I was quite taken aback by the theology that was realized through the materials and the skill with which the work was undertaken. For example, one woman had painted a large piece of paper with twisting and flowing ink colors and the words of the Athanasian Creed swirling around. She had cut out three dancers in motion from tracing paper and placed them, one on top of the other, against the swirling background. The dancers were clearly distinct and yet overlapped and interpenetrated each other, evoking the idea of *perichorēsis* in the graceful "dance of the Trinity." There were many other examples that I could mention, and those whose work was not technically brilliant still greatly benefited from the activity.

14. The only thing about the whole experiment that didn't quite work was the order of the rooms. It would have worked better to have the Spirit room first, then the Son, then the Father.

Music

Apart from congregational hymn and chorus singing, music can be used in other ways to draw people into the Trinity in worship. Most obviously, a congregation could listen to a piece of music that somehow, verbally or non-verbally, communicated something of the tri-unity of God. Alternatively worshippers could be involved in the very creation of such music. In one Trinitarian music workshop I saw in action once, a small group of people with varied musical abilities were brought together to explore ways of expressing the Trinity musically. One group of three musicians who were able to play instruments worked as a team, and each person took on the role of a person of the Trinity. Each one then had to reflect on the person they were representing and the relation of that person to the other two. Each would ask, "How can I communicate something of the Father (or whichever person) through my instrument? How can I bring out some of the interactions within the Trinity by the interactions with the other instruments?" How, in other words, could they image the Godhead in a small way through their music? I never actually heard the finished result, but it is clear that there are an infinite number of paths on which their creativity could have taken them here and one could easily imagine any number of powerful musical results that express something of the truth of the Trinity. The musical styles could be anything from classical to improvised jazz; from hip hop to a cappella, from Gregorian chants to folk music. Another group explored the Trinity through (wordless) vocals and percussion. They too sought to bring out some of the interrelatedness and joy of the Trinity. Not everyone will find such music-making helpful, but many will—and not only those who think of themselves as musical. Even those who can't sing and have no skill on any instrument can find a sense of exhilaration and release when taking part in such activities.

Clearly creating such music can be, for certain kinds of people at least, an act of worship and exploration of the Trinity. But even those who cannot easily worship through creating such music may find that listening to it stirs praise for the Trinity within their hearts. Although musical tastes vary widely, there are few people who will find that music does not deeply touch and shape their spiritual lives in some way. This is clear enough from the role that singing has played in Christian history. We all know what difference a tune we like can make to the impact a song has on us. A congregation can be invited to contemplate a piece of music that reflects the Trinity either in its words or in the wordless ways I mentioned above. When using wordless music it may be helpful for someone to guide the congregation in making sense of it, since not everyone finds interpreting music easy. The art of quietly reflecting on music in worship is a learned skill, but one that is worth fostering. It is also worth considering the use of music to accompany dance and the visual arts in worship.

POETRY AND CREATIVE WRITING

Poetry is a powerful medium for celebrating the Trinity, because in poetry words can open up stunning new ways of seeing reality. I often feel awed by how a good poet or song lyricist can deploy words in such economical yet evocative ways. There are many people in churches who have more poetic talents than we (or even they themselves) realize, and churches should do more to encourage people to do some creative writing and to try writing poetry. Many Christians (myself included) can testify to how much fun and how releasing poetry writing can be. Now it has to be said that much that is called poetry, both inside and outside the church, is pretty poor quality (and I include my own "poetry" here). Although such poetry is great for those who write it and ought to be encouraged in private devotion, it is usually not best used in public worship. But there are some poets among us who are exceptionally gifted by God, and such people would be able to write some stunning Trinitarian poetry that could be used in worship. Non-poetic creative writing is also an avenue worth exploring. Here is an example of some creative writing by a pastor from Basingstoke called Phil Norris. This is the prose that was used to open the "dance of the Trinity" discussed earlier:

> Father, Son, and Spirit existing in perfect love and harmony. Enjoying one-another. Honoring one-another. Loving one another. Perfect peace. Perfect happiness. Perfect contentment. One God, yet three persons. Three persons, yet one God. Barely distinguishable as they move, perfectly united, perfectly harmonious, perfectly loving. Moving and dancing together. None out of step. None doing their own thing. All united. The dance of the Trinity. The dance of God.
>
> From this dance the Father speaks. "Let's create." And from the Father's idea, the Word of the Son and the brooding of the Spirit, this wonderful world and its creatures come forth. Culminating in

men and women, formed from the earth, yet made to reflect this harmonious image of the Trinity. Created from the dance.

Yet what was intended for perfection falls into imperfection. What was made for glory turns to sin. But the dance continues. Father sends the Son to his creation. The Son glorifies the Father. The Spirit fills the Son. Perfect co-operation, harmony, and love continue.

And from this dance, the circle of the Trinity expands, to invite those created in his image into the circle. This is not a dance only for the Godhead. This is a dance for all. Invited by the Spirit and through the Son to the Father. To reject one is to reject all three. To receive one is to receive all three. To enter the dance. The enjoyment, love, and harmony of the Godhead are shared. Participation in the dance of the Trinity is enjoyed. The life of God becoming our life, as we dance and move with him.

WORSHIP OUTSIDE THE BOX

I hope that this chapter has opened up some new possibilities for engaging with the Trinity in worship. We aptly respond to, and reflect, the dynamic, creative dance of the Trinity in our dynamic, creative worship. Most of us so easily find ourselves stuck in a rut, and we need the Spirit-inspired creative energies of the artists to bring new life and color to worship. We also need to realize the Trinitarian potential of those more "normal" aspects of our weekly public worship. Creative Trinitarian worship can take any number of forms, and the ideas in this chapter are intended as no more than sparks to light new ideas in your own minds. Whatever your context, I would encourage you to think carefully and creatively about your public worship. How can you celebrate the Trinity where you are and with the resources you have in your church? How can the people God has put you with be released to use their gifts to God's glory in public worship? The challenge is simply this: dare to worship the Trinity outside the box.

Epilogue

Avoiding a Trinitarian Fad

How CAN I SUM up this book in a single paragraph? How about this: Christian worship should seek to bring God's church into a dynamic encounter with the Christian God—the Holy Trinity. Such worship will ceaselessly and effortlessly move back and forth between the threeness of God and the unity of God. It will shift focus from Father to Son to Spirit and back again in a restless celebration of divine love and mystery. It will also highlight the perichoretic relations within the Godhead by not allowing the worshippers to lose sight of any of the persons. At times the worship will draw the Father into focus, however the Son and Spirit will still be there—out of focus but within our field of awareness. At other times the Son will attract our attention, but not in such a way that we do not see the Father and the Spirit as well. When the Spirit attracts our worshipping attention it will always be as the Spirit of the Father and the Spirit of the Son. Worship that makes us aware of the interrelationships within God is fully Trinitarian worship. Trinitarian worship is always "through the Son" and "in the Spirit," but it is woven from an ever-changing mosaic of songs, prayers, Bible readings, testimonies, Spirit-gifts, sermons, Holy Communion, drama, dance, art, and more besides. The variety is endless and the possibilities infinite, but at the heart of it all stands the mystery of the Holy Trinity. That is what Christian worship *is*.

Many church leaders and worship leaders are very keen to shape their communal and individual worship in Trinitarian ways. I think that the vision behind this book will resonate with many people because I am not saying anything new but simply calling Christians to remember something that they have always known anyway. However, I am worried about the long-term sustainability of the vision. Anyone familiar with the contemporary worship scene in the modern Protestant West will know just how fast-changing it is. Yesterday's must-use song is today's must-not-use song. Few songs have a shelf life beyond five years. Indeed, most never last longer than a year. One sees fashions and fads in Christian worship music just as in secular popular music. You may recall the glut of songs about rivers that coincided with the Toronto Blessing in the mid-1990s. They're now water under the bridge, if you'll excuse the pun. I can imagine something similar with Trinitarian worship. I can see it becoming all the rage and then, after a year or so, being replaced by the newer, sexier thing. Such a danger needs to be anticipated and steps need to be taken to ensure that Trinitarian worship does not fall victim to fashion.

The journey beyond the fad begins with our discussion of the Trinitarian syntax of Christian faith in chapter 7. I have argued throughout this book that the Trinity is so deeply embedded within Christian thought and living that no authentic Christian utterance about God can violate this syntax. I have also argued that we need to bring the Trinitarian structure of our beliefs and experience into full view when we speak of, and to, God. It is grasping the very foundational level of this syntax of the Trinity that offers the first step towards hope for the long-term sustainability of overt Trinitarian worship. You see, I actually have little problem with the fast-changing nature of contemporary worship songs because there is nothing sacrosanct about singing the same songs forever and ever. To be honest, I find a fair few hymns to be both lyrically impenetrable and musically murderous! Old is not necessarily better. And when it comes to musical style, few things turn me off more than a church organ (apologies to fans of the organ—it's just a personal thing). I have no problem with changing theological emphases in songs either. Indeed, it will be important to adjust the emphases of our songs if our worship is to connect with what God is doing and if it is to be culturally relevant. However, the Trinity does not float on the surface of Christianity like oil on water. The Trinity is more akin to the hydrogen in the water—it is a constituent part such that, were it removed, the water would cease to be water. It is precisely because the Trinity runs deep down to the very roots of our faith that it can sustain itself by being of universal relevance. Whatever time period the church lives in, whatever culture it contextualizes itself in, whatever new moves of God there may be influencing our songs, the Trinity will *always* and *everywhere* be at the centre of our worship. Once this vision is grasped and understood, then imagining the Trinity falling out of focus is equivalent to imagining a de-generation of Christian worship—and nobody wants that. In this epilogue I simply wish to make some initial suggestions for avoiding the danger of a Trinitarian fad.

Train worship leaders and songwriters in Trinitarian theology. We charis-matics train our worship leaders in being Spirit-sensitive, in the art of the sound system, in how to link songs well, in the use of PowerPoint, and in personal intimacy with God. Why don't we also teach a robust Trinitarian theology as well as a theology of worship as an essential component of their craft? Basic Christian theology is the stuff of songs and prayers so it should be obvious that some training is required here. I am not saying that we need to train them to be *academic* theologians, but merely that theology should be a regular component of training. The kinds of ideas contained in this book need to be taught regularly as an essential part of leading wor-ship if the Trinitarian vision is to work its way like leaven into the heart of our worship. How to shape a worship meeting so that the congregation becomes aware of meeting with the Father through the Son in the Spirit is an essential practical skill, and yet I have never seen it taught. Writing songs with overt Trinitarian syntax is a great need in our day, but how is one to do it? Songwriters need practical help here. If we wish to see change, then we need to offer training.

(a) Organizations that put on training days for worship leaders and songwriters need to have theological training as an essential compo-nent in any program.

(b) Churches may wish to provide in-house training for their worship leaders and songwriters if they feel that they can do it adequately.

(c) Educational institutions, particularly Christian colleges and uni-versities, need to put together accredited courses in worship lead-ing and song writing, and churches need to encourage those with a worship ministry to go on such courses. While there are some very good courses in this area, there is definitely a need for more. In these contexts, the centrality of the Trinity should be taught.

(d) Web-based courses provide great opportunities for training those worship leaders whose lives require the flexibility such courses offer.

Team up songwriters and theologians. Few people combine the gifts of songwriter and theologian in the way of a Charles Wesley or a Graham Kendrick and so Christian songwriters should, as a matter of course, ask for advice on their lyrics from those with more theological understanding. This is simply recognizing the fact that God has shaped his *ekklēsia* so that we all have different strengths and weaknesses. Not everyone is called to be a theologian, but those who are gifted in this way are given for the edification of the whole community—including the songwriters. Songwriters need theologians to offer inspiration and guidance in their work as lyricists. Making use of capable Christian poets would also help lift our lyrics above the mundane. In the same way theologians, along with all Christians, need songwriters to weave the words and notes of praise into a tapestry of song that they can take upon their own lips.

Trinitarian teaching.

Education within churches—from the Sunday school to the sermon to the discussion group or the Bible study—needs to recover overt Trinitarian syntax. Changes in worship practice need to be reinforced by changes in educational practice. This means that our Bible teachers and those who produce the material we use need to think in a more Trinitarian way. They also may well need some retraining. To that end, there is a good case to be made for some formal teaching on the Trinity of the kind found in chapter 4 of this book. I do not believe that such teaching is of much use if the rest of our teaching and worship lacks overt Trinitarian syntax, but if we can recover the Trinity in *all* we do then some formal teaching occasionally would be helpful. There is much to be said, for example, for including the Trinity in beginners' courses for new Christians. However, I remain convinced that the far more urgent task is to make the overt Trinitarian syntax omnipresent. It is also important that we think through introductions to the Christian faith such as the Alpha and Christianity Explored courses, and particularly courses for new Christians, so as to bring out this syntax. For instance, when we speak of the cross we should not simply speak of Jesus, nor even of Jesus and the Father who sent him. One is not enough, and two won't get the job done. We should speak of the "blood of Christ, who through the eternal Spirit offered himself without blemish to God" (Heb 9:14). Every phase of the biblical metanarrative and every area of Christian dogmatics will need to have its Trinitarian skeletal structure recovered.

RESOURCES

There is an urgent need for the dissemination of resources for those who wish to explore the Trinitarian dimensions of worship. Books of resources would be helpful, but perhaps websites dedicated to the "re-Trinitarianiz-ing" of worship would be better still because they are: (a) free; (b) instantly accessible all over the world; and (c) flexible enough to keep up to date with the fast-changing worship scene.[1] They could alert us to good songs, good prayers, good poems, good meditations, good resources to use with kids, good books, good sermons, and good imaginative ideas for highlighting the Trinity in communal worship. A discussion board on relevant issues would also be very helpful. It would also be good if existing worship web-sites took the issue seriously and took steps to include it as a major issue. I recently visited a very large and excellent website for worship leaders and songwriters called hairyworship.com (name changed to protect the site's identity). I did a search on the word "Trinity" and found that out of the vast mass of articles and products available on the site only two items were flagged up—neither of which had anything other than a passing reference to the Trinity. Suitably modified, excellent websites such as hairyworship .com could become tools for a Trinitarian renewal of worship.

PERSONAL SPIRITUALITY

We need to encourage and resource people in our congregations to develop their own spiritual lives in Trinitarian ways. Helping people to pray and read Scripture so that they see the Trinity is important. Here set prayers can be very helpful—even for those who prefer spontaneous extempore prayers. Set prayers can teach patterns of prayer that can form habits that shape a more Trinitarian spontaneity. Church leaders need to think about how to assist the Trinitarian spiritual formation of those in their care. Those who produce Bible reading notes and other resources for personal devotions also need to give the issue careful thought.

---

1. In fact, it is the evangelical, Pentecostal, and charismatic worship scenes that are the fastest changing. More liturgical traditions are much more stable.

FRESH THOUGHT AND LOCAL THOUGHT

All Christian theology is influenced by our culture and context, and that is as it should be. The presentation in this book is not intended as the *final* word on Trinitarian worship or as the *universal* manual for such worship in all cultures. Even for my own context it is hardly anything more than a first step. It is intended as a kick-start for others to reflect on the issue in their own contexts. Christians will need to keep on reshaping and refreshing their theology and worship, and this book is no more than one contribution to that ongoing process. Worship and the way Trinitarian worship looks may differ from one generation to the next or from one culture to another, but however it looks it will still be recognizably Trinitarian and have the same basic shape found in this book. My hope is that *Worshipping Trinity* at least provides resources for some people to pick up where my reflections leave off and to follow the Spirit's lead in their own communal and individual dances with the Trinity. As with any dance, things just won't stand still.

Appendix 1

Family Prayers

I WROTE THE FOLLOWING daily prayers (one for each day of the week) for my family to use after meal times (which is why it is set out for four people, A to D). The basic idea was to pray our way, week by week, through the whole biblical story in a Trinitarian way. Such prayer can play a role in helping us to indwell that story—to live out of it. I also wanted to make historic orthodoxy, as embodied by the Nicene Creed, central to our spirituality. Thus six of the days make explicit use of extracts from that creed.

I did not write these prayers for public use and I do not offer them as *the* way to do Trinitarian prayer. They are simply offered as *one* way that our family has tried to do it. (And, I should add that our use of them has been "on and off" over the years.) If you find them helpful then that's great. If you don't then that's fine. You are welcome to use them, to change them, or to ignore them as you see fit. My hope is that they will at least inspire the prayerful imaginations of some readers as they seek to know God for themselves in prayer.

◈ Day 1: Creation

A: We come to you Father, along the path opened up by Jesus and with the guiding help of the Spirit.

All: Forgive us our sins as we forgive those who sin against us. Lord have mercy.

All: *"We believe in one God, the Father, the Almighty, maker of heaven and earth, of all that is, seen and unseen."* (Nicene Creed)

B: Father, creator God, thank you for the beautiful world you have created. All things that exist come from you.

C: Jesus, creator God, the Father created all things that exist *through* you and *for* you. You hold the universe in existence from moment to moment.

D: Holy Spirit, life-giver, you bring life to God's creation. You are the presence of God in the world. Everywhere we could go, you are there.

All: Lord God, the Three-in-One, we thank you for all the many environments you have created:

A: For mountains, for fields, for deserts, for ice caps, for forests, and for cities;

B: For rivers, for lakes, for seas, and for oceans;

C: For the sky full of light and clouds and stars.

All: Lord God, the Three-in-One, we thank you for all the vastness and all the detail of the world:

D: For the unthinkably huge number of planets, stars, and galaxies in this vast and awesome universe;

A: For the amazing detail of the tiny creatures, of the living cell, of DNA, of molecules, atoms, and particles smaller still.

All: Lord God, the Three-in-One, we thank you for the wonder and the beauty of the life you have created:

B: Thank you for the creatures of the air, from the insect to the bird;

C: Thank you for the creatures of the earth, from the reptile to the mammal;

D: Thank you for the creatures of the sea, from the crustacean to the fish;

A: Thank you for the creatures in the heavens: cherubim and seraphim and all the armies of angels.

All: Lord God, the Three-in-One, we thank you for the wonder and the beauty of humanity:

B: We are made of the dust yet we are made in your image;

C: We are insignificant and yet objects of your tender care;

D: We are a part of the world and yet clothed with your glory.

All: Lord God, the Three-in-One, we thank you for the wonder and the beauty of human life:

A: Thank you for family, for school, for work, and for leisure;

B: Thank you for religion, for politics, for business, and for science.

C: Thank you for emotions, for thought, for spirit, and for our bodies;

D: Thank you for music, for books, for dance, for craft, and for art.

A: Creator God, we pray your blessing on [insert your own intercessions here . . .]

All: In the name of the Father and of the Son and of the Holy Spirit. Amen.

▧ Day 2: God's Way with Israel

All: We come to you Father, along the path opened up by Jesus and with the guiding help of the Spirit.

All: Forgive us our sins as we forgive those who sin against us. Lord have mercy.

A: Adonai, God of Israel, you are *our* God and we love you.

B: We thank you Adonai for your covenant relationship with our father Abraham.

C: We thank you Adonai for hearing the cries of Israel when they were suffering as slaves in Egypt.

D: We thank you Adonai for guiding your people Israel by your wise words and your Holy Spirit.

A: We thank you Adonai for providing food and water for Israel when they wandered in the desert after leaving Egypt.

B: We thank you Adonai for giving your good and holy law to Moses.

C: We thank you Adonai for being present with your people in the pillar of cloud and of fire.

D: We thank you Adonai that your holy, awesome presence was in the midst of Israel in the Jerusalem temple.

A: We thank you Adonai that you provided a system of sacrifices so that your people could have their sins removed.

B: We thank you Adonai for your patience with Israel when they sinned and for your corrective punishments.

C: We thank you Adonai for appointing priests and for sending prophets to guide your people and to keep them on the right path.

D: We thank you Adonai for the exile and restoration of Israel.

A: We thank you Adonai for sending Israel's Messiah, Jesus, to deliver them from sin and to lead them into a renewed covenant relationship with you.

B: We thank you Adonai for uniting us Gentiles with your people Israel through Jesus, the Messiah.

C: We thank you Adonai for preserving the Jewish people through centuries of persecution. Forgive us for the role that Christians have played in afflicting them. Have mercy on us Lord.

D: We thank you Adonai that you still love the many Jews who have not yet recognized Jesus as their Messiah. Help us to love and honor them too.

All: We thank you Adonai that one day all Israel will embrace the Messiah and will be saved.

All: God of Abraham, Isaac, and Jacob;
God of Moses, of David, and of the prophets;
God of Jesus, the Messiah;
You are *our* God.
We worship you.

All: We pray for peace in the Middle East;

We pray for peace and security for Israel and justice
for the suffering Palestinians.

We pray that Messianic Jews and Christian Palestinians
would love each other as brothers and sisters.

All: In the name of the Father and of the Son and of the Holy Spirit.
Amen.

◈ DAY 3: THE LIFE OF JESUS

A: We come to you Father, along the path opened up by Jesus, and with the guiding help of the Spirit.

All: Forgive us our sins as we forgive those who sin against us. Lord have mercy.

All: *"We believe in one Lord, Jesus Christ, the only Son of God,*
Eternally begotten of the Father,
God from God
Light from Light,
true God from true God,
begotten, not made,
of one being with the Father.
Through him all things were made.
For us humans and for our salvation he came down from heaven;
By the power of the Holy Spirit he became incarnate of the virgin
Mary, and was made man." (Nicene Creed)

B: Father, we praise you that you loved the world so much that you sent your one and only Son to come among us as a human being.

C: Father, we thank you that Jesus spoke your wise words and did your powerful deeds—when we see his heart revealed we can see your heart revealed.

D: Father, we praise you for your deep, eternal love for Jesus.

A: Holy Spirit, we thank you for miraculously enabling Mary to conceive and give birth to Jesus.

B: Holy Spirit, praise you for working through Jesus as he walked among us—revealing the Father to him, empowering him to speak the Father's words and to do the Father's deeds.

C: Holy Spirit, we honor you for your deep, eternal love for Jesus.

D: Jesus, we praise you that although you shared divine glory in heaven with the Father from all eternity, you laid it aside and entered our world as a human being.

A: Jesus, we thank you that although in heaven you were rich, for our sakes you became poor so that through your poverty we might become "rich."

B: Thank you Jesus that you were not ashamed to take on our humanity and to know us as your brothers and sisters. You are forever our brother.

C: Jesus, we worship you for your merciful acts of kindness: signs of the coming kingdom of God; pictures of the age to come.

D: Jesus, thank you that you welcomed the outcasts, the rejected, the unlovely, the damaged, the sinners. Help us to be like you.

A: Jesus, help us to listen carefully to your challenging and radical words of wisdom.

B: Jesus, please help us, by your Spirit, to follow you as disciples all the days of our lives.

C: Jesus, our Messiah, our King, our Lord, and our God—we worship you.

D: Jesus, gentle Master, friend of sinners, Good Shepherd—we love you.

A: Jesus, healer of wounds, bringer of hope, Lord of creation—we trust in you.

All: We pray for [. . .]

All: In the name of the Father and of the Son and of the Holy Spirit. Amen.

◈ Day 4: The Death and Burial of Jesus

A: We come to you Father, along the path opened up by Jesus, and with the guiding help of the Spirit.

All: Forgive us our sins as we forgive those who sin against us. Lord have mercy.

All: *"For our sake [Jesus] was crucified under Pontius Pilate; he suffered death and was buried."* (Nicene Creed)

B: Thank you Father that you loved the world so much that you gave your one and only Son to be crucified by sinful men in order that whoever believes in him may not perish but have everlasting life.

C: Father, you loved your Son from all eternity so the cross must have cost you dearly. Thank you that you were willing to pay that price for us.

D: Thank you Holy Spirit that you gave Jesus the strength to face his cross of pain and humiliation.

A: Thank you Holy Spirit that as Jesus suffered you groaned with him in his pain.

B: Jesus, our Good Shepherd, you love your sheep and laid down your life for them. Praise you for your love.

C: Jesus, we honor you because although you were in very nature God you did not seek to cling to your divine rights. Instead you humbled yourself and became obedient to death, even the shameful death of a cross.

D: Jesus, we love you because you stood in your place—you suffered the consequences of our sins even though you had done no wrong. You embraced our suffering, our pain, our shame, our separation from God. You descended into Hades.

A: Jesus, you have brought us into a relationship with the Father. You have made peace through your blood shed on Calvary.

B: Jesus, to many people the cross is a sign of failure and weakness but we see that it's God's victory over sin and death and his power to save us.

C: Jesus, to many people the cross is a sign of your foolishness and humiliation but we see that it's a sign of God's wisdom and it is your glory.

D: Jesus, many see the cross as proof of the evils of humanity but we see that it is also a proof of the love of God for his broken world.

A: Jesus, gracious Savior, we worship you for the cross.

B: Jesus, closest friend, we love you for the price you paid for us.

C: Jesus, crucified Lord, we honor you—enthroned on Calvary.

D: Jesus, Servant King, we bow at your pierced feet.

All: We pray for [. . .]

All: In the name of the Father and of the Son and of the Holy Spirit. Amen.

⬚ Day 5: Resurrection and Ascension

A: We come to you Father, along the path opened up by Jesus and with the guiding help of the Spirit.

All: Forgive us our sins as we forgive those who sin against us. Lord have mercy.

All: *"On the third day he rose again in accordance with the Scriptures; he ascended into heaven and is seated at the right hand of the Father."* (Nicene Creed)

B: Father, you reached down into the grave of Jesus and, by your Holy Spirit, raised him from the dead.

C: Holy God, you would not surrender your beautiful world to sin, to decay, to death, and to the tomb.

D: Lord, the end of Jesus's story was not "death" but "everlasting life"; not "the tomb" but "the resurrection."

A: Jesus, when God raised you from death he transformed your mortal body into an indestructible one made alive by the Spirit.

B: Jesus, we praise you that you are alive for evermore and so your rule will know no end.

C: Father, thank you that one day you will resurrect our bodies in the same way that you transformed Jesus' body. Thank you that the end of our story is not death and a grave but resurrection and eternal life. Thank you that the future of the whole universe is "resurrection."

D: An empty tomb—Life has triumphed and death has been defeated.

A: Resurrection—Grace has triumphed and sin has been defeated.

B: A risen Lord—God has triumphed and evil has been defeated.

C: Jesus, you have been raised to the highest place and given the name above every name. You sit at the right hand of God the Father.

D: Praise you Jesus that you rule over all things from God's throne in heaven.

A: We worship you risen Christ. We join with all your people around the world and down through the ages to praise your name.

B: One day, Lord Jesus, every creature in the universe will love and worship you. May that day come soon!

C: Thank you that you know the difficulties we sometimes face in our lives and you understand them.

D: Thank you that you pray to the Father for us every day.

A: Thank you that you are with us right now through the person of your Spirit.

All: We pray for [. . .]

All: In the name of the Father and of the Son and of the Holy Spirit. Amen.

❖ Day 6: The Sending of the Spirit

A: We come to you Father, along the path opened up by Jesus and with the guiding help of the Spirit.

All: Forgive us our sins as we forgive those who sin against us. Lord have mercy.

All: *"We believe in the Holy Spirit, the Lord, the Giver of Life, who proceeds from the Father. With the Father and the Son he is worshipped and glorified. He has spoken through the prophets. We believe in one, holy, catholic, and apostolic church. We acknowledge one baptism for the forgiveness of sins."* (Nicene Creed)

B: Father, you gave the Holy Spirit to Jesus when he ascended to heaven and Jesus has poured him out upon the church.

C: Jesus, thank you so much for the gift of the Holy Spirit to your people.

D: Your Spirit is a gift too wonderful for words.

A: He is the *very presence of God* given to us.

B: Your Spirit—God before us.

C: Your Spirit—God beside us.

D: Your Spirit—God within us.

B: Holy Spirit, you are to us a refreshing stream and a powerful flood.

C: Holy Spirit, you are to us a gentle breeze and a mighty rushing wind.

D: Holy Spirit, you are to us fire from on high and rain from heaven.

A: Holy Spirit, you bring to us the presence of the Father and the presence of Jesus.

B: Lord Spirit, we thank you that you teach us about Jesus and guide us in his ways.

C: Lord Spirit, we thank you that you give us the power and courage we need to proclaim the good news.

D: Lord Spirit, we thank you that you give each of us different gifts to build up the Christian community.

A: Lord Spirit, we thank you that you change us day by day to become more like Jesus.

B: Lord Spirit, we thank you that one day you will transform our mortal bodies in the same way that you transformed Jesus' body. You will raise us to eternal life.

C: We welcome you today and every day—come and fill our lives.

D: We open our hearts to you—please make us like Christ.

A: We need your power and love and wisdom.

All: Please fill us today, lovely Spirit of God.

All: We pray for […]

All: In the name of the Father and of the Son and of the Holy Spirit. Amen.

▨ DAY 7: THE RENEWED CREATION

A: We come to you Father, along the path opened up by Jesus and with the guiding help of the Spirit.

All: Forgive us our sins as we forgive those who sin against us. Lord have mercy.

All: *"[Jesus] will come again in glory to judge the living and the dead, and his kingdom will have no end . . . We look for the resurrection of the dead and the life of the world to come. Amen."* (Nicene Creed)

B: King Jesus, the day is coming when you will return from heaven to earth and every eye will see you in all your radiant glory.

C: You will crush evil, sin, and death forever. Old things will pass away and God will make all things new.

D: Father, you will raise your people from the dead and we will rule with Christ forever and ever.

A: This lovely universe that you created will be set free from death and decay. It will be transformed, resurrected, and filled full of your presence and glory.

B: Father, we thank you so much for refusing to hand this world over to sin and death. Even though it so often rejects you, you refuse to throw the world away and begin again. Instead you will bring it to a wonderful future.

C: Lord God, one day we will see you face to face. We will "dance" with the Trinity. You will be our God and we will be your people.

D: Father, you will wipe every tear from our eyes. There will be no more pain or sorrow for the old order of things will have passed away.

A: You will heal the old wounds between people and between nations. There will be peace and not war.

B: There will be life and not death.

C: There will be joy and not misery.

D: There will be freedom and not captivity.

A: There will be justice, mercy, love, forgiveness, goodness, liberty, and worship.

B: Every knee will bow before you, Jesus. Every tongue in heaven, on earth, and under the earth will sing your praise. We long to see the world at last offer you the worship you deserve.

C: Father, this is the future you have planned for the cosmos.

D: Jesus, this is the future that your death and resurrection make possible.

A: Spirit, this is the future that you are guiding the world towards.

B: Although we see terrible things around us—dreadful wickedness and suffering—we thank you God that creation is in *your* hands.

C: You have not lost control of your world, Father. The future is in safe hands.

D: Jesus—your resurrection is the shape of things to come.

All: We pray for [...]

All: In the name of the Father and of the Son and of the Holy Spirit. Amen.

Appendix 2

"Two Men and an It?"
Is the Triune God Male?

WHEN I WAS A teenager I remember going to a party at one of my friends' houses. Her mother was a keen feminist and on the kitchen wall she had pinned up a newspaper article about the Trinity. The headline was "Two Men and an It." BAM! I got the point instantly. That was the first time that I became conscious of the issues raised by the dominance of male language for God within the Judeo-Christian tradition. Language such as *Father* and *Son* and *King* and *Lord* were simply the lens through which I looked at God. I had never stopped to look at the lens itself. Was it a good lens?

Feminists—both Christian feminists and anti-Christian feminists—did look at the lens and raised some very important questions about it. The central worry was that God was presented as being male (or if not literally being male then as being more like men than women). And, as Mary Daly famously wrote, "If God is male then the male is God."[1] On top of that is the fact that many people have suffered terrible abuse at the hands of their human fathers and thinking of God as the Father can be *very* difficult for them. All of this presents a challenge for traditional Christianity.

In this little appendix I wish to do no more than offer a few brief thoughts on this important issue.

---

1. Daly, *Beyond God the Father*, 19. Daly is at the radical extreme of feminism with little time for Christian feminists.

IS GOD MALE?

The first issue to be clear about is this—God is *not* male. Indeed Christian orthodoxy has always emphatically denied that God is male. God is not male; God is not female; God is not a blend of both. God transcends sexuality. So language about God as "the Father" and as "the Son" was always understood, when applied to God, in such a way as to strip away the literal male dimension of it. This much is undisputed.

However, some theologians have argued that while God is not male God *is* masculine. By this they mean that God has more (so-called) masculine qualities than (so-called) feminine qualities. Consequently it is more truthful to present him using male metaphors than female ones.[2] I confess to being highly skeptical about such claims. In the first instance, although biology obviously plays an important role, what we consider to be "masculine" and "feminine" is, to quite some extent, culturally shaped rather than universal. Secondly, the list of masculine qualities that God is said to possess usually includes items such as loving his children, caring for them, being protective them, disciplining them, providing for them, and so on. But surely none of us really think that love of one's children is a masculine trait or that providing for, protecting, and disciplining children is what fathers *but not mothers* do. Third, this approach also has the problematic consequence that men *really are* more like God than women; more "in his image" than women. So I do not think of God as masculine or feminine—not literally. If we do wish to designate certain qualities as masculine and feminine (and if culturally contextualized this is perfectly appropriate) then I would say that God possesses attributes that are analogous to *both masculine and feminine* qualities.[3] I have no interest in a "feminized" God but I also have no interests in a "macho" God. The God of biblical faith is neither.

2. Consider, for instance, John Piper's comments at the 2012 Desiring God conference for pastors. "God has revealed himself to us in the Bible *pervasively* as King, not Queen, and as Father, not Mother. The second person of the Trinity is revealed as the eternal Son. The Father and the Son created man and woman in his image, and gave them together the name of the man, *Adam* (Gen 5:2) . . . The Son of God comes into the world as a man, not a woman . . . From all of this, I conclude that God has given Christianity a masculine feel. And, being a God of love, he has done it for the maximum flourishing of men *and women*." The talk sets forth eight traits of masculine ministry (reflecting God's masculine qualities). The full text can be found here: http://www.desiringgod.org/resource-library/conference-messages/the-frank-and-manly-mr-ryle-the-value-of-a-masculine-ministry.

3. So I have no objections to most of Piper's traits of "masculine ministry"—indeed, they are (mostly) commendable. I just think that we also need to hear about the

Here's the thing: God is beyond our language—God is what theologians call "transcendent."[4] You can't put God in a box, even a language box, and hope that God'll be contained. "The heavens, even the highest heavens, cannot contain you" (2 Chr 2:6). So when human language is applied to God it is not used in exactly the same way that we use it in ordinary contexts. The Bible draws on all sorts of created things and uses them as windows through which to better understand the God who is beyond understanding. Thus God is said to be a shepherd, a king, an angry she-bear robbed of her cubs, a light, a warrior, and so on. Of course, God is not *literally* any of these things but all these metaphors point to different aspects of the reality of God and God's relationship with creation. So they are true but we must not collapse the difference between God and the metaphor. When we say "God is a shepherd" there is an implicit but unspoken "but not literally" in the silence that follows. Well, the language of "Father" and "Son" is the same in this regard. The language is drawn from the human world of family relationships and used as a window through which to better understand God. But it is metaphorical language.[5]

In some ways this is a disturbing idea—God seems to slip out of our grasp when we realize this. But it is also a liberating idea that snaps us out of thinking that we "comprehend" God. It lets God be God. Remember that Yhwh himself forbids the making of images, *either male or female*: "Therefore watch yourselves very carefully. Since you saw no form on the day that the LORD spoke to you at Horeb out of the midst of the fire, beware lest

---

(culturally contextualized) "feminine" traits of Christianity to go alongside the (culturally contextualized) masculine ones.

4. The person who has influenced me the most here is Thomas Aquinas. His discussions on human language and the transcendent God are still central to theological discussion today (see *Summa Theologiae* I.qq.2–26).

5. The language of "Spirit" is also a metaphor. Both the Greek and Hebrew words translated "spirit" are the words used for "breath" and "wind" and the idea of an invisible force suggested by those words was used to make sense of the third person of the Trinity. I ought to add a qualification here, from Aquinas again. Some language about God is not metaphorical but analogical. God is wise, good, loving, just, and the like, in a primary way. God is, for instance, *goodness itself*. Human goodness is but a dim reflection of God's goodness. But human language has been developed to pick out the qualities of goodness in humans so it only *indirectly* points to the supereminent goodness of God. When we use such language of God we need to be aware that it is not metaphorical but nor it is conventional: it is functioning *analogically* and does not mean exactly the same as when applied to created things. We can know that God *really is* good, but we need to appreciate that his goodness is not just a bigger version of our own; it is a different order of goodness that we only glimpse "in a glass darkly."

you act corruptly by making a carved image for yourselves, in the form of any figure, the likeness of *male or female* . . ." (Deut 4:15–16). We need to be careful not to allow our verbal images to become like idols.

Understanding "Father" and "Son" Language

Ancient Judaism emerged from a pagan environment in which the cultures around them had many gods and goddesses and sexuality was built-in to the notion of the divine. So Israel was familiar with male and female ways of imagining God.[6] Given its context, why did biblical religion avoid female metaphors for God? I shall offer two quick suggestions.

First, ancient Israel conceptualized God as "one" and as transcending sexuality. God did not create by mating with a goddess; God simply spoke . . . "and it was." So the dominance of masculine images for God was not an attempt to make God male but an *attempt to desexualize the notion of God* (without depersonalizing God into an "it"). In the polytheistic context in which Israel was situated there was a very real danger that if male and female metaphors were mixed and balanced this would be understood as introducing sexuality to the notion of God and ordinary Israelites would be led into paganism. Given that male metaphors were not focused on the *gender* aspect, it may not be a coincidence that the Bible never seeks to draw lessons for human fathers from God the Father. God's fatherhood is, weird as it may sound, gender-neutral.

Second, Israel was a patriarchal society and so the public roles were almost entirely occupied by men. Thus language used to communicate ideas of divine rule, justice, protection, and the like necessarily drew on masculine images—king, judge, warrior, lord, etc. As Stephen Barton notes, "The predominance of masculine images of God in both Scripture and tradition has to do with the patriarchal structure of the societies in and for which those images were developed, not with the gender of God."[7]

6. As an aside, it should be noted that the fact that these cultures had male and female gods did not make them egalitarian. Pagan polytheism with its goddesses remained as patriarchal as Israel itself and this ought to make us suspicious of any simplistic connection between female images of deity and the equality of women.

7. Quoted by Stanley Grenz in his essay "Is God Sexual?" in Kimmel, *This Is My Name Forever*, 199–200. It is worth stating that although biblical cultures were patriarchal it does not follow that this is a divinely sanctioned social order. See the essays in Sloan, *Tamar's Tears*.

Language of God as *Father* needs to be understood, in the first instance, in its ancient and biblical contexts. In ancient Palestine a father was seen as the "source" of the family and very much a figure of authority in the family. He was also one who loved, protected, provided for, and passed on an inheritance to his children. As such, he was to be loved, honored, and obeyed. So talk of God as the Father has those connotations in Scripture.

We should, however, observe that God is not Father and "Son" but *the* Father and "*the* Son."[8] The word *the* is important because it says, *this particular* Father; *this particular* Son. In this way generic nouns (*father* and *son*) come to serve as something like a personal proper name. So it is not enough to understand the meanings of the words father and son in their ancient context (although that provides a way in); we also need to see how *this particular* Father and *this particular* Son relate to each other and to human beings. Thus, although the human words do shape how we see God, God, in turn, reshapes how those words work in theological contexts. And *this* Father and *this* Son do not lord it over women or abuse women.[9]

The notion of God as the Father is filled out by the biblical contexts in which it is used. So Yhwh is the Father to Israel in that he promises to redeem Israel out of his steadfast love and his covenant faithfulness. The idea of God as the Father here has a *future dimension*—the blessings that God will one day bring about for his children. That dimension comes out in the New Testament as well. The Father is the origin of his children; he loves his children; he provides for them; he protects them; he calls his children to live together as one family; and he promises them redemption, a future inheritance—the kingdom of God. As Marianne Meye Thompson notes, "to speak of God as Father is to evoke a narrative of birth, care, and provision, love and mercy, and of promise and redemption."[10]

8. I owe this point to R. Kendall Soulen's essay, "The Name of the Holy Trinity."

9. It is worth noting that the New Testament does not use the idea of God as "the Father" as a basis for supporting male privilege.

10. Thompson, *The Promise of the Father*, 166. We should add that language of "the Son" also needs to be defined in terms of the different ways that the Bible fills it out. "To speak of Jesus as the Son is to speak of him in a diverse and multifaceted way. Jesus is the firstborn Son who is preeminent, the heir of all things, and has a unique relationship with God. He is the first raised from the dead. As Son-king, he is the promised messianic king, the son of David, who has God's authority and establishes God's eternal kingdom. As Son-prophet, he is in a unique position to image, reveal, and represent God. As Son-priest, he is holy and blameless, and so he can secure salvation for his people. Jesus is the obedient Son to his Father—even to the end of history, when he gives all things to his Father. As Son, he is God embodied. There is a progressive heightening of his sonship:

But Yhwh is not simply the Father of the community of God (Israel and the church). He is the Father of *Jesus*. This theme is common across the NT—and was clearly *central* to Jesus's own relationship with God—but is strongest in John's Gospel where the Father-Son relationship reaches new heights. Here the metaphor points to something *unique* and *eternal* in the relationship between God and Jesus. Jesus is "the Son" in a way distinct from that in which anyone else is "son." The metaphor, though, still has the connotations drawn from its ancient family context (God as Jesus' "source," who loves him and will bless him with an inheritance; who is to be loved and honored and obeyed). But the church *never* understood this relationship as biological (God *literally* as Jesus's father) and soon made clear that it was not even something that began in time. In other words, if this relationship is eternal (as Scripture indicates) then there never was a *time* when God begat Jesus. So, in the language of the early church, Jesus is *"eternally begotten of the Father."* Obviously this Father-Son relationship is different from any human father-son relationship. And gender is simply not the issue in the way that the Bible deploys this imagery.[11]

Now obviously Jesus was a male but we cannot read Jesus' maleness back into God. The church's creeds have always been at pains to keep a clear distinction between Jesus' human and divine natures. So while Jesus (as human) is male, the divine Word that is incarnate as Jesus is not. Indeed it is interesting to note that teaching about Jesus' divinity found in John 1:1–18 and Colossians 1:15–20 draws on the Old Testament wisdom traditions. Jesus is the very "wisdom of God" made flesh (1 Cor 1:24). Yet in Israel's wisdom tradition this divine wisdom is personified *as a female* (e.g., Proverbs 8). Of course, this does not make the divine wisdom *literally* female, but it alerts us to the fact that the second person of the Trinity—the Son—is not male in his divinity but only in his humanity. And, in my opinion, even then there was no *theological necessity* for divine Word to be incarnate as a male. The most critical thing, theologically speaking, was that the Word become a *human being* and be *Jewish*. Of course, there may have been very good *pragmatic* reasons why the Word became a *male* human but the point is that this was not a theological necessity.

---

from the incarnation, through baptism, resurrection, to is exaltation." Williams, *The Maleness of Jesus*, 184.

11. It is worth adding that in ancient Jewish culture the inheritance was usually passed to the firstborn son and so the language of *son* connotes the important notion of inheritance in a way that *child* or *daughter* would not have done. But, again, the point of comparison in the metaphor is the idea of *inheritance* and not gender.

We should also bear in mind that the Bible does, in fact, draw on some female similes and metaphors to speak of Yhwh. For instance, God is like a woman crying out in childbirth (Isa 42:14); a mother who *gave birth* to Israel (Deut 32:18; Num 11:12; cf. the role of the Spirit in "giving birth" in John 3:5); a mother suckling her children (Num 11:12);[12] a mother that can never forget or forsake her child (Isa 49:15) and who comforts her child (Isa 66:13). God is like a woman mixing dough (Matt 13:33); a woman seeking a lost coin (Luke 15:8–9); a seamstress making clothes for Israel (Neh 9:21); a midwife (Ps 22:9–10a; 71:6; Isa 46:3; 66:9). God is like a female animal—a mother bird (Deut 32:11–12; Pss 17:8; 36:7; 57:1; 91:1, 4; Isa 31:5); an angry mother bear (Hos 13:8); and Jesus is like a mother hen desiring to gather her chicks (Matt 23:37). Obviously my point is not that God is female![13] I am simply noting that drawing on female images is not inherently problematic. After all, women are created in the image of God (Gen 1:27)!

Naming the Trinity—A Proposal

Theologian R. Kendall Soulen, in his book *The Divine Name(s) and the Holy Trinity*, has made a thought-provoking suggestion for naming the Trinity that I think is worth explaining in this context. Soulen argues that in the Bible and in Christian history there is not only *one* pattern for naming the Trinity (e.g., Father, Son, and Spirit) but *three* different patterns, each associated with one of the persons.

1. *The theological (God) pattern:* The God-pattern is tied to the unique name of God, Yhwh. The first person of the Trinity is the one whose name this is. The first person bestows this sacred name upon the second person, and the third person seeks to bring glory and honor to the name of the first person in the second. For instance, in Philippians 2 God gives Jesus the "name above every name" (i.e., the name

---

12. This passage (Num 11:10–15) is interesting in that Moses claims that God (and not Moses) is the mother that *conceived* Israel, *gave birth* to Israel, and *carried Israel in his bosom* (v. 12). Then he says "if *you* will treat me like this, kill me at once" (v. 15). Yet in the Hebrew the word *you* that Moses uses of God is a second person *feminine* singular pronoun. If the text is not corrupt then this is the only instance in the Bible in which God is referred to with a feminine pronoun. It's possible and interesting but not certain.

13. None of these texts claims that God is female! For instance, if you put 42:14 in context you will see that the prophet is mixing his metaphors and Yhwh is presented as a "man of war."

"Yhwh") the Spirit draws out a response of worship of Jesus to the glory of God the Father. There is a lot to say about this important naming-pattern but we must move on.

2. *The christological (Christ) pattern:* The Christ-pattern is the one that we are most familiar with. This makes use of the fixed language of "the Father, the Son, and the Spirit."

3. *The pneumatological (Spirit) pattern:* The Spirit-pattern is open-ended and vastly diverse. Here all the wide range of biblical images for the persons springs to mind (e.g., Jesus as light, as a door, as a shepherd, as a king; the Spirit as fire, as wind, as water, as oil; God like a warrior, a judge, a rock, dry rot, and so on). Here too are all the many different images of the three that do not fit the first two patterns. For instance: God, Christ, Spirit (New Testament); God, Word, Breath (New Testament); Root, Tree, Fruit (Tertullian); Lover, Beloved, Love (Augustine); Rose, Flower, Fragrance (John of Damascus); Power, Wisdom, Goodness (Peter Abelard); Almighty, Fountain of Bliss, River of Raptures (Charles Wesley); Mother-Sophia, Jesus-Sophia, Spirit-Sophia (Elizabeth Johnson).

Soulen claims that all three patterns speak the truth about the Trinity but do so from different vantage points. The God-pattern has an overall focus on *divine mystery*, as represented by the unspeakable name Yhwh; the Christ-pattern has a focus on *divine presence*, focused in the Son, Emmanuel (God with us); and the Spirit-pattern has a focus on the richness of *divine blessing*.

Now, says Soulen, it is also really important that we see that the three patterns should be related to each other in *Trinitarian* ways. What this means is that we need to appreciate that they are:

a) *Distinct:* Just as we do not collapse the three persons into one (that's Modalism, see chapter 4) so too we must also not seek to collapse the patterns into one. For instance, some feminist theologians wish to absorb the Christ-pattern into the Spirit-pattern. They see Father, Son, and Spirit language as just another set of metaphors that works in some contexts but not in others and which can be dropped and exchanged for new sets. But it cannot. This naming pattern is grounded in Jesus' own life and ministry and was bequeathed by him to the *ekklēsia*. It has always been central to Christian spirituality because it

is a pattern laid down by Jesus himself and Christian faith is grounded in the particular history of Jesus.

b) *Equal:* Just as we do not subordinate any of the persons to the others
(that is a heresy known as subordinationism) so too we do not subordinate any of the patterns to the others. Here traditional Christians
have been at fault. We have often subordinated the Spirit-pattern to
the Christ-pattern, making "Father, Son, and Spirit" *the* privileged
way to speak of the persons.

The most appropriate way to speak of the Trinity is to hold all three patterns
together and to allow them to "illuminate each other, supplement each
other, and protect each other from misunderstanding."[14]

So can we abandon talk of Father, Son, and Spirit? No. Christian faith
is rooted in the particulars of history—God's election of a *particular* people
(Israel) and incarnation as a *particular* human being (Jesus). Particularity
really matters and this *particular* God (Yhwh) incarnate as this *particular*
human (Jesus) gifted us this *particular* naming-pattern and the church has
always maintained it as central. To abandon such talk would create a major
breach with all earlier forms of the faith (including its very root, Jesus). But
we do need to do a better job of explaining this pattern so that people do
not read off it ideas of God as male or as more like men than women or take
it to imply that men should rule women.

Can we speak of God by using female metaphors and similes? Yes, and
doing so can help protect us against taking the male metaphors literally.[15]
But we need to do so in such a way that we do not inadvertently reintroduce

14. E-mail to me dated January, 23, 2012. I am well aware of the fact that this book
itself does not reflect the equality of the patterns adequately. To a large extent this is
because one of the strengths of the Christ-pattern is that it is fixed and simple and thus
works well in teaching contexts. If I kept flipping the language with which I referred to
the different persons it could be confusing for readers.

15. I would note that I do not think that they would or should be as dominant as male
metaphors. The reason for this is, firstly, because particularity is so important in Christianity and the particulars of Jesus' own relationship with God rightly become thematic
for Christian spirituality. Secondly, female metaphors occupy only the third naming-
pattern (although they *could* be used in the first) and they share that with a plethora of
non-female images. Male metaphors are guaranteed by the Christ-pattern. Thus, even
a balance between the Christ-pattern and the Spirit-pattern will not lead to a balance
between male and female language for God.

And is it OK to pray, "Our Mother in heaven?" No. But not because it is inherently
wrong to speak of God using feminine metaphors but because the Lord's Prayer was
given to the community of disciples by Jesus himself and we are not at liberty to modify
it in such ways.

sexuality into God. This is a real danger to be guarded against but it can be done. For instance, in William Young's bestselling novel, *The Shack*, the first person of the Trinity appears to Mackenzie Phillips as an African American woman called Papa and yet there is no confusion because she explains: "Mackenzie, I am neither male nor female, even though both genders are derived from my nature. If I choose to appear to you as a man or a woman, it's because I love you. For me to appear as a woman and suggest that you call me Papa is simply to mix metaphors, to help you keep from falling so easily back into your religious conditioning."[16]

16. Young, *The Shack*, 93. We see just this kind of odd mixing of metaphors in a very early Christian hymn from the *Odes of Solomon* 19:1–4 (which speaks of the milk from the Father's breasts) and from the Council of Toledo in 675 (which declared that "the Son was . . . from the womb of the Father"). On the *Odes of Solomon* see Charlesworth, *The Earliest Christian Hymnbook*.

Bibliography

Angelici, Ruben, translator. *Richard of Saint Victor, On the Trinity*. Eugene, OR: Cascade Books, 2011.

Athanasius. *On the Incarnation*. Crestwood, NY: St. Vladimir's Seminary Press, 2003.

Augustine. *The Trinity: De Trinitate*. Introduction, translation, and notes by Edmund Hill. Hyde Park, NY: New City, 1991.

Barth, Karl. *Church Dogmatics* III/3. Translated by A. T. McKay, et al. Edinburgh: T. & T. Clark, 1961.

Basil the Great, Saint. *On the Holy Spirit*. Crestwood, NY: St. Vladimir's Seminary Press, 1980.

Bauckham, Richard. "God's Self-Identification with the Godforsaken in the Gospel of Mark." In *Jesus and the God of Israel: God Crucified and Other Studies on the New Testament's Christology of Divine Identity*, 254–68. Milton Keynes, UK: Paternoster, 2008.

———. *Jesus and the God of Israel: God Crucified and Other Studies on the New Testament's Christology of Divine Identity*. Milton Keynes, UK: Paternoster, 2008

Boyd, Gregory. *Seeing Is Believing: Experience Jesus through Imaginative Prayer*. Grand Rapids: Baker, 2004.

Brown, Rosalind. *How Hymns Shape Our Lives*. Grove Spirituality Series. Cambridge: Grove, 2001.

Brueggemann, Walter. "The Costly Loss of Lament." *Journal for the Study of the Old Testament* 36 (1986) 57–71.

Buxton, Graham. *Dancing in the Dark: The Privilege of Participating in the Ministry of Christ*. Carlisle, UK: Paternoster, 2001.

Castello, Daniel. *The Apathetic God: Exploring the Contemporary Relevance of Divine Impassibility*. Paternoster Theological Monographs. Milton Keynes, UK: Paternoster, 2009.

Charlesworth, James H. *The Earliest Christian Hymnbook: The Odes of Solomon*. Eugene, OR: Cascade Books, 2009.

Cocksworth, Christopher. *Holy, Holy, Holy: Worshipping the Trinitarian God*. London: Darton, Longman & Todd, 1997.

Cohen, David J., and Michael Parsons. *In Praise of Worship: An Exploration of Text and Practice*, 143–61. Eugene, OR: Pickwick Publications, 2010.

Daly, Mary. *Beyond God the Father: Toward a Philosophy of Women's Liberation*. Boston: Beacon, 1973.

The Divine Liturgy of Our Father among the Saints John Chrysostom: The Greek Text Together with a Translation into English. Translated by the Very Reverend Archimandrite Ephraim Lash. Milton under Wychwood, UK: Lynn, 2011.

Bibliography

Eberhart, Christian A. *The Sacrifice of Jesus: Understanding Atonement Biblically*. Facets. Minneapolis: Fortress, 2011.

Ephraim, Archimandrite. "The Trinity in Contemporary Eucharistic Liturgy." In *The Forgotten Trinity 3: A Selection of Papers Presented to the BCC Study Commission on Trinitarian Doctrine Today*, 47–61. London: British Council of Churches, 1991.

Fee, Gordon. *God's Empowering Presence: The Holy Spirit in the Letters of Paul*. Peabody, MA: Hendrickson, 1994.

Fretheim, Terence E. *The Suffering of God: An Old Testament Perspective*. Overtures to Biblical Theology. Philadelphia: Fortress, 1984.

Gavrilyuk, Paul. *The Suffering of the Impassible God: The Dialectics of Patristic Thought*. Oxford Early Christian Studies. Oxford: Oxford University Press, 2004.

Grant, Jamie. "Psalm 44 and a Christian Spirituality of Lament." Unpublished paper given as the Tyndale Old Testament Lecture, July 2007.

Gregory of Nazianzus, Saint. *On God in Christ: The Five Theological Orations*. St. Vladimir's Seminary Press Popular Patristics Series. Crestwood, NY: St. Vladimir's Seminary Press, 2002.

Gunton, Colin. *Father, Son, and Holy Spirit: Toward a Fully Trinitarian Theology*. London: T. & T. Clark, 2003.

Hart, Trevor. *Regarding Karl Barth*. Carlisle, UK: Paternoster, 1999.

Hauerwas, Stanley. "Carving Stone or Learning to Speak Christian." In *Living Out Loud: Conversations about Virtue, Ethics, and Evangelicalism*, edited by Luke Bretherton and Russell Rook, 60–79. Milton Keynes, UK: Paternoster, 2010.

———. "How We Lay Bricks and Make Disciples." In *Living Out Loud: Conversations about Virtue, Ethics, and Evangelicalism*, edited by Luke Bretherton and Russell Rook, 39–59. Milton Keynes, UK: Paternoster, 2010.

Hilborn, David. "Glossolalia as Communication: A Linguistic-Pragmatic Perspective." In *Speaking in Tongues: Multi-Disciplinary Perspectives*, edited by Mark J. Cartledge, 111–46. Milton Keynes, UK: Paternoster, 2006.

Hulme, Bruce. "Hillsong Christology." Unpublished paper, 2004.

Hurtado, Larry. *At the Origins of Christian Worship*. Didsbury Lectures. Carlisle, UK: Paternoster, 1999.

———. *Lord Jesus Christ: Devotion to Jesus in Earliest Christianity*. Grand Rapids: Eerdmans, 2003.

Julian of Norwich, Saint. *Showings*. Edited by E. Colledge. Classics of Western Spirituality. New York: Paulist, 1978.

Kimmel, Alvin F., editor. *This Is My Name Forever: The Trinity & Gender Language for God*. Downers Grove, IL: InterVarsity, 2001.

Kinzer, Mark S. *Postmissionary Messianic Judaism: Redefining Christian Engagement with the Jewish People*. Grand Rapids: Brazos, 2005.

LaCugna, Catherine Mowry. *God for Us: The Trinity and Christian Life*. New York: HarperCollins, 1991.

Leach, John. *Living Liturgy: A Practical Guide to Using Liturgy in Spirit-Led Worship*. Rev. ed. Eastbourne, UK: Kingsway, 1997.

Liebengood, Kelly D. "'Don't Be Like Your Fathers': Reassessing the Ethnic Identity of 1 Peter's 'Elect Sojourners.'" Paper presented at the British New Testament Conference, University of Durham, 4 September 2008.

Lossky, Vladimir. *The Mystical Theology of the Eastern Church*. London: James Clarke, 1957.

Man, Ron. *Proclamation and Praise: Hebrews 12:2 and the Christology of Worship*. Eugene, OR: Wipf & Stock, 2007.

Marsh, Richard, editor. *Prayers from the East: Traditions in Eastern Christianity*. Minneapolis: Fortress, 2004.

Marshall, Bruce D. "Israel: Do Christians Worship the God of Israel?" In *Knowing the Triune God: The Work of the Spirit in the Practices of the Church*, edited by J. J. Buckley and D. S. Yeago, 231–64. Grand Rapids: Eerdmans, 2001.

McConville, J. Gordon. *Judgment and Promise: An Interpretation of the Book of Jeremiah*. Leicester, UK: Apollos, 1993.

Meek, Donald E. *The Quest for Celtic Christianity*. Edinburgh: Handsel, 2000.

Moffitt, David M. "Blood, Life, and Atonement: Reassessing Hebrews' Christological Appropriation of Yom Kippur." In *The Day of Atonement: Its Interpretations in Early Jewish and Christian Traditions*, edited by Thomas Hieke and Tobias Nicklas, 211–24. Themes in Biblical Narrative: Jewish and Christian Traditions 15. Leiden: Brill, 2011.

Moltmann, Jürgen. *The Crucified God*. London: SCM, 1974.

Ngien, Dennis. *Gifted Response: The Triune God as the Causative Agency of our Responsive Worship*. Milton Keynes, UK: Paternoster, 2008.

Noble, Tom. *Holy Trinity: Holy People: The Historic Doctrine of Christian Perfecting*. The Didsbury Lectures Series. Eugene, OR: Cascade, 2013.

Northumbria Community. *Celtic Daily Prayer: From the Northumbria Community*. Rev. ed. London: HarperCollins, 2000.

Parry, Robin A. "The Trinity and Lament." In *In Praise of Worship: An Exploration of Text and Practice*, edited by David J. Cohen and Michael Parsons, 143–61. Eugene, OR: Pickwick Publications, 2010.

————. "Wrestling with Lamentations in Christian Worship." In *Great Is Thy Faithfulness?: Reading Lamentations as Sacred Scripture*, edited by Robin A. Parry and Heath A. Thomas, 175–97. Eugene, OR: Pickwick Publications, 2011.

Page, Nick. *And Now Let's Move into a Time of Nonsense: Why Worship Songs are Failing the Church*. Milton Keynes, UK: Authentic Media, 2004.

Peterson, Eugene H. "Evangelical Spirituality." In *The Futures of Evangelicalism: Issues and Prospects*, edited by Craig Bartholomew et al., 241–42. Leicester, UK: InterVarsity, 2003.

Pseudo-Dionysius. *Pseudo-Dionysius: The Complete Works*. The Classics of Western Spirituality. Translated by Colm Luibheid. New York: Paulist, 1987.

Rae, Michael. "The Trinity." In *The Oxford Handbook of Philosophical Theology*, edited by Thomas P. Flint and Michael C. Rea, 403–29. Oxford Handbooks. Oxford: Oxford University Press, 2009.

Rahner, Karl. *The Trinity*. London: Burns & Oates, 1970.

Rauser, Randal. *Finding God in "The Shack."* Colorado Springs: Paternoster, 2009.

Resner, A. "Lament: Faith's Response to Loss." *Restoration Quarterly* 32/3 (1990) 129–42.

Sloan, Andrew, editor. *Tamar's Tears: Evangelical Engagements with Feminist Old Testament Hermeneutics*. Eugene, OR: Pickwick Publications, 2011.

Smail, Tom. *Like Father, Like Son: The Trinity Imaged in Our Humanity*. Milton Keynes, UK: Paternoster, 2005.

Soulen, R. Kendall. *The Divine Name(s) and the Holy Trinity*. Vol. 1, *Distinguishing the Voices*. Louisville: Westminster John Knox, 2011.

————. *The God of Israel and Christian Theology*. Minneapolis: Fortress, 1996.

Bibliography

————. "The Name of the Holy Trinity: A Triune Name." *Theology Today* 59 (2002) 244–61.

Steven, James H. S. *Worship in the Spirit: Charismatic Worship in the Church of England.* Studies in Evangelical History and Thought. Carlisle, UK: Paternoster, 2002.

Swinton, John. *Raging with Compassion: Pastoral Responses to the Problem of Evil.* Grand Rapids: Eerdmans, 2007.

Thiselton, Anthony C. *The First Epistle to the Corinthians.* New International Greek Testament Commentary. Grand Rapids: Eerdmans, 2000.

Thomas Aquinas, Saint. *New English Translation of St. Thomas Aquinas's Summa Theologiae (Summa Theologica).* Translated by Alfred J. Freddoso. Online: http://www.nd.edu/~afreddos/summa-translation/TOC-part1.htm/.

Thomas, Viv. *Paper Boys: A Vision for the Contemporary Church—From Delivery to Dance through God as Trinity.* Milton Keynes, UK: Authentic, 2004.

Thompson, Marianne Meye. *The Promise of the Father: Jesus and God in the New Testament.* Louisville: Westminster John Knox, 2000.

Torrance, Alan. "Does God Suffer? Incarnation and Impassibility." In *Christ in Our Place: The Humanity of God in Christ for the Reconciliation of the World,* edited by Trevor Hart and Daniel Thimell, 345–68. Exeter, UK: Paternoster, 1989.

Torrance, James B. *Worship, Community, and the Triune God of Grace.* Didsbury Lectures 1994. Carlisle, UK: Paternoster, 1996.

Torrance, Thomas F. *Atonement: The Person and Work of Christ.* Edited by Robert T. Walker. Milton Keynes, UK: Paternoster, 2009.

————. *Incarnation: The Person and Life of Christ.* Edited by Robert T. Walker. Milton Keynes, UK: Paternoster, 2008.

Tozer, A. W. *The Counselor: Straight Talk about the Holy Spirit from a 20th-Century Prophet.* Camp Hill, PA: Christian, 1993.

Tripp, David. "Hymnody and Liturgical Theology: Hymns as an Index of the Trinitarian Character of Worship in Some Western Christian Traditions." In *The Forgotten Trinity 3: A Selection of Papers Presented to the BCC Study Commission on Trinitarian Doctrine Today,* 63–88. London: British Council of Churches, 1991.

Waggoner, Berten. "Leading Trinitarian Worship." *Inside Worship* 52 (February 2004) 5–6.

Ward, Pete. *Liquid Church.* Carlisle, UK: Paternoster, 2002.

————. *Selling Worship: How What We Sing Has Changed the Church.* Milton Keynes, UK: Paternoster, 2005.

Warren, Rick. *The Purpose Driven Church: Growth without Compromising Your Message and Mission.* Grand Rapids: Zondervan, 1995.

Webb, William J. *Slaves, Women & Homosexuals: Exploring the Hermeneutics of Cultural Analysis.* Downers Grove, IL: InterVarsity, 2001.

Webber, Robert E. "Is Our Worship Adequately Triune?" *Reformation and Revival Journal* 9/3 (2000) 121–29.

White, Susan. *Whatever Happened to the Father? The Jesus Heresy in Modern Worship.* Ilfracombe, UK: The Methodist Sacramental Fellowship, 2002.

Williams, Neil H. *The Maleness of Jesus: Is It Good News for Women?* Eugene, OR: Cascade Books, 2011.

Wolterstorff, Nicholas. *Lament for a Son.* Grand Rapids: Eerdmans, 1987.

Wood, Susan. "The Liturgy: Participatory Knowledge of God in the Liturgy." In *Knowing the Triune God: The Work of the Spirit in the Practices of the Church,* edited by J. J. Buckley and D. S. Yeago, 95–118. Grand Rapids: Eerdmans, 2001.

Young, William. *The Shack*. Newbury Park, CA: Windblown Media, 2007.

Zizioulas, John. *Being as Communion: Studies in Personhood and the Church*. Contemporary Greek Theologians 4. Crestwood, NY: St. Vladimir's Seminary Press, 1985.

———. "The Doctrine of God the Trinity Today: Suggestions for an Ecumenical Study." In *The Forgotten Trinity 3: A Selection of Papers Presented to the BCC Study Commission on Trinitarian Doctrine Today*, 19–32. London: British Council of Churches, 1991.

Lightning Source UK Ltd.
Milton Keynes UK
UKOW050637100513

210472UK00001B/9/P